THE BEQUEST

TIM SEELEY

FREDDIE E. WILLIAMS II

JEREMY COLWELL

MARSHALL DILLON

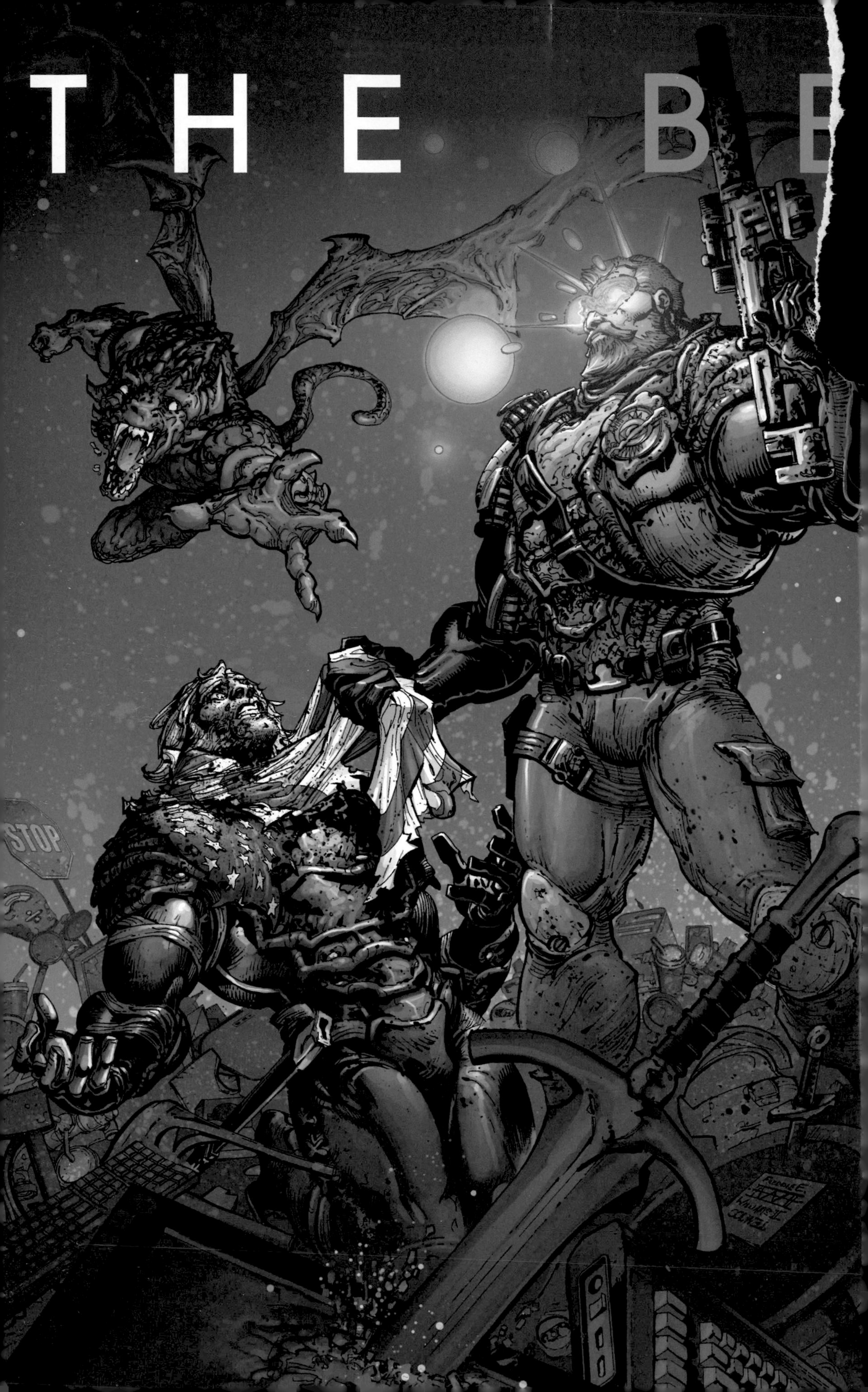
THE B
STOP

Q U E S T

TIM SEELEY writer

FREDDIE E. WILLIAMS II artist

JEREMY COLWELL colorist

MARSHALL DILLON letterer

FREDDIE E. WILLIAMS II w/ **JEREMY COLWELL** front & original covers

CHRIS CAMPANA & **TYLER WALPOLE** variant covers

DAVE SHARPE logo designer

CHARLES PRITCHETT issue #1 backmatter designer

COREY BREEN book designer

MIKE MARTS editor

created by **TIM SEELEY** & **FREDDIE E. WILLIAMS II**

AFTERSHOCK™

MIKE MARTS - Editor-in-Chief • **JOE PRUETT** - Publisher/CCO • **LEE KRAMER** - President • **JON KRAMER** - Chief Executive Officer
STEVE ROTTERDAM - SVP, Sales & Marketing • **DAN SHIRES** - VP, Film & Television UK • **CHRISTINA HARRINGTON** - Managing Editor
MARC HAMMOND - Sr. Retail Sales Development Manager • **RUTHANN THOMPSON** - Sr. Retailer Relations Manager
KATHERINE JAMISON - Marketing Manager • **KELLY DIODATI** - Ambassador Outreach Manager • **BLAKE STOCKER** - VP, Finance
AARON MARION - Publicist • **LISA MOODY** - Finance • **RYAN CARROLL** - Director, Comics/Film/TV Liaison • **JAWAD QURESHI** - Technology Advisor/Strategist
RACHEL PINNELAS - Social Community Manager • **CHARLES PRITCHETT** - Design & Production Manager • **COREY BREEN** - Collections Production
TEODORO LEO - Associate Editor • **STEPHANIE CASEBIER** & **SARAH PRUETT** - Publishing Assistants

AfterShock Logo Design by **COMICRAFT**
Publicity: contact **AARON MARION** (aaron@publichausagency.com) & **RYAN CROY** (ryan@publichausagency.com) at **PUBLICHAUS**
Special thanks to: **ATOM! FREEMAN, IRA KURGAN, MARINE KSADZHIKYAN, KEITH MANZELLA, ANTHONY MILITANO, ANTONIA LIANOS, STEPHAN NILSON** & **ED ZAREMBA**

INTRODUCTION

When I was eleven years old, I took a test. The test results indicated I was qualified for "The Gifted & Talented" program in my school district. This meant I could leave my tiny rural school in the wilds of Wisconsin, and go to a totally different tiny rural school in the wilds of Wisconsin. But at *this* school, I'd be surrounded by students like me. Gifted. Talented.

Nerds.

And, thus, as my awkward, lonely, country bumpkin-ass stumbled to make new friends among mathletes and child prodigies, did I discover Dungeons & Dragons.

Every recess during the long Wisconsin winter, my new friends and I opted out of frostbite to become fighters, wizards and hot female elves. We fought demons and devils that would surely have rattled all the Satanic Panickers in our conservative community. We escaped, and told each other awesome stories while we played the roles of heroes with dice and graphs. Since the rules books were expensive, I exported the game home to my two little brothers by creating a similar, but almost entirely rule-less game called Caverns & Creatures. I read *Drizzt* novels and *Dragonlance* and painted miniatures. I was hooked.

For, like, four years.

And then I got a girlfriend, a fast-food job, a car and another girlfriend. D&D took a distant back seat to Whopper Wednesday shifts and make-out sessions in the rear of my '85 Chevy Cavalier.

Many years later, I was reading a news article about internet conspiracies and Facebook-fueled cults that were destroying the fabric of American democracy. And I thought that all these people wanted was an escape from their lives. From the difficulty of accepting change and the sadness of not being what you thought you would be. They wanted to be a part of something and make friends. And I thought...it's too bad they don't just play D&D.

And, thus, the nugget for THE BEQUEST was conceived. I dug out an old pitch where I'd envisioned fantasy heroes becoming superheroes on modern Earth (that was a weird one), cut out the superheroes and started writing a story about fantasy world adventurers in a strife-ridden modern America. It was good...but my art wasn't cutting it. So, it sat.

Then Freddie Williams, who I had just worked with on *Injustice vs Masters of the Universe*, asked me if I had anything fun to pitch. I shrieked with joy. I had, as they say, my axe.

Thus did my talented Art Bard friend and I embark on a quest to tell our tale, enlisting to our side the Wizard of Hues, Jeremy Colwell; Diviner of Punctuation, Marshall Dillon; Assassin of Bad Grammar, Christina Harrington; Barbarian of the Editorial Wastes, Mike Marts; and the able warriors of the AfterShock Citadel.

Sorry. Like I said...

Nerds.

Whether you've ever shaken the dice or not, I hope you enjoy this brief escape from a lonely, stressful world into a land of heroes, magic and six metal barrels of the finest brew that can be had for a sheet of green paper.

And, while you're at...stay off Facebook.

TIM SEELEY
August 2021

1

ROLE INITIATIVE

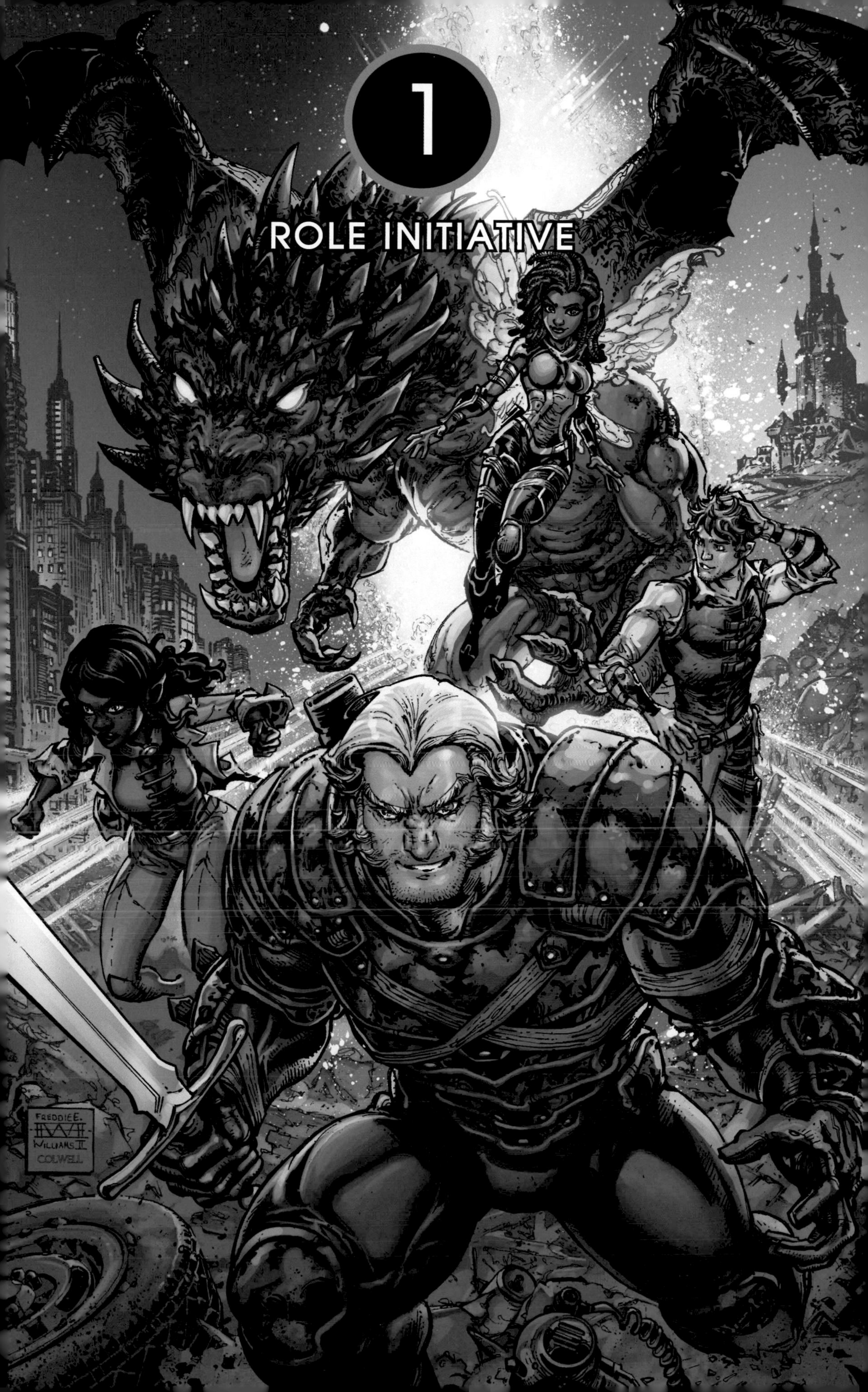
FREDDIE E.
WILLIAMS II
COLWELL

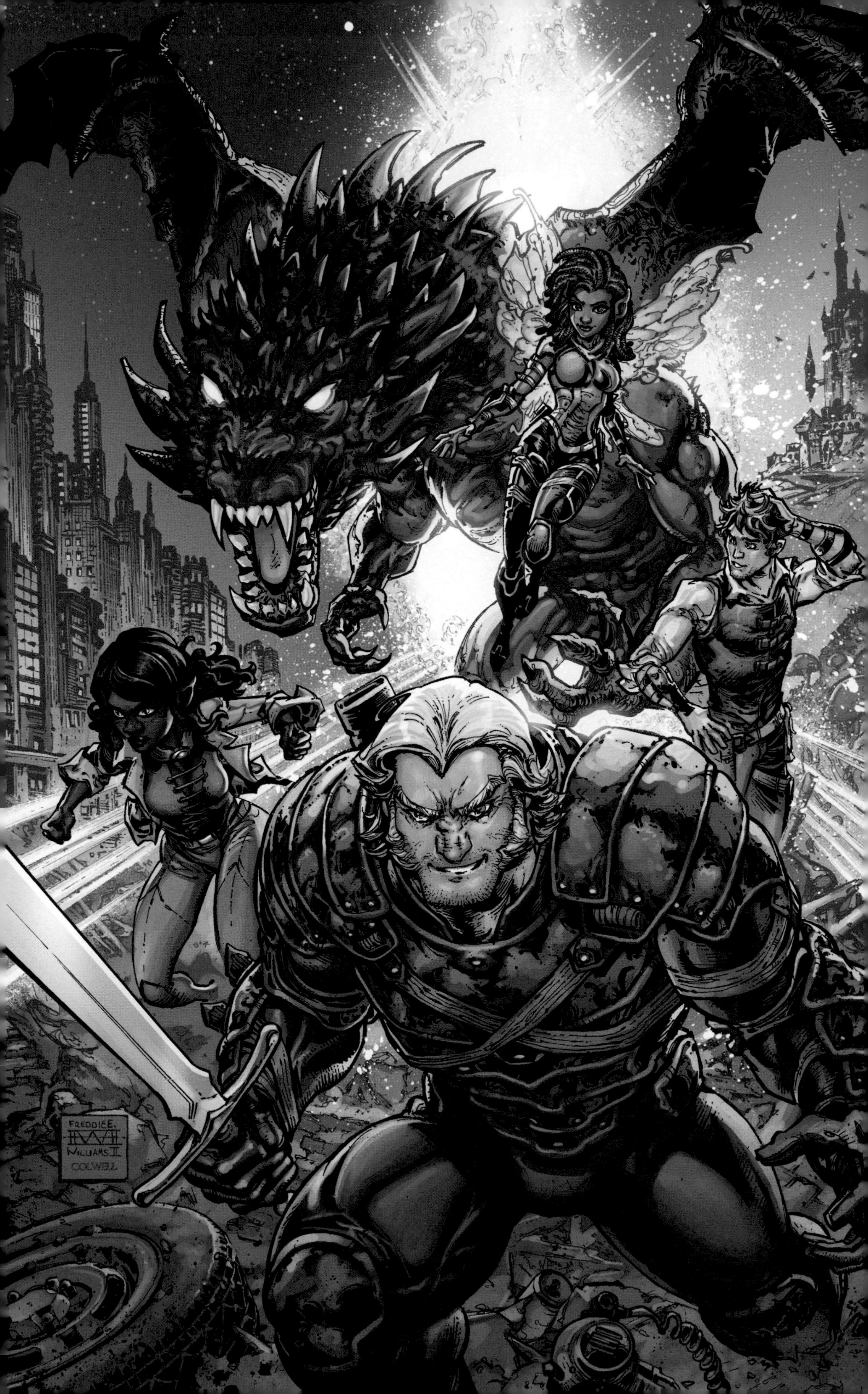
FREDDIE E.
WILLIAMS II
COLWELL

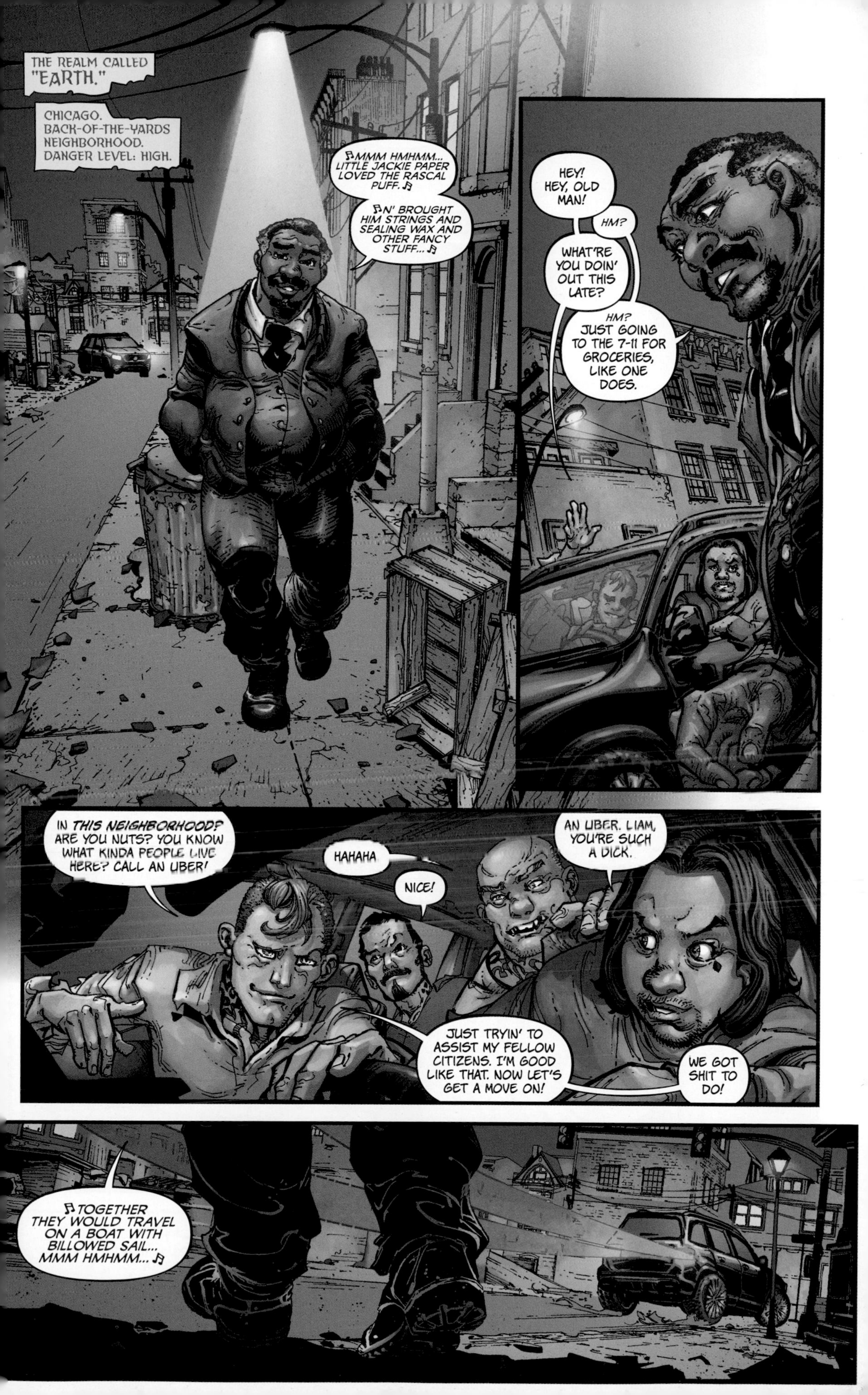
THE REALM CALLED "EARTH."
CHICAGO. BACK-OF-THE-YARDS NEIGHBORHOOD. DANGER LEVEL: HIGH.
♫MMM HMHMM... LITTLE JACKIE PAPER LOVED THE RASCAL PUFF.♫
♫N' BROUGHT HIM STRINGS AND SEALING WAX AND OTHER FANCY STUFF...♫
HEY! HEY, OLD MAN!
HM?
WHAT'RE YOU DOIN' OUT THIS LATE?
HM? JUST GOING TO THE 7-11 FOR GROCERIES, LIKE ONE DOES.
IN THIS NEIGHBORHOOD? ARE YOU NUTS? YOU KNOW WHAT KINDA PEOPLE LIVE HERE? CALL AN UBER!
HAHAHA
NICE!
AN UBER. LIAM, YOU'RE SUCH A DICK.
JUST TRYIN' TO ASSIST MY FELLOW CITIZENS. I'M GOOD LIKE THAT. NOW LET'S GET A MOVE ON!
WE GOT SHIT TO DO!
♫TOGETHER THEY WOULD TRAVEL ON A BOAT WITH BILLOWED SAIL... MMM HMHMM...♫

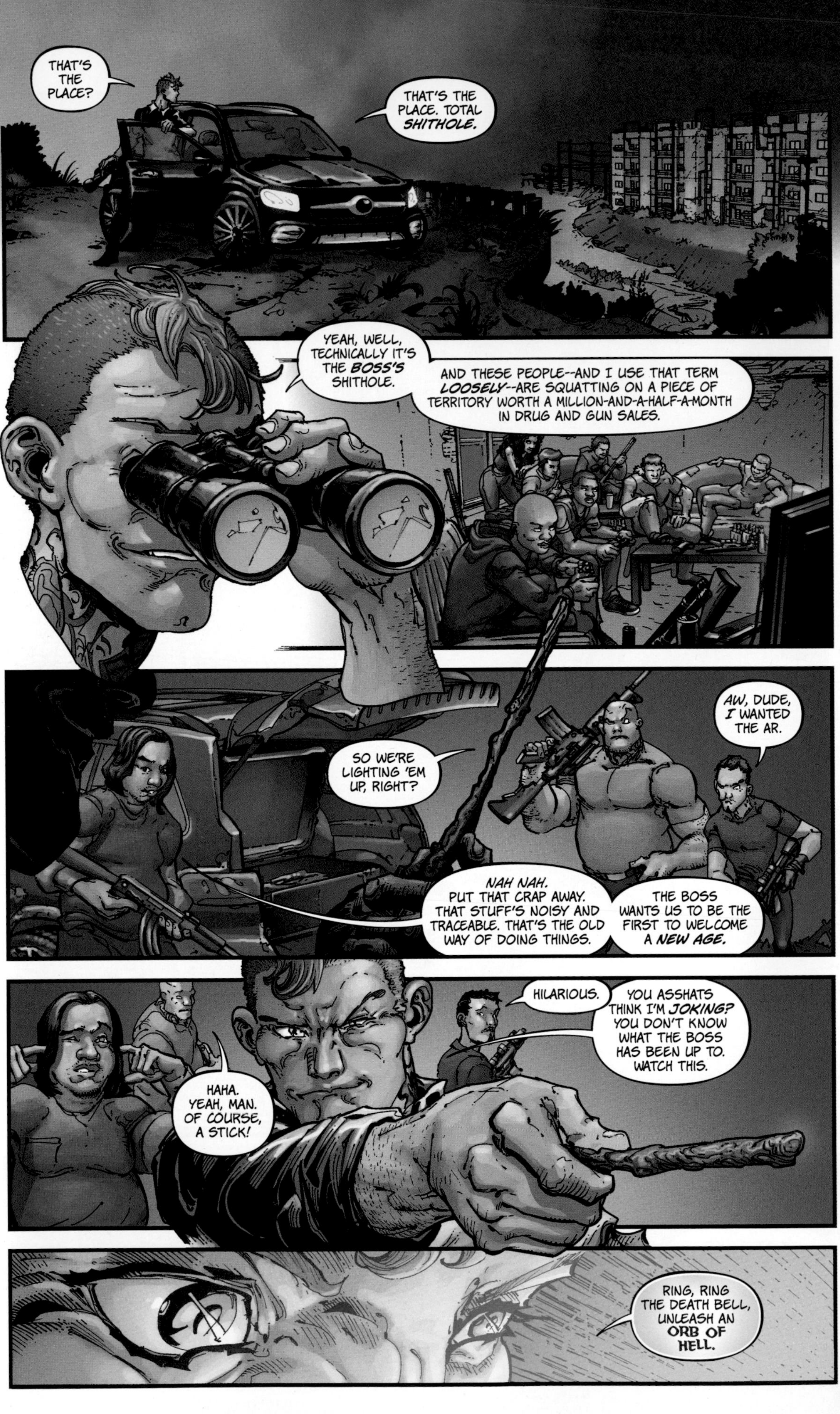

THAT'S THE PLACE?
THAT'S THE PLACE. TOTAL SHITHOLE.
YEAH, WELL, TECHNICALLY IT'S THE BOSS'S SHITHOLE.
AND THESE PEOPLE--AND I USE THAT TERM LOOSELY--ARE SQUATTING ON A PIECE OF TERRITORY WORTH A MILLION-AND-A-HALF-A-MONTH IN DRUG AND GUN SALES.
SO WE'RE LIGHTING 'EM UP, RIGHT?
AW, DUDE, I WANTED THE AR.
NAH NAH. PUT THAT CRAP AWAY. THAT STUFF'S NOISY AND TRACEABLE. THAT'S THE OLD WAY OF DOING THINGS.
THE BOSS WANTS US TO BE THE FIRST TO WELCOME A NEW AGE.
HAHA. YEAH, MAN. OF COURSE, A STICK!
HILARIOUS.
YOU ASSHATS THINK I'M JOKING? YOU DON'T KNOW WHAT THE BOSS HAS BEEN UP TO. WATCH THIS.
RING, RING THE DEATH BELL, UNLEASH AN ORB OF HELL.

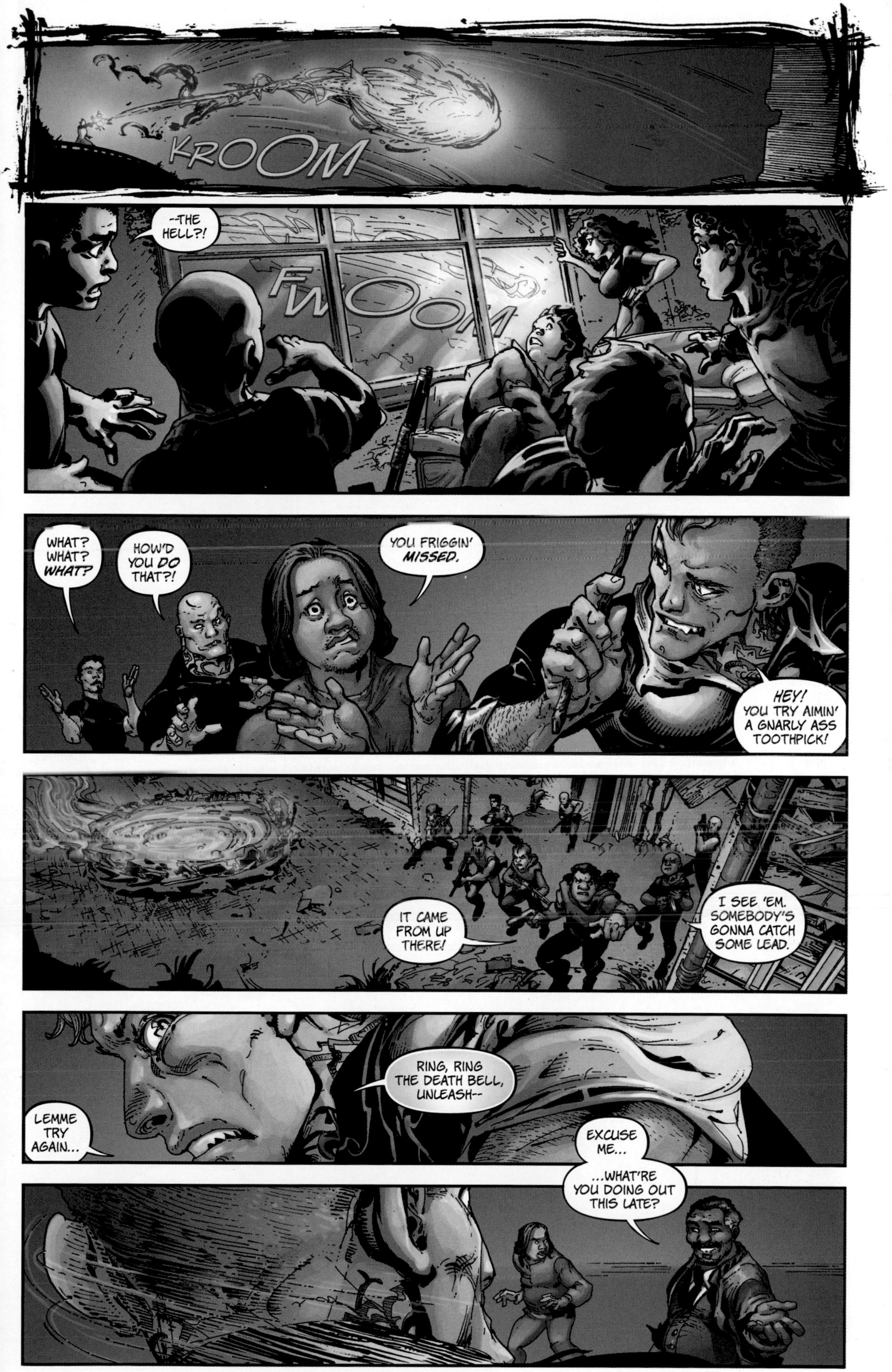
KROOM
--THE HELL?!
FWOOM
WHAT? WHAT? WHAT?
HOW'D YOU DO THAT?!
YOU FRIGGIN' MISSED.
HEY! YOU TRY AIMIN' A GNARLY ASS TOOTHPICK!
IT CAME FROM UP THERE!
I SEE 'EM. SOMEBODY'S GONNA CATCH SOME LEAD.
LEMME TRY AGAIN...
RING, RING THE DEATH BELL, UNLEASH--
EXCUSE ME...
...WHAT'RE YOU DOING OUT THIS LATE?

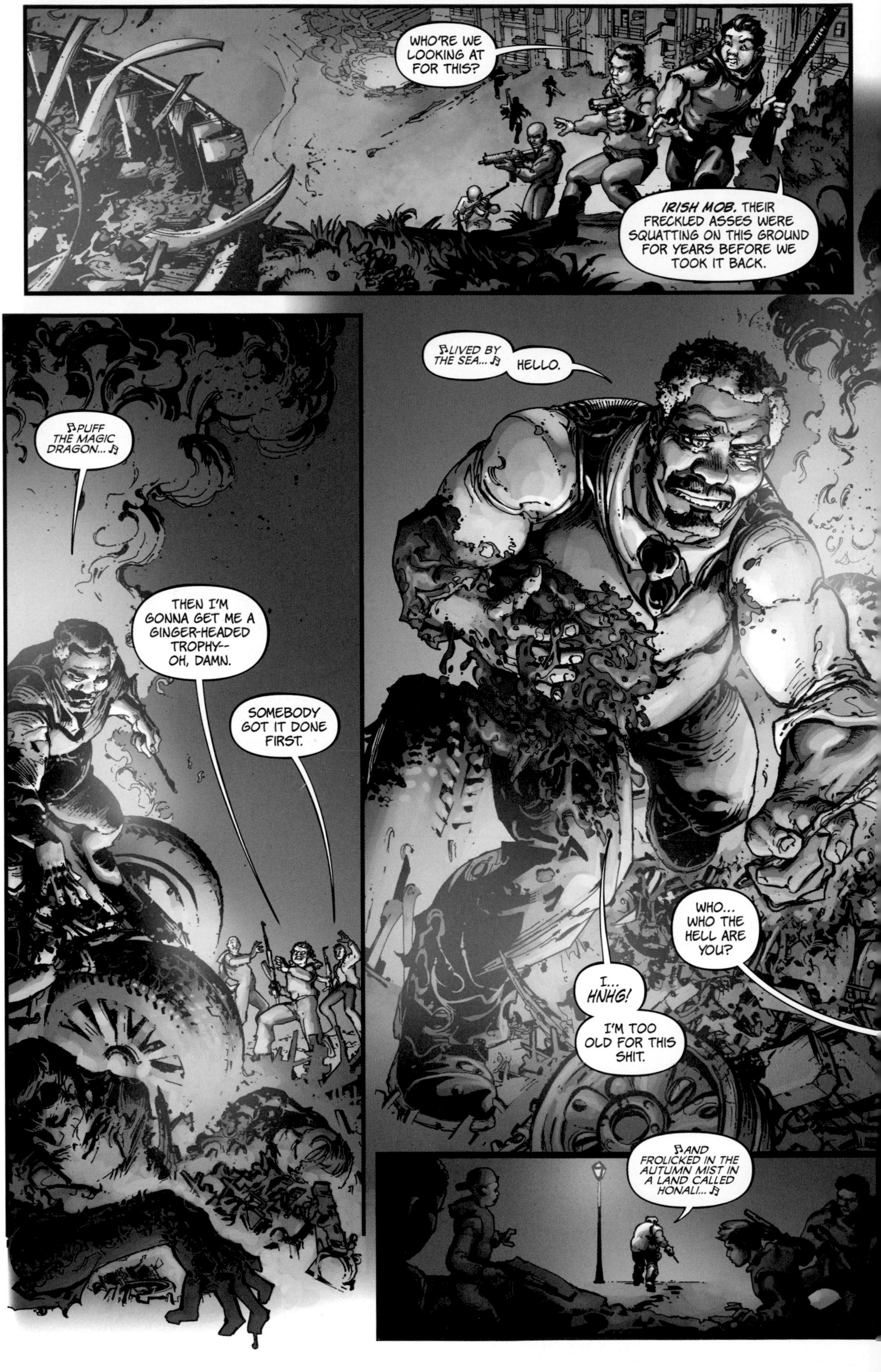
WHO'RE WE LOOKING AT FOR THIS?
IRISH MOB. THEIR FRECKLED ASSES WERE SQUATTING ON THIS GROUND FOR YEARS BEFORE WE TOOK IT BACK.
♫PUFF THE MAGIC DRAGON...♫
THEN I'M GONNA GET ME A GINGER-HEADED TROPHY-- OH, DAMN.
SOMEBODY GOT IT DONE FIRST.
♫LIVED BY THE SEA...♫
HELLO.
WHO... WHO THE HELL ARE YOU?
I... HNHG!
I'M TOO OLD FOR THIS SHIT.
♫AND FROLICKED IN THE AUTUMN MIST IN A LAND CALLED HONALI...♫

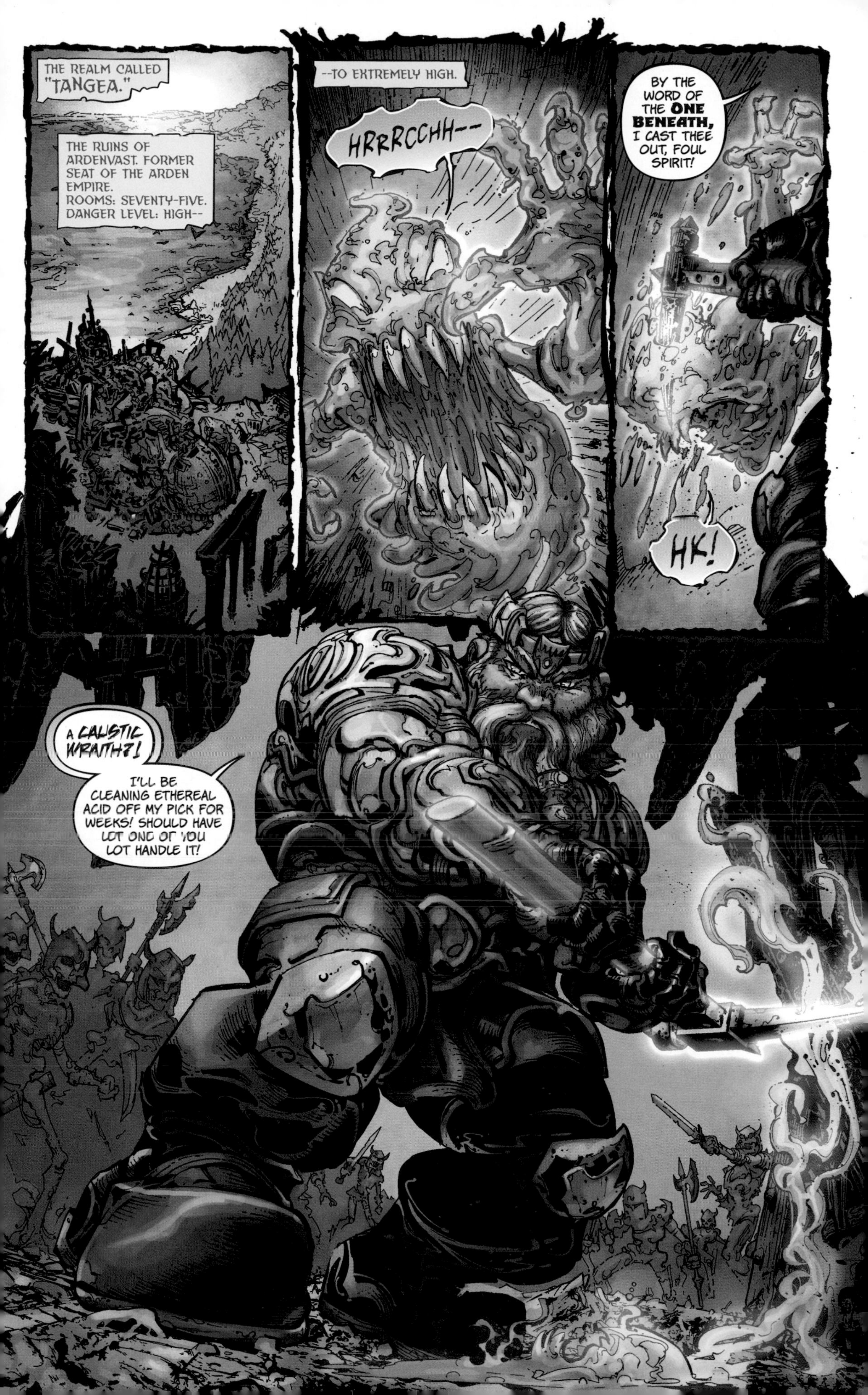
THE REALM CALLED "TANGEA."
THE RUINS OF ARDENVAST. FORMER SEAT OF THE ARDEN EMPIRE.
ROOMS: SEVENTY-FIVE.
DANGER LEVEL: HIGH--
--TO EXTREMELY HIGH.
HRRRCCHH--
BY THE WORD OF THE ONE BENEATH, I CAST THEE OUT, FOUL SPIRIT!
HK!
A CAUSTIC WRATH?!
I'LL BE CLEANING ETHEREAL ACID OFF MY PICK FOR WEEKS! SHOULD HAVE LET ONE OF YOU LOT HANDLE IT!

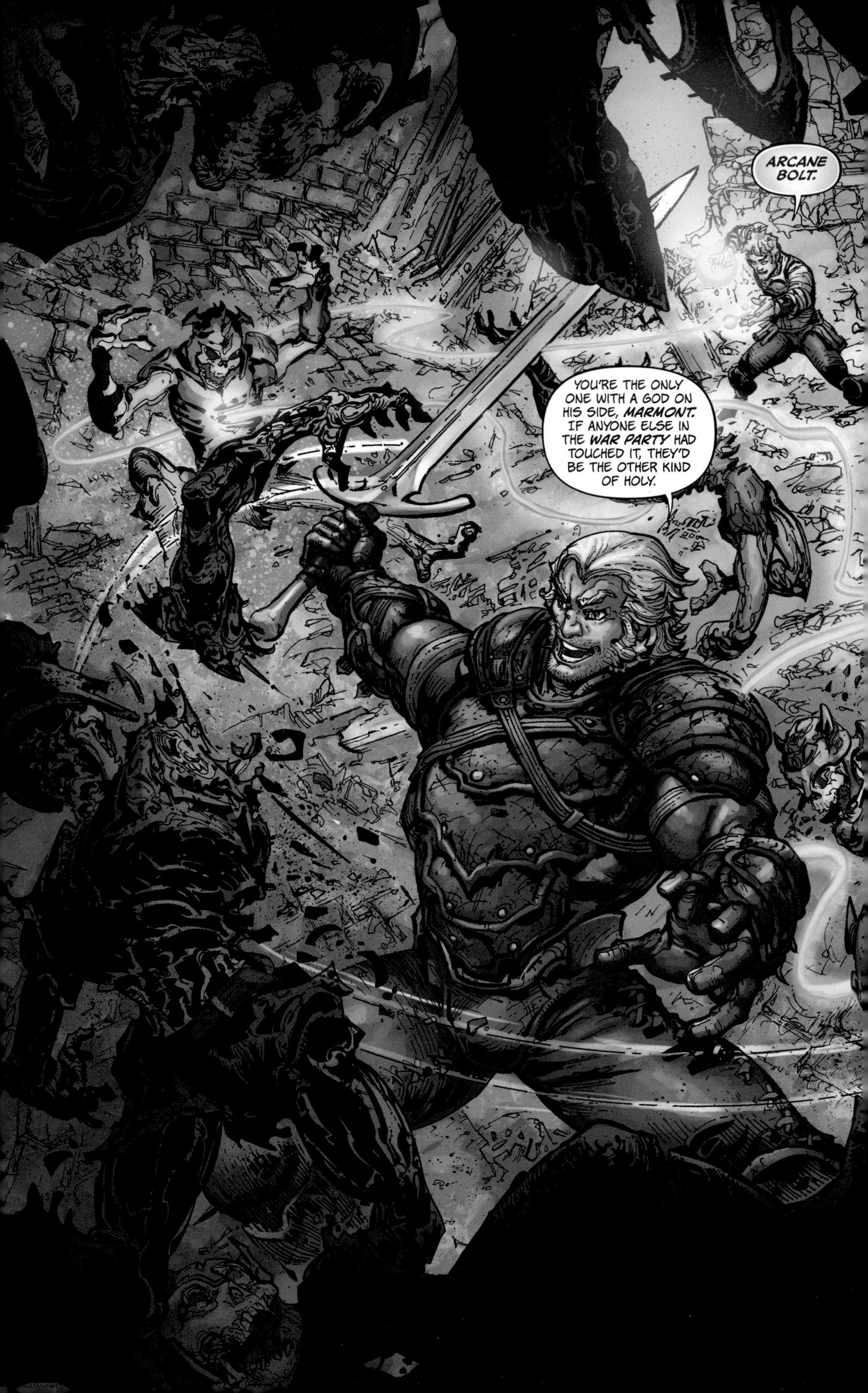
ARCANE BOLT.
YOU'RE THE ONLY ONE WITH A GOD ON HIS SIDE, MARMONT. IF ANYONE ELSE IN THE WAR PARTY HAD TOUCHED IT, THEY'D BE THE OTHER KIND OF HOLY.

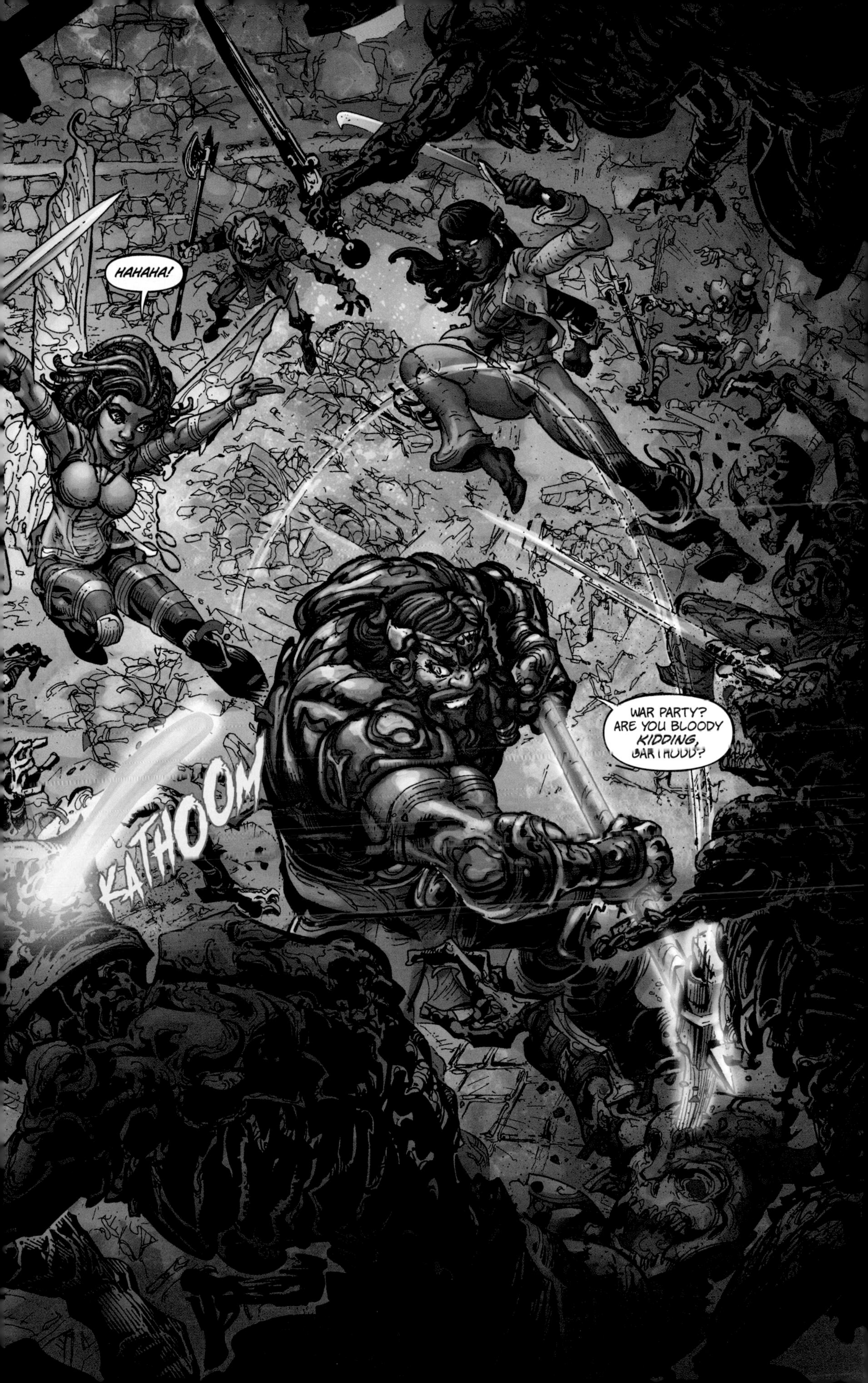
HAHAHA!
WAR PARTY? ARE YOU BLOODY *KIDDING,* BARTHOOD?
KATHOOM

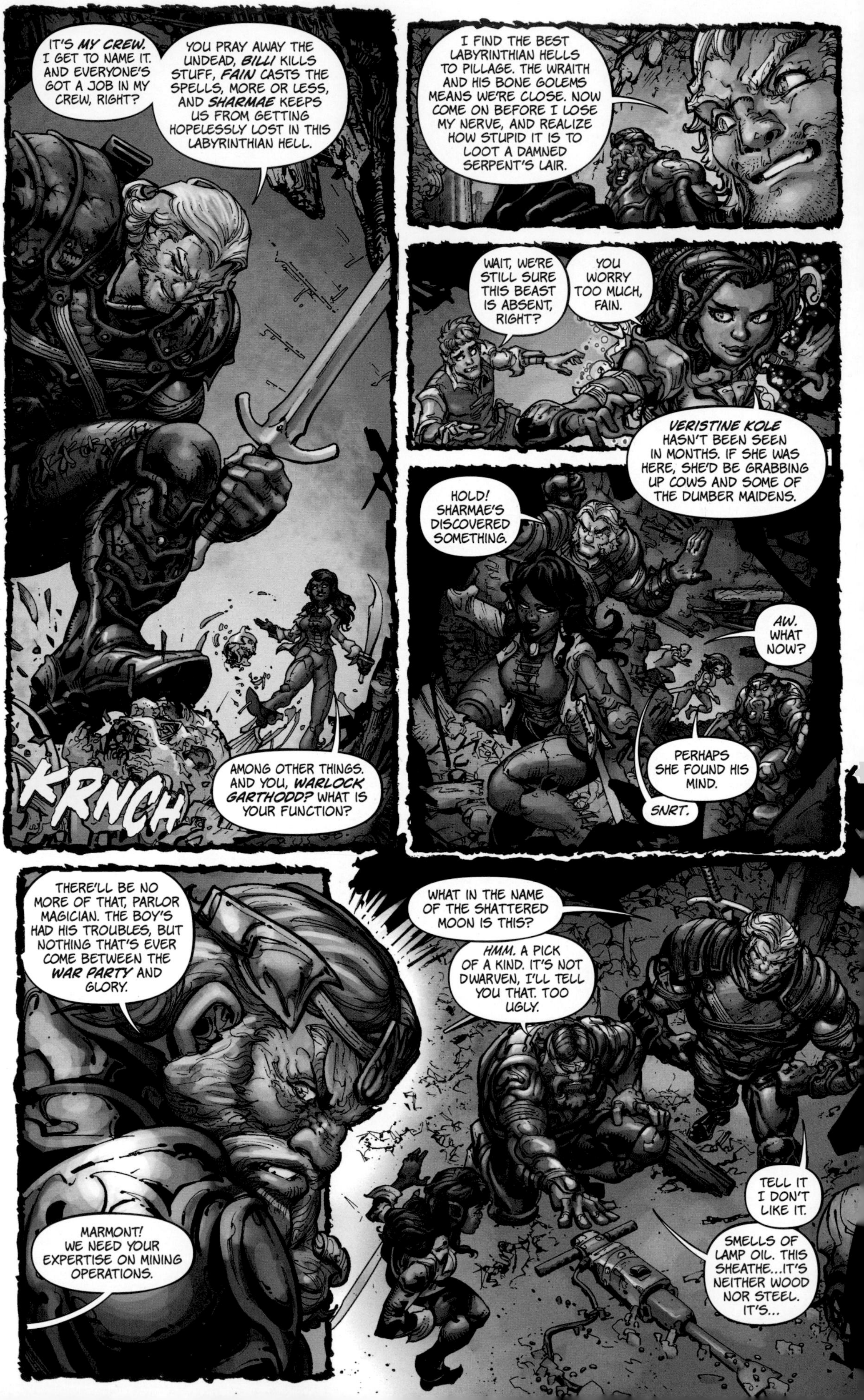
IT'S MY CREW. I GET TO NAME IT. AND EVERYONE'S GOT A JOB IN MY CREW, RIGHT?
YOU PRAY AWAY THE UNDEAD, BILLI KILLS STUFF, FAIN CASTS THE SPELLS, MORE OR LESS, AND SHARMAE KEEPS US FROM GETTING HOPELESSLY LOST IN THIS LABYRINTHIAN HELL.
KRNCH
AMONG OTHER THINGS. AND YOU, WARLOCK GARTHODD? WHAT IS YOUR FUNCTION?
I FIND THE BEST LABYRINTHIAN HELLS TO PILLAGE. THE WRAITH AND HIS BONE GOLEMS MEANS WE'RE CLOSE. NOW COME ON BEFORE I LOSE MY NERVE, AND REALIZE HOW STUPID IT IS TO LOOT A DAMNED SERPENT'S LAIR.
WAIT, WE'RE STILL SURE THIS BEAST IS ABSENT, RIGHT?
YOU WORRY TOO MUCH, FAIN.
VERISTINE KOLE HASN'T BEEN SEEN IN MONTHS. IF SHE WAS HERE, SHE'D BE GRABBING UP COWS AND SOME OF THE DUMBER MAIDENS.
HOLD! SHARMAE'S DISCOVERED SOMETHING.
AW. WHAT NOW?
PERHAPS SHE FOUND HIS MIND.
SNRT.
THERE'LL BE NO MORE OF THAT, PARLOR MAGICIAN. THE BOY'S HAD HIS TROUBLES, BUT NOTHING THAT'S EVER COME BETWEEN THE WAR PARTY AND GLORY.
MARMONT! WE NEED YOUR EXPERTISE ON MINING OPERATIONS.
WHAT IN THE NAME OF THE SHATTERED MOON IS THIS?
HMM. A PICK OF A KIND. IT'S NOT DWARVEN, I'LL TELL YOU THAT. TOO UGLY.
TELL IT I DON'T LIKE IT.
SMELLS OF LAMP OIL. THIS SHEATHE...IT'S NEITHER WOOD NOR STEEL. IT'S...

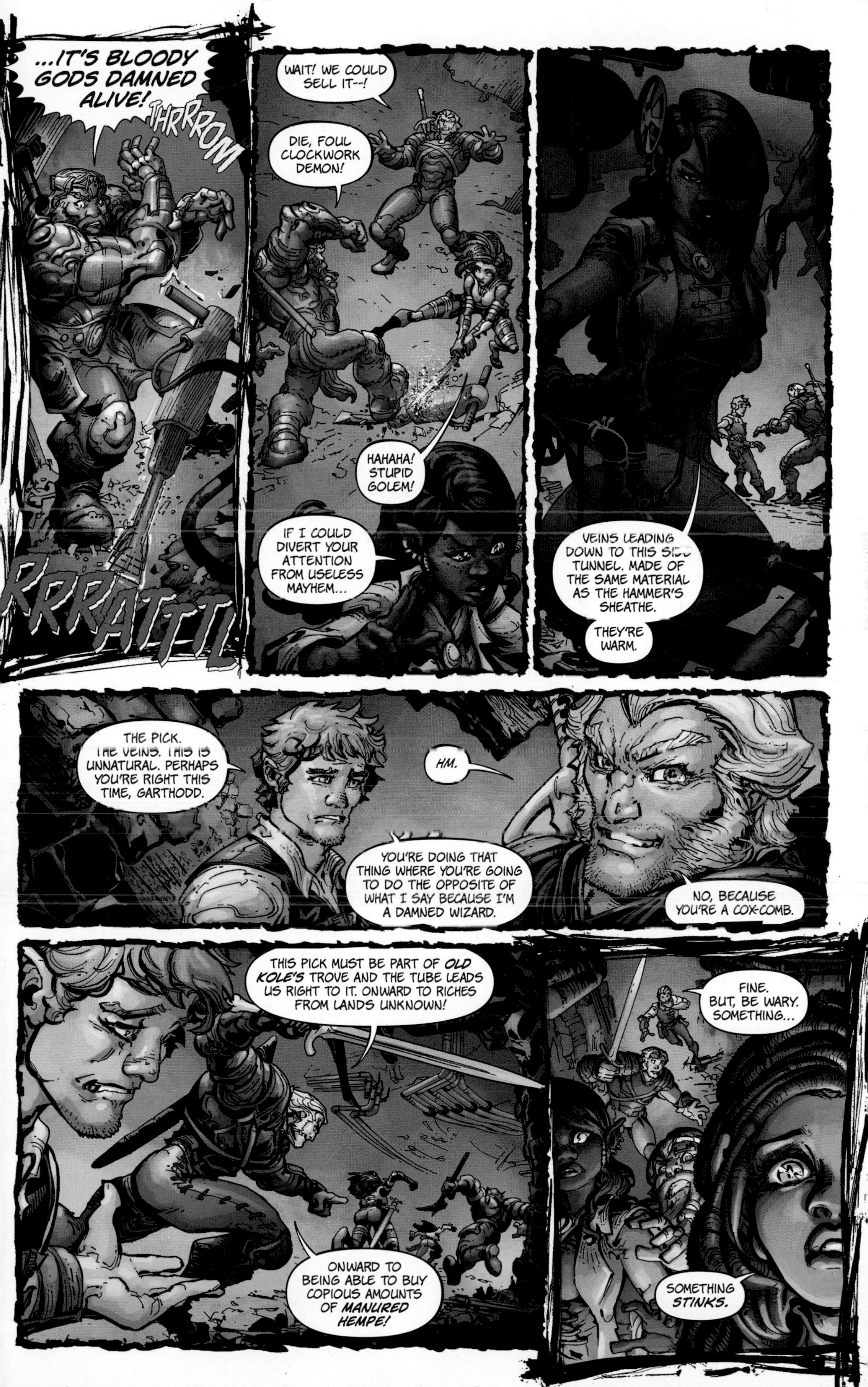
...IT'S BLOODY GODS DAMNED ALIVE!
THRRROM
RRRATTTL
WAIT! WE COULD SELL IT--!
DIE, FOUL CLOCKWORK DEMON!
HAHAHA! STUPID GOLEM!
IF I COULD DIVERT YOUR ATTENTION FROM USELESS MAYHEM...
VEINS LEADING DOWN TO THIS SIDE TUNNEL. MADE OF THE SAME MATERIAL AS THE HAMMER'S SHEATHE.
THEY'RE WARM.
THE PICK. THE VEINS. THIS IS UNNATURAL. PERHAPS YOU'RE RIGHT THIS TIME, GARTHODD.
HM.
YOU'RE DOING THAT THING WHERE YOU'RE GOING TO DO THE OPPOSITE OF WHAT I SAY BECAUSE I'M A DAMNED WIZARD.
NO, BECAUSE YOU'RE A COX-COMB.
THIS PICK MUST BE PART OF *OLD KOLE'S* TROVE AND THE TUBE LEADS US RIGHT TO IT. ONWARD TO RICHES FROM LANDS UNKNOWN!
ONWARD TO BEING ABLE TO BUY COPIOUS AMOUNTS OF ***MANURED HEMPE!***
FINE. BUT, BE WARY. SOMETHING...
SOMETHING *STINKS.*

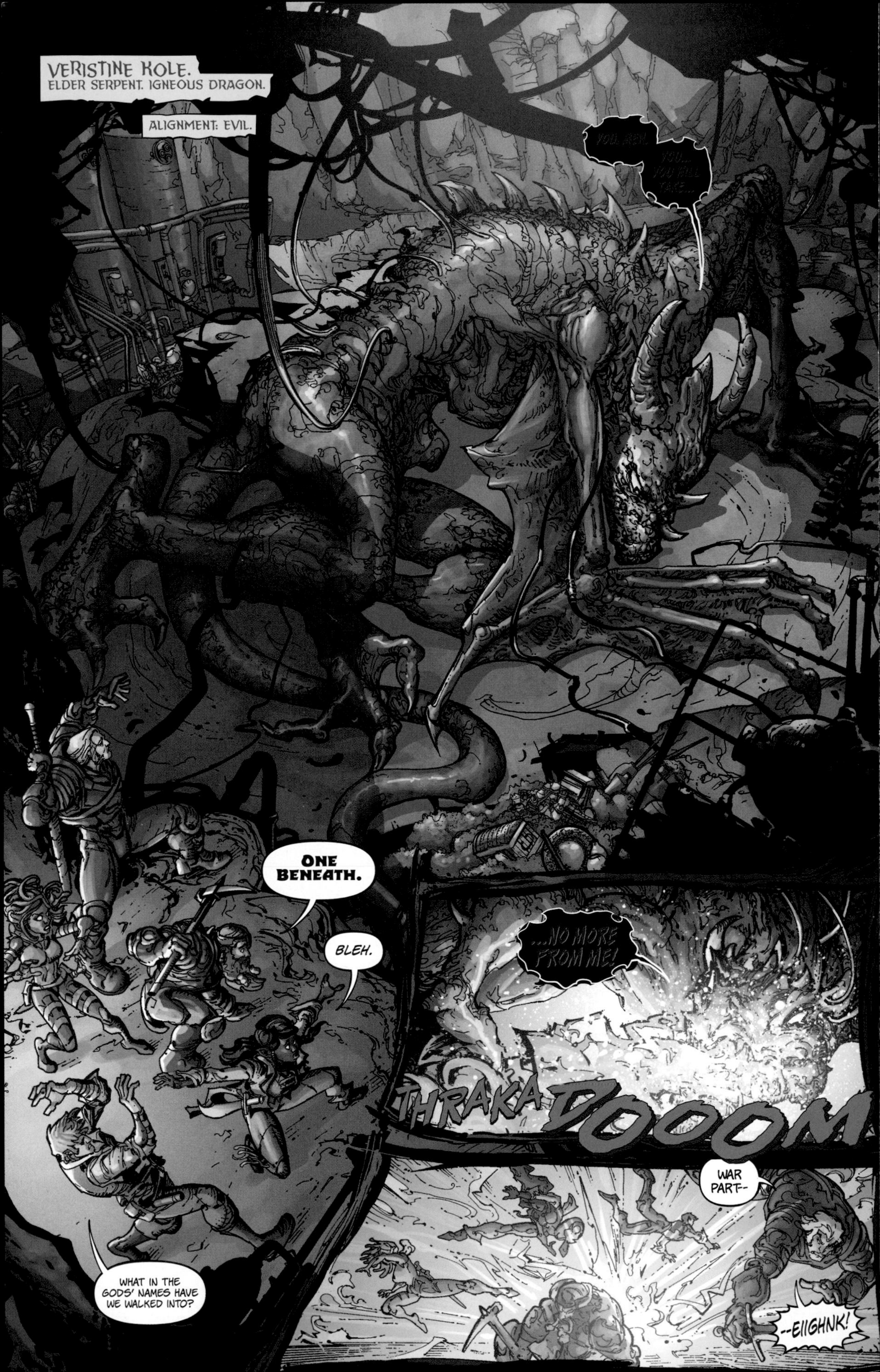
VERISTINE KOLE.
ELDER SERPENT. IGNEOUS DRAGON.
ALIGNMENT: EVIL.
YOU. KEN.
YOU... YOU WILL TAKE...
ONE BENEATH.
BLEH.
WHAT IN THE GODS' NAMES HAVE WE WALKED INTO?
...NO MORE FROM ME!
THRAKADOOOOM
WAR PART-
--EIIGHNK!

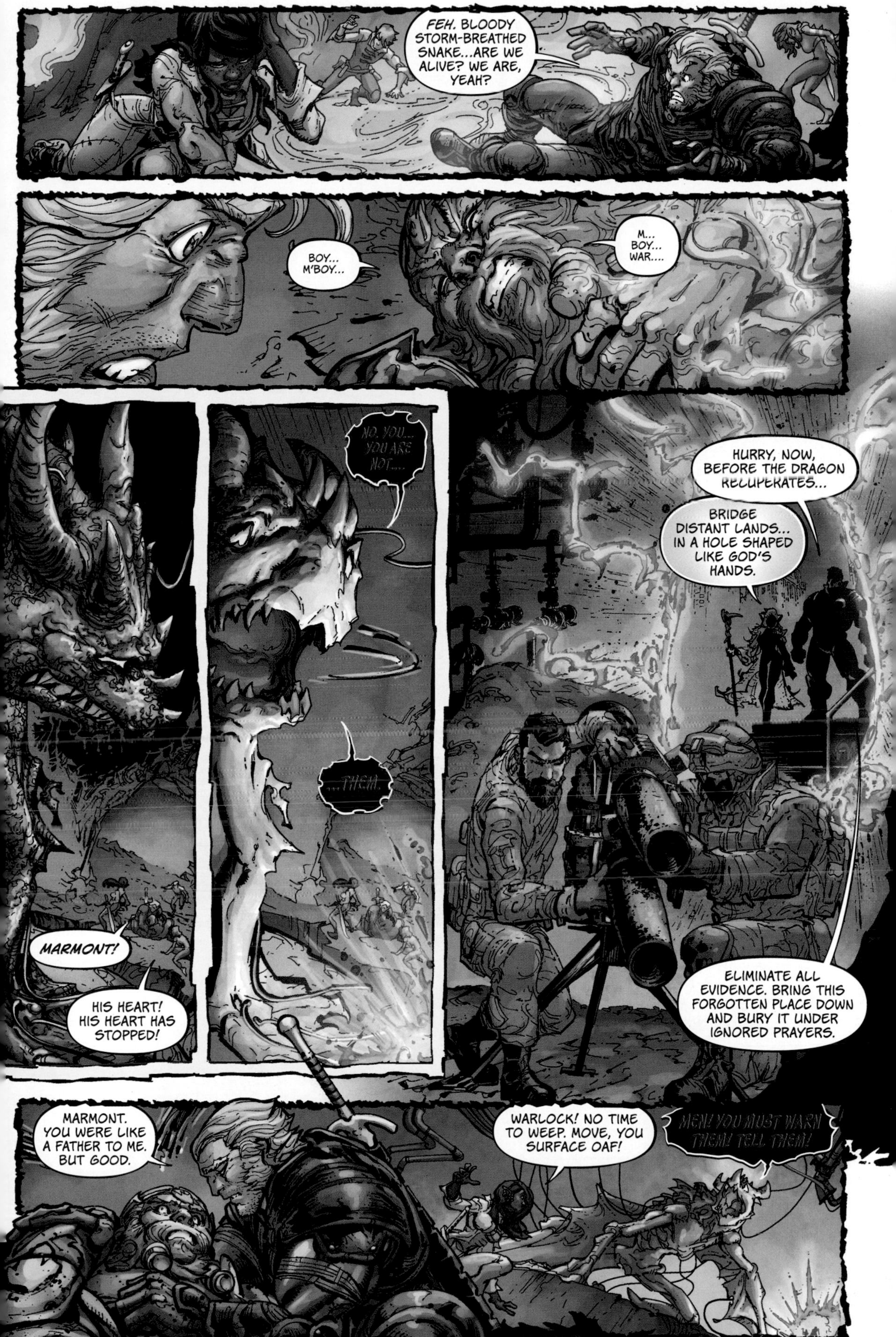
FEH. BLOODY STORM-BREATHED SNAKE...ARE WE ALIVE? WE ARE, YEAH?
BOY... M'BOY...
M... BOY... WAR....
NO. YOU... YOU ARE NOT....
...THEM.
MARMONT!
HIS HEART! HIS HEART HAS STOPPED!
HURRY, NOW, BEFORE THE DRAGON RECUPERATES...
BRIDGE DISTANT LANDS... IN A HOLE SHAPED LIKE GOD'S HANDS.
ELIMINATE ALL EVIDENCE. BRING THIS FORGOTTEN PLACE DOWN AND BURY IT UNDER IGNORED PRAYERS.
MARMONT. YOU WERE LIKE A FATHER TO ME. BUT GOOD.
WARLOCK! NO TIME TO WEEP. MOVE, YOU SURFACE OAF!
MEN! YOU MUST WARN THEM! TELL THEM!

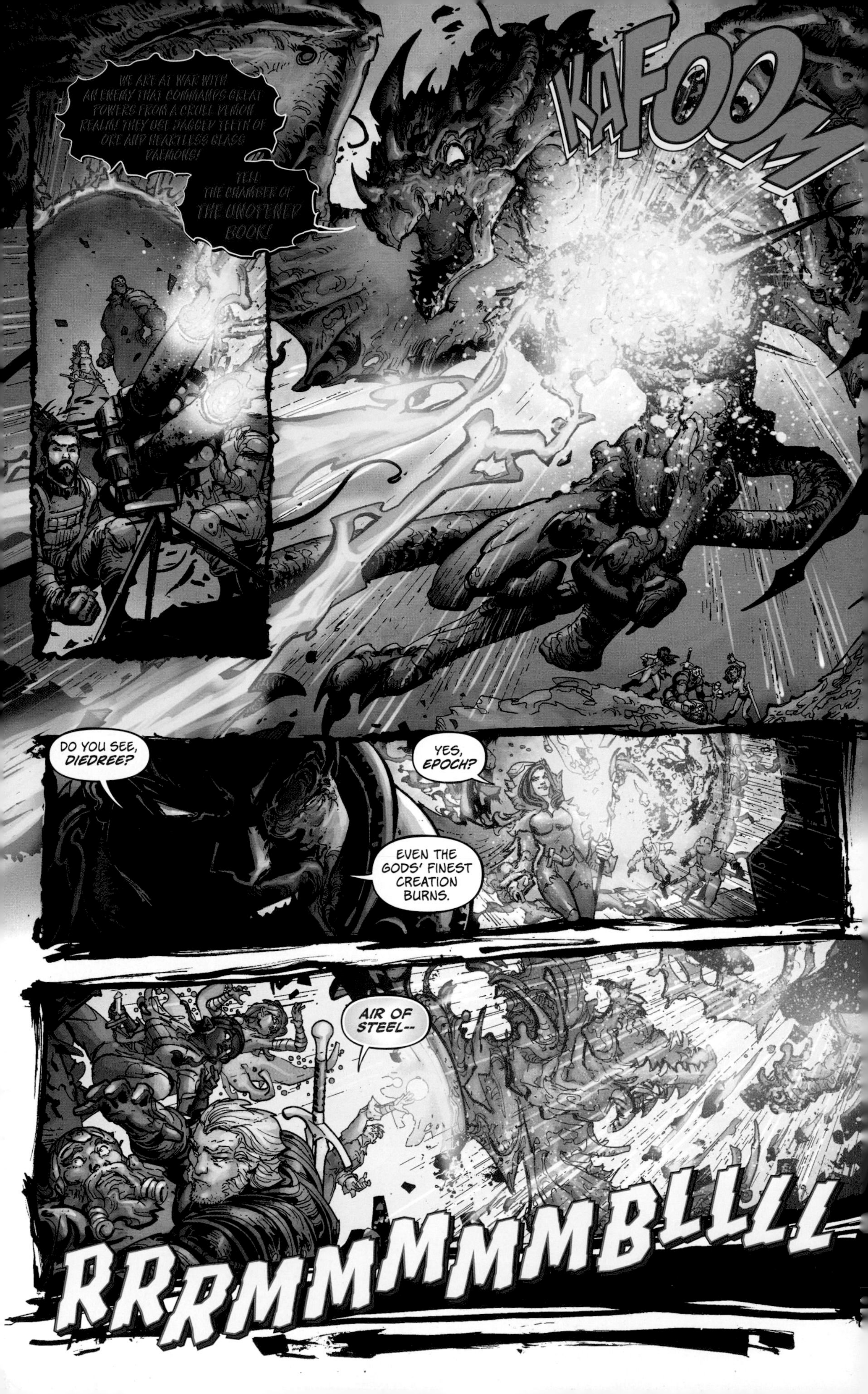
WE ARE AT WAR WITH AN ENEMY THAT COMMANDS GREAT POWERS FROM A CRUEL DEMON REALM! THEY USE JAGGED TEETH OF ORE AND HEARTLESS GLASS DAEMONS!
TELL THE CHAMBER OF THE UNOPENED BOOK!
KAFOOM
DO YOU SEE, DIEDREE?
YES, EPOCH?
EVEN THE GODS' FINEST CREATION BURNS.
AIR OF STEEL--
RRRMMMMMMBLLLL

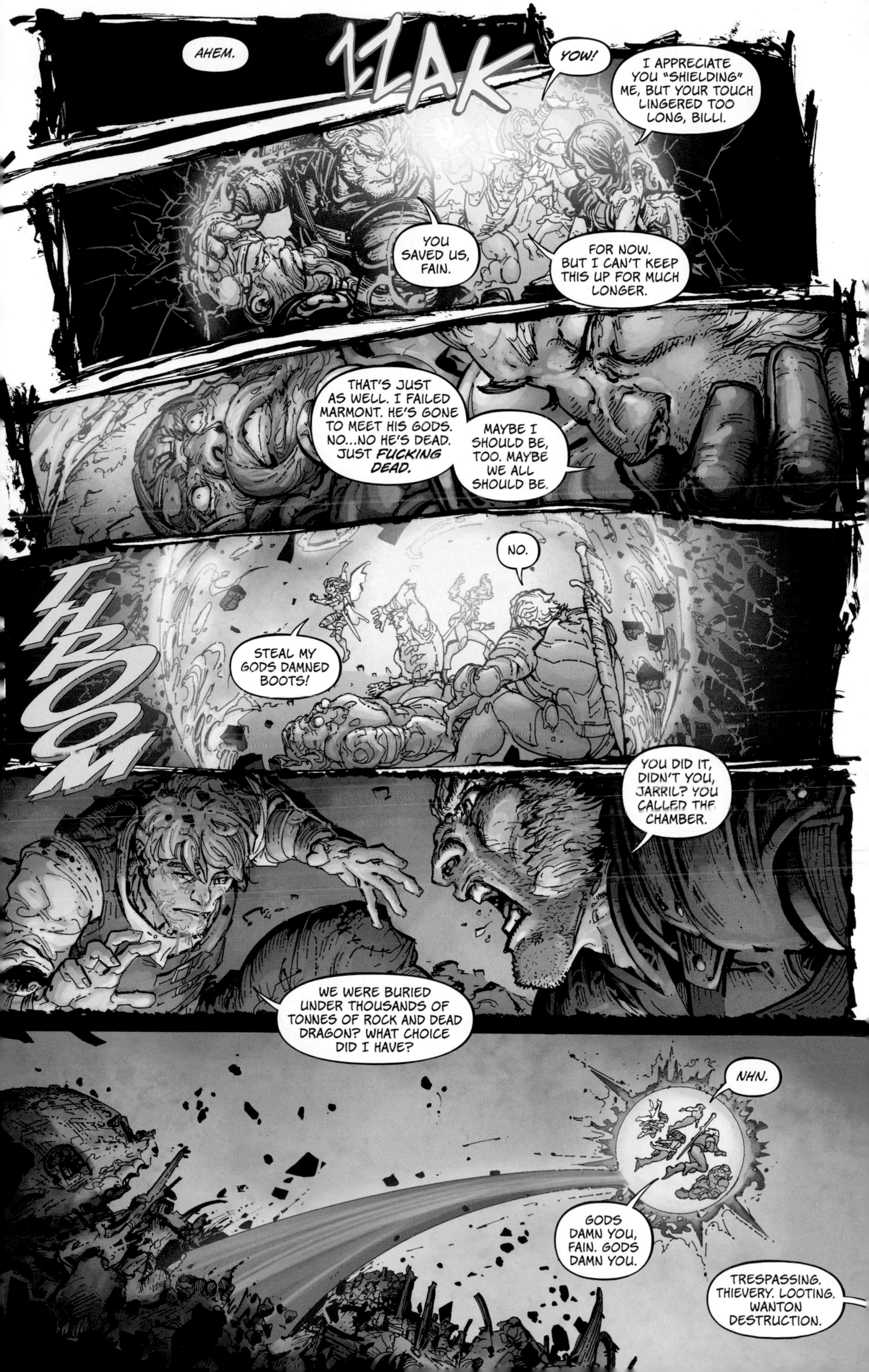
AHEM.
ZZAK
YOW!
I APPRECIATE YOU "SHIELDING" ME, BUT YOUR TOUCH LINGERED TOO LONG, BILLI.
YOU SAVED US, FAIN.
FOR NOW. BUT I CAN'T KEEP THIS UP FOR MUCH LONGER.
THAT'S JUST AS WELL. I FAILED MARMONT. HE'S GONE TO MEET HIS GODS. NO...NO HE'S DEAD. JUST FUCKING DEAD.
MAYBE I SHOULD BE, TOO. MAYBE WE ALL SHOULD BE.
THROOM
NO.
STEAL MY GODS DAMNED BOOTS!
YOU DID IT, DIDN'T YOU, JARRIL? YOU CALLED THE CHAMBER.
WE WERE BURIED UNDER THOUSANDS OF TONNES OF ROCK AND DEAD DRAGON? WHAT CHOICE DID I HAVE?
NHN.
GODS DAMN YOU, FAIN. GODS DAMN YOU.
TRESPASSING. THIEVERY. LOOTING. WANTON DESTRUCTION.

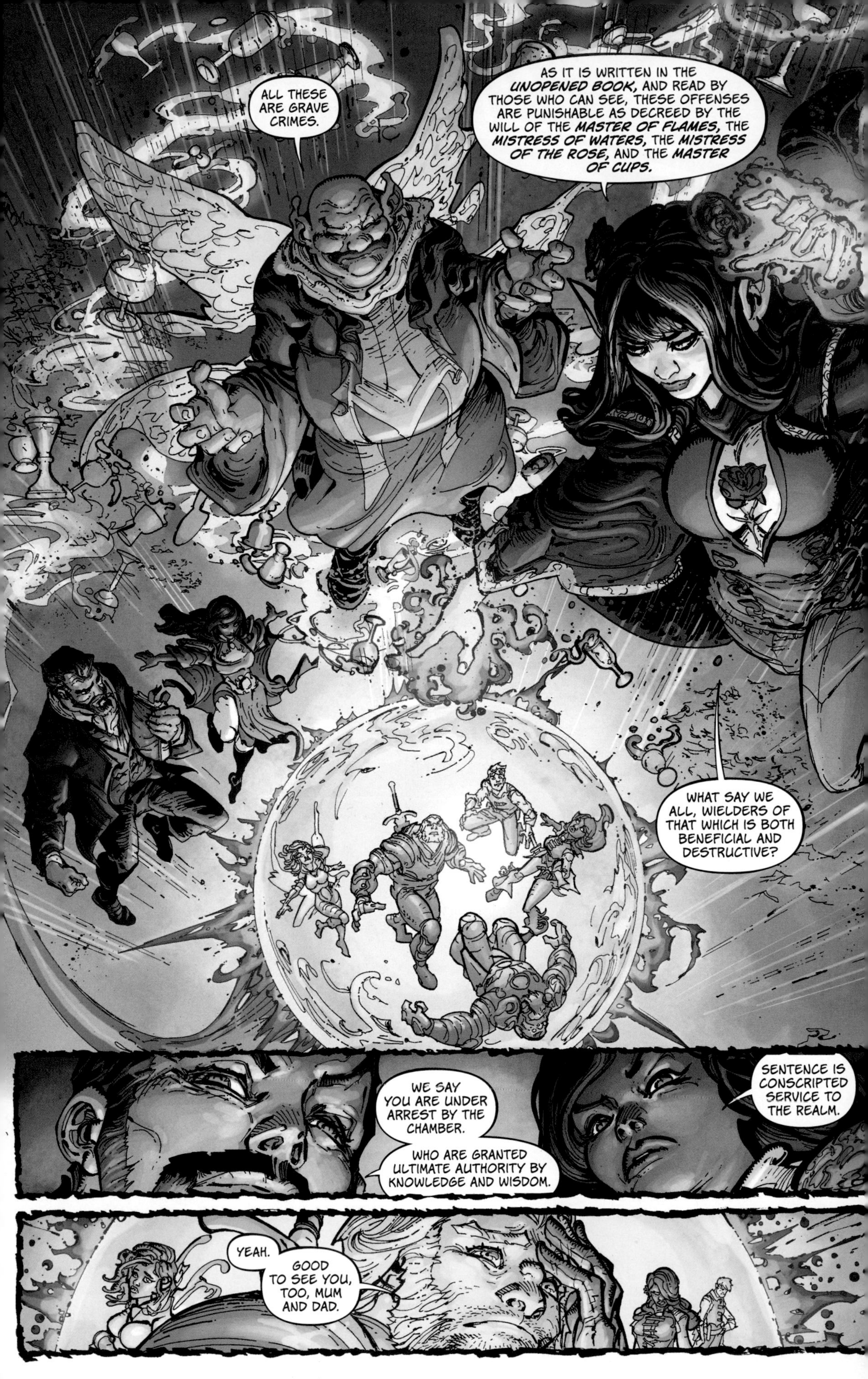
ALL THESE ARE GRAVE CRIMES.
AS IT IS WRITTEN IN THE UNOPENED BOOK, AND READ BY THOSE WHO CAN SEE, THESE OFFENSES ARE PUNISHABLE AS DECREED BY THE WILL OF THE MASTER OF FLAMES, THE MISTRESS OF WATERS, THE MISTRESS OF THE ROSE, AND THE MASTER OF CUPS.
WHAT SAY WE ALL, WIELDERS OF THAT WHICH IS BOTH BENEFICIAL AND DESTRUCTIVE?
WE SAY YOU ARE UNDER ARREST BY THE CHAMBER.
WHO ARE GRANTED ULTIMATE AUTHORITY BY KNOWLEDGE AND WISDOM.
SENTENCE IS CONSCRIPTED SERVICE TO THE REALM.
YEAH.
GOOD TO SEE YOU, TOO, MUM AND DAD.

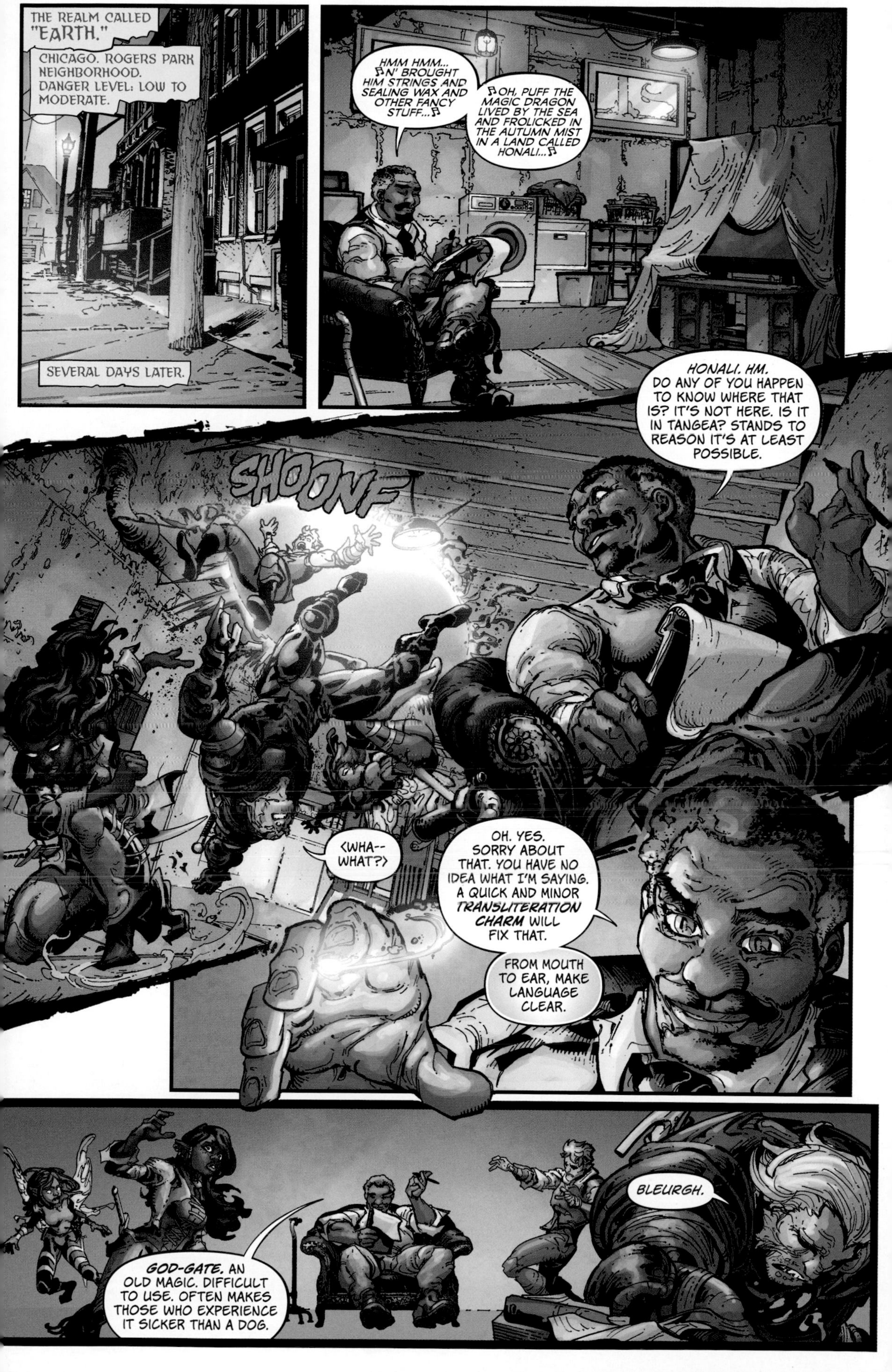
THE REALM CALLED "EARTH."
CHICAGO. ROGERS PARK NEIGHBORHOOD. DANGER LEVEL: LOW TO MODERATE.
SEVERAL DAYS LATER.
HMM HMM... ♫N' BROUGHT HIM STRINGS AND SEALING WAX AND OTHER FANCY STUFF...♫
♫OH, PUFF THE MAGIC DRAGON LIVED BY THE SEA AND FROLICKED IN THE AUTUMN MIST IN A LAND CALLED HONALI...♫
HONALI. HM. DO ANY OF YOU HAPPEN TO KNOW WHERE THAT IS? IT'S NOT HERE. IS IT IN TANGEA? STANDS TO REASON IT'S AT LEAST POSSIBLE.
SHOONF
<WHA-- WHAT?>
OH. YES. SORRY ABOUT THAT. YOU HAVE NO IDEA WHAT I'M SAYING. A QUICK AND MINOR TRANSLITERATION CHARM WILL FIX THAT.
FROM MOUTH TO EAR, MAKE LANGUAGE CLEAR.
GOD-GATE. AN OLD MAGIC. DIFFICULT TO USE. OFTEN MAKES THOSE WHO EXPERIENCE IT SICKER THAN A DOG.
BLEURGH.

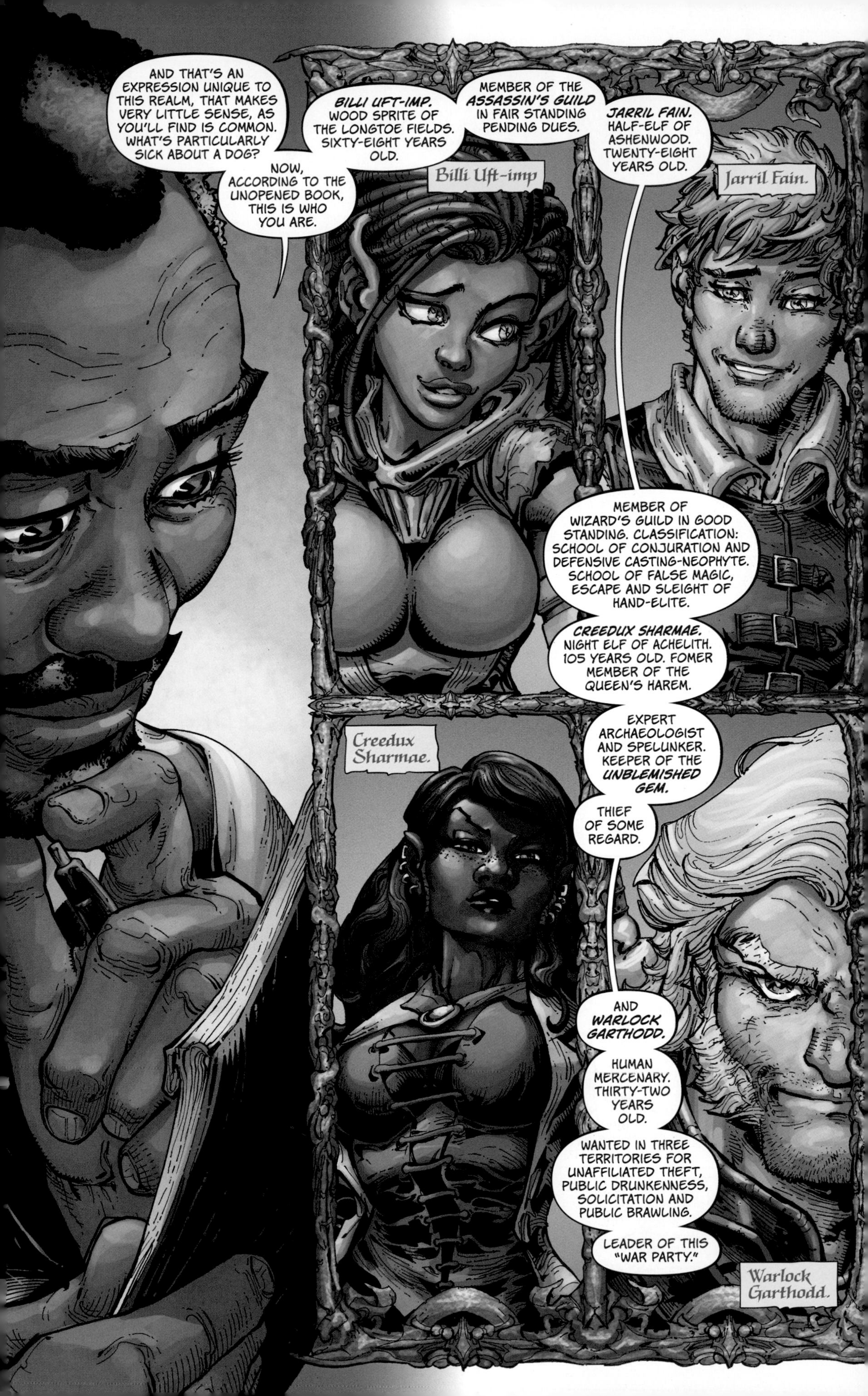

AND THAT'S AN EXPRESSION UNIQUE TO THIS REALM, THAT MAKES VERY LITTLE SENSE, AS YOU'LL FIND IS COMMON. WHAT'S PARTICULARLY SICK ABOUT A DOG?
NOW, ACCORDING TO THE UNOPENED BOOK, THIS IS WHO YOU ARE.
BILLI UFT-IMP. WOOD SPRITE OF THE LONGTOE FIELDS. SIXTY-EIGHT YEARS OLD.
MEMBER OF THE ASSASSIN'S GUILD IN FAIR STANDING PENDING DUES.
Billi Uft-imp
JARRIL FAIN. HALF-ELF OF ASHENWOOD. TWENTY-EIGHT YEARS OLD.
Jarril Fain.
MEMBER OF WIZARD'S GUILD IN GOOD STANDING. CLASSIFICATION: SCHOOL OF CONJURATION AND DEFENSIVE CASTING-NEOPHYTE. SCHOOL OF FALSE MAGIC, ESCAPE AND SLEIGHT OF HAND-ELITE.
CREEDUX SHARMAE. NIGHT ELF OF ACHELITH. 105 YEARS OLD. FOMER MEMBER OF THE QUEEN'S HAREM.
Creedux Sharmae.
EXPERT ARCHAEOLOGIST AND SPELUNKER. KEEPER OF THE UNBLEMISHED GEM.
THIEF OF SOME REGARD.
AND WARLOCK GARTHODD.
HUMAN MERCENARY. THIRTY-TWO YEARS OLD.
WANTED IN THREE TERRITORIES FOR UNAFFILIATED THEFT, PUBLIC DRUNKENNESS, SOLICITATION AND PUBLIC BRAWLING.
LEADER OF THIS "WAR PARTY."
Warlock Garthodd.

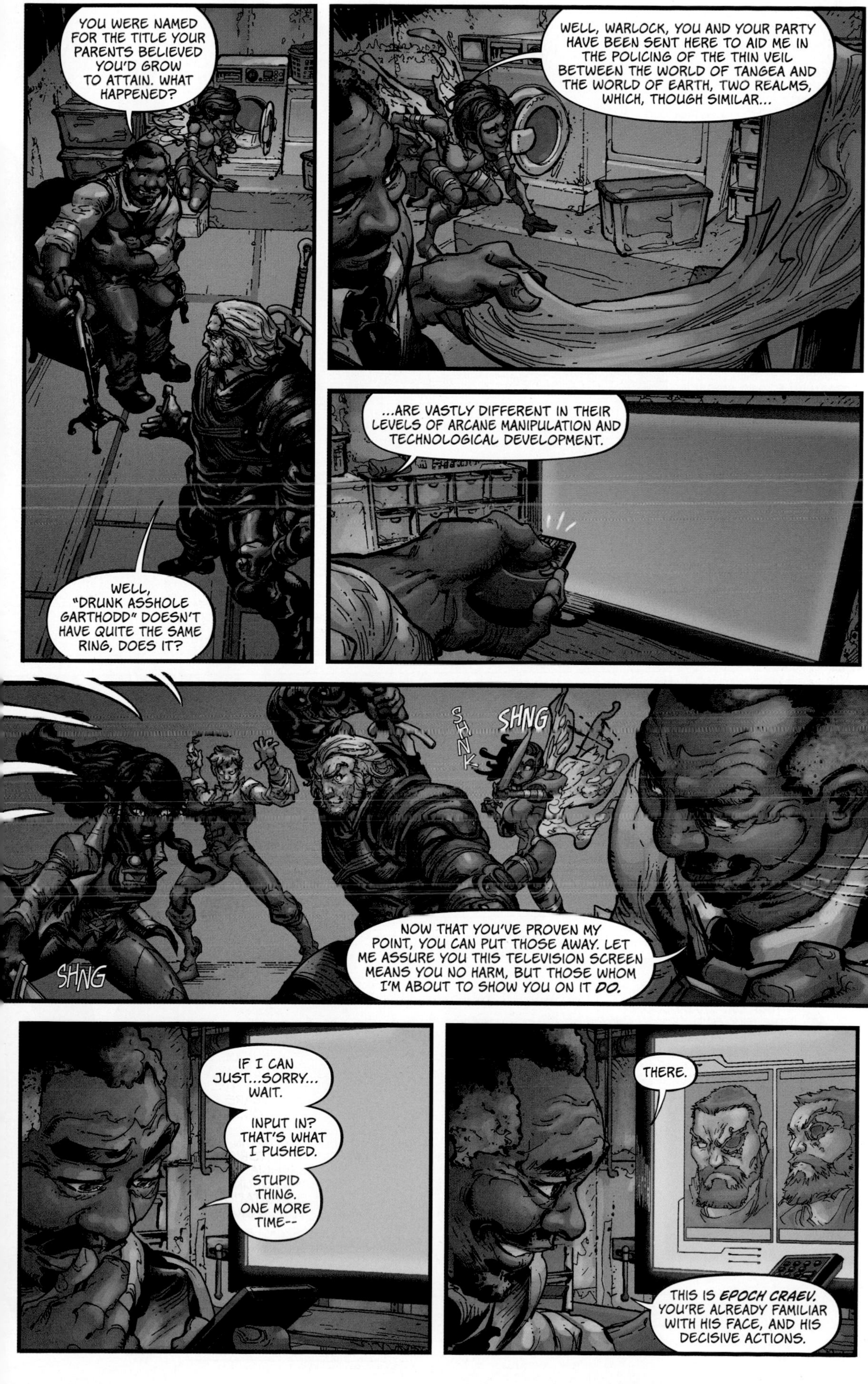
YOU WERE NAMED FOR THE TITLE YOUR PARENTS BELIEVED YOU'D GROW TO ATTAIN. WHAT HAPPENED?
WELL, "DRUNK ASSHOLE GARTHODD" DOESN'T HAVE QUITE THE SAME RING, DOES IT?
WELL, WARLOCK, YOU AND YOUR PARTY HAVE BEEN SENT HERE TO AID ME IN THE POLICING OF THE THIN VEIL BETWEEN THE WORLD OF TANGEA AND THE WORLD OF EARTH, TWO REALMS, WHICH, THOUGH SIMILAR...
...ARE VASTLY DIFFERENT IN THEIR LEVELS OF ARCANE MANIPULATION AND TECHNOLOGICAL DEVELOPMENT.
SHNK
SHNG
SHNG
NOW THAT YOU'VE PROVEN MY POINT, YOU CAN PUT THOSE AWAY. LET ME ASSURE YOU THIS TELEVISION SCREEN MEANS YOU NO HARM, BUT THOSE WHOM I'M ABOUT TO SHOW YOU ON IT DO.
IF I CAN JUST...SORRY... WAIT.
INPUT IN? THAT'S WHAT I PUSHED.
STUPID THING. ONE MORE TIME--
THERE.
THIS IS EPOCH CRAEV. YOU'RE ALREADY FAMILIAR WITH HIS FACE, AND HIS DECISIVE ACTIONS.

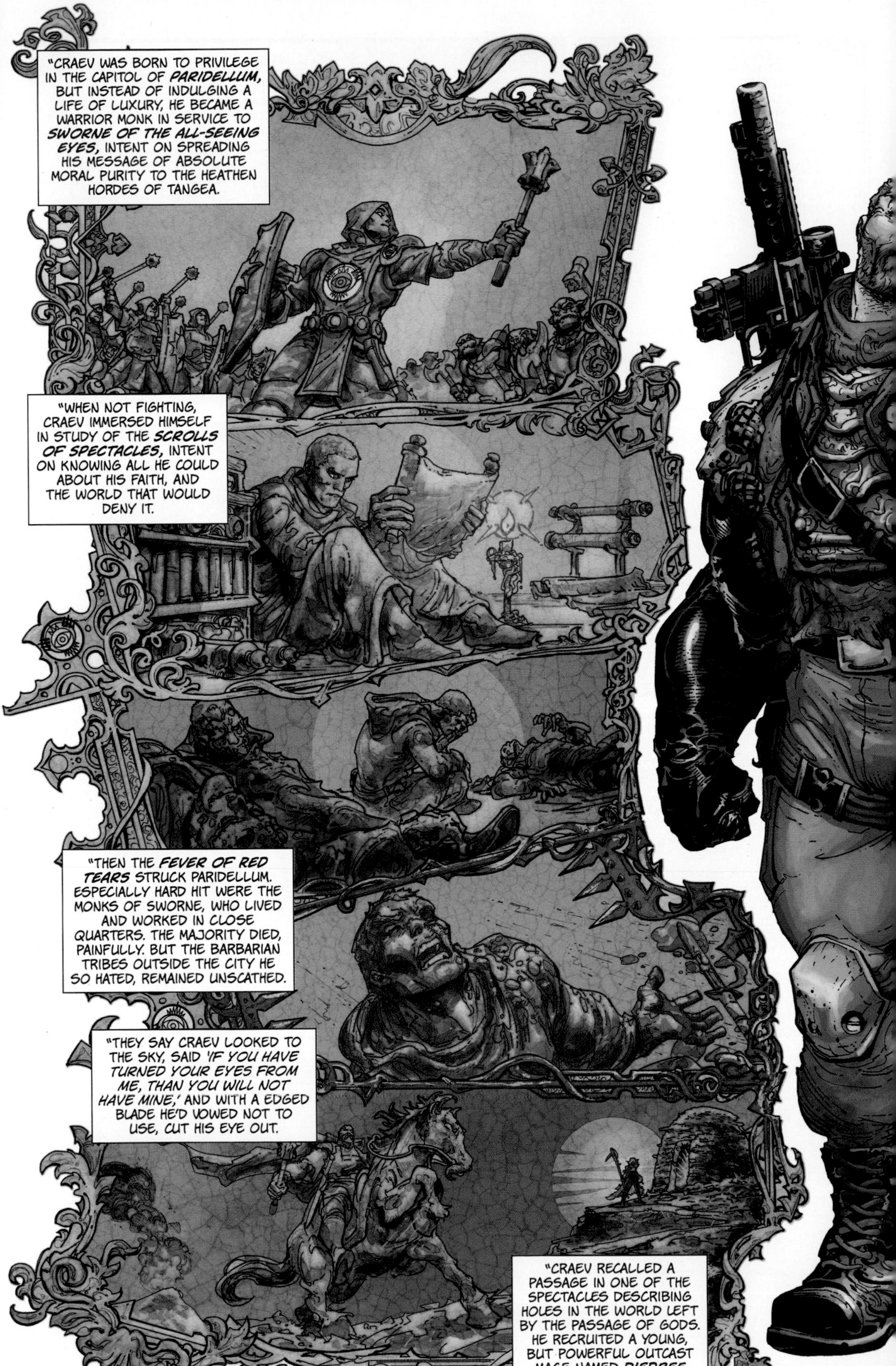
"CRAEV WAS BORN TO PRIVILEGE IN THE CAPITOL OF *PARIDELLUM,* BUT INSTEAD OF INDULGING A LIFE OF LUXURY, HE BECAME A WARRIOR MONK IN SERVICE TO *SWORNE OF THE ALL-SEEING EYES,* INTENT ON SPREADING HIS MESSAGE OF ABSOLUTE MORAL PURITY TO THE HEATHEN HORDES OF TANGEA.
"WHEN NOT FIGHTING, CRAEV IMMERSED HIMSELF IN STUDY OF THE *SCROLLS OF SPECTACLES,* INTENT ON KNOWING ALL HE COULD ABOUT HIS FAITH, AND THE WORLD THAT WOULD DENY IT.
"THEN THE *FEVER OF RED TEARS* STRUCK PARIDELLUM. ESPECIALLY HARD HIT WERE THE MONKS OF SWORNE, WHO LIVED AND WORKED IN CLOSE QUARTERS. THE MAJORITY DIED, PAINFULLY. BUT THE BARBARIAN TRIBES OUTSIDE THE CITY HE SO HATED, REMAINED UNSCATHED.
"THEY SAY CRAEV LOOKED TO THE SKY, SAID *'IF YOU HAVE TURNED YOUR EYES FROM ME, THAN YOU WILL NOT HAVE MINE,'* AND WITH A EDGED BLADE HE'D VOWED NOT TO USE, CUT HIS EYE OUT.
"CRAEV RECALLED A PASSAGE IN ONE OF THE SPECTACLES DESCRIBING HOLES IN THE WORLD LEFT BY THE PASSAGE OF GODS. HE RECRUITED A YOUNG, BUT POWERFUL OUTCAST MAGE NAMED *DIEDREE DOHL.*

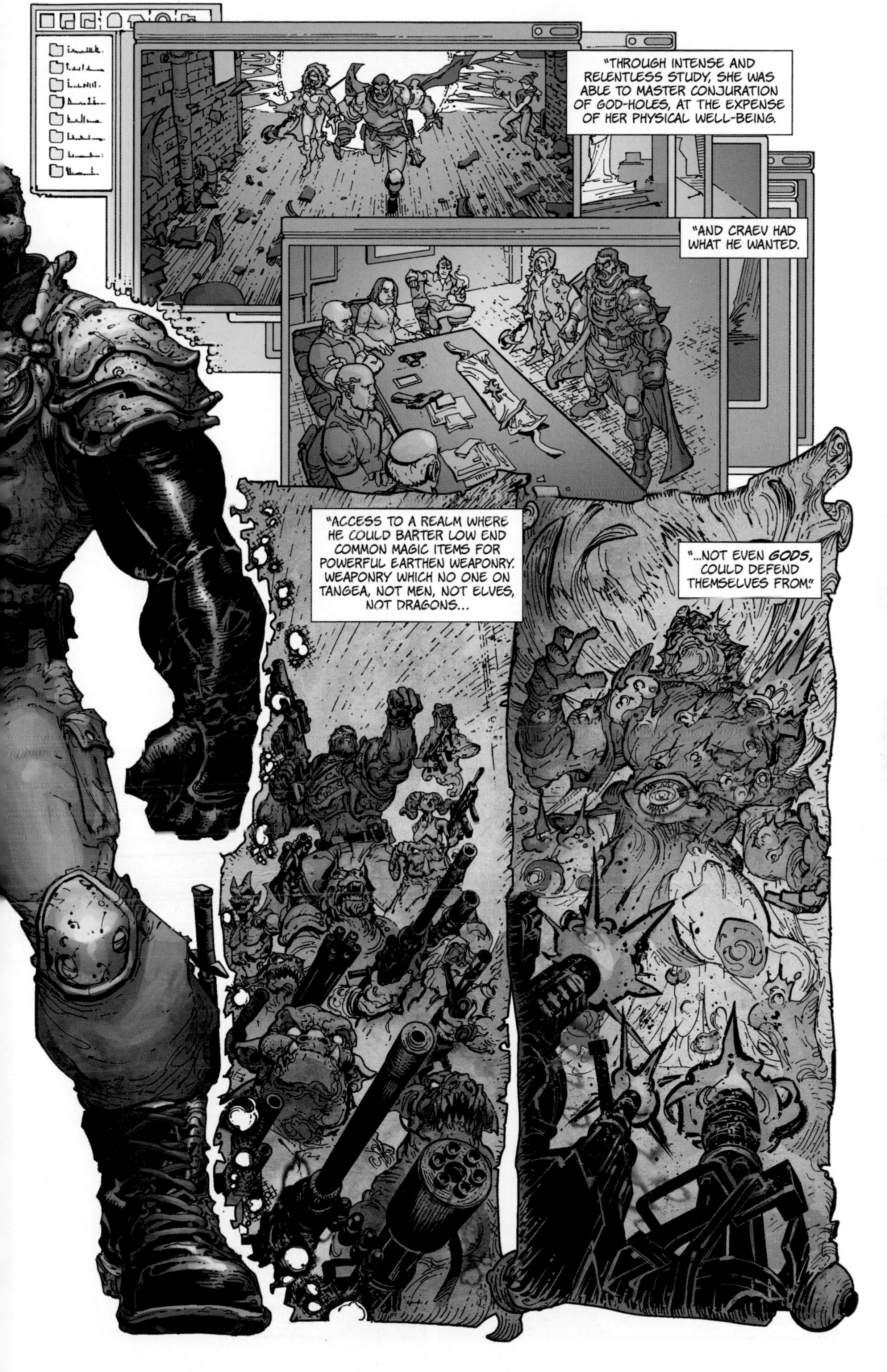
"THROUGH INTENSE AND RELENTLESS STUDY, SHE WAS ABLE TO MASTER CONJURATION OF GOD-HOLES, AT THE EXPENSE OF HER PHYSICAL WELL-BEING.
"AND CRAEV HAD WHAT HE WANTED.
"ACCESS TO A REALM WHERE HE COULD BARTER LOW END COMMON MAGIC ITEMS FOR POWERFUL EARTHEN WEAPONRY. WEAPONRY WHICH NO ONE ON TANGEA, NOT MEN, NOT ELVES, NOT DRAGONS...
"...NOT EVEN *GODS*, COULD DEFEND THEMSELVES FROM."

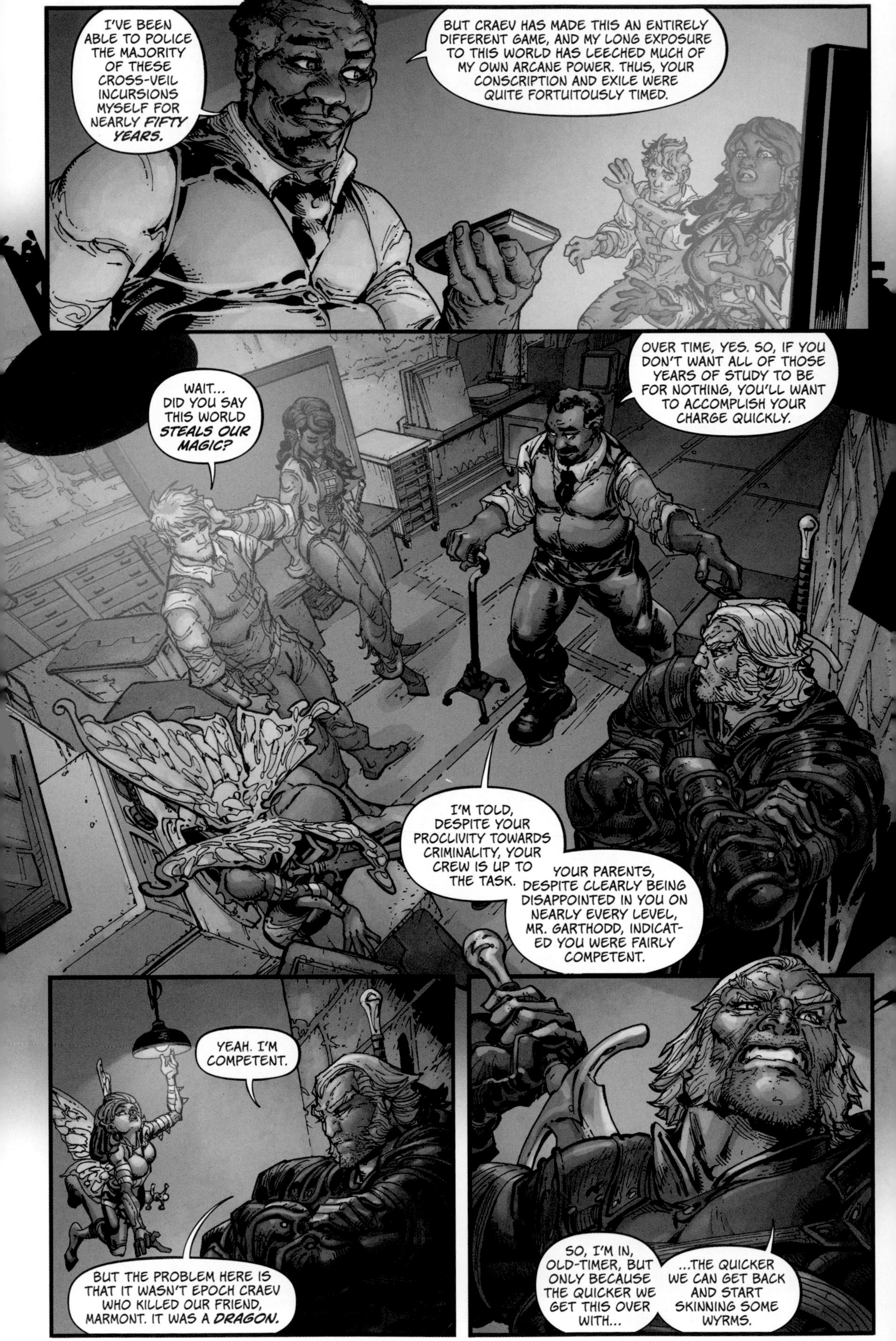
I'VE BEEN ABLE TO POLICE THE MAJORITY OF THESE CROSS-VEIL INCURSIONS MYSELF FOR NEARLY FIFTY YEARS.
BUT CRAEV HAS MADE THIS AN ENTIRELY DIFFERENT GAME, AND MY LONG EXPOSURE TO THIS WORLD HAS LEECHED MUCH OF MY OWN ARCANE POWER. THUS, YOUR CONSCRIPTION AND EXILE WERE QUITE FORTUITOUSLY TIMED.
WAIT... DID YOU SAY THIS WORLD STEALS OUR MAGIC?
OVER TIME, YES. SO, IF YOU DON'T WANT ALL OF THOSE YEARS OF STUDY TO BE FOR NOTHING, YOU'LL WANT TO ACCOMPLISH YOUR CHARGE QUICKLY.
I'M TOLD, DESPITE YOUR PROCLIVITY TOWARDS CRIMINALITY, YOUR CREW IS UP TO THE TASK.
YOUR PARENTS, DESPITE CLEARLY BEING DISAPPOINTED IN YOU ON NEARLY EVERY LEVEL, MR. GARTHODD, INDICATED YOU WERE FAIRLY COMPETENT.
YEAH. I'M COMPETENT.
BUT THE PROBLEM HERE IS THAT IT WASN'T EPOCH CRAEV WHO KILLED OUR FRIEND, MARMONT. IT WAS A DRAGON.
SO, I'M IN, OLD-TIMER, BUT ONLY BECAUSE THE QUICKER WE GET THIS OVER WITH...
...THE QUICKER WE CAN GET BACK AND START SKINNING SOME WYRMS.

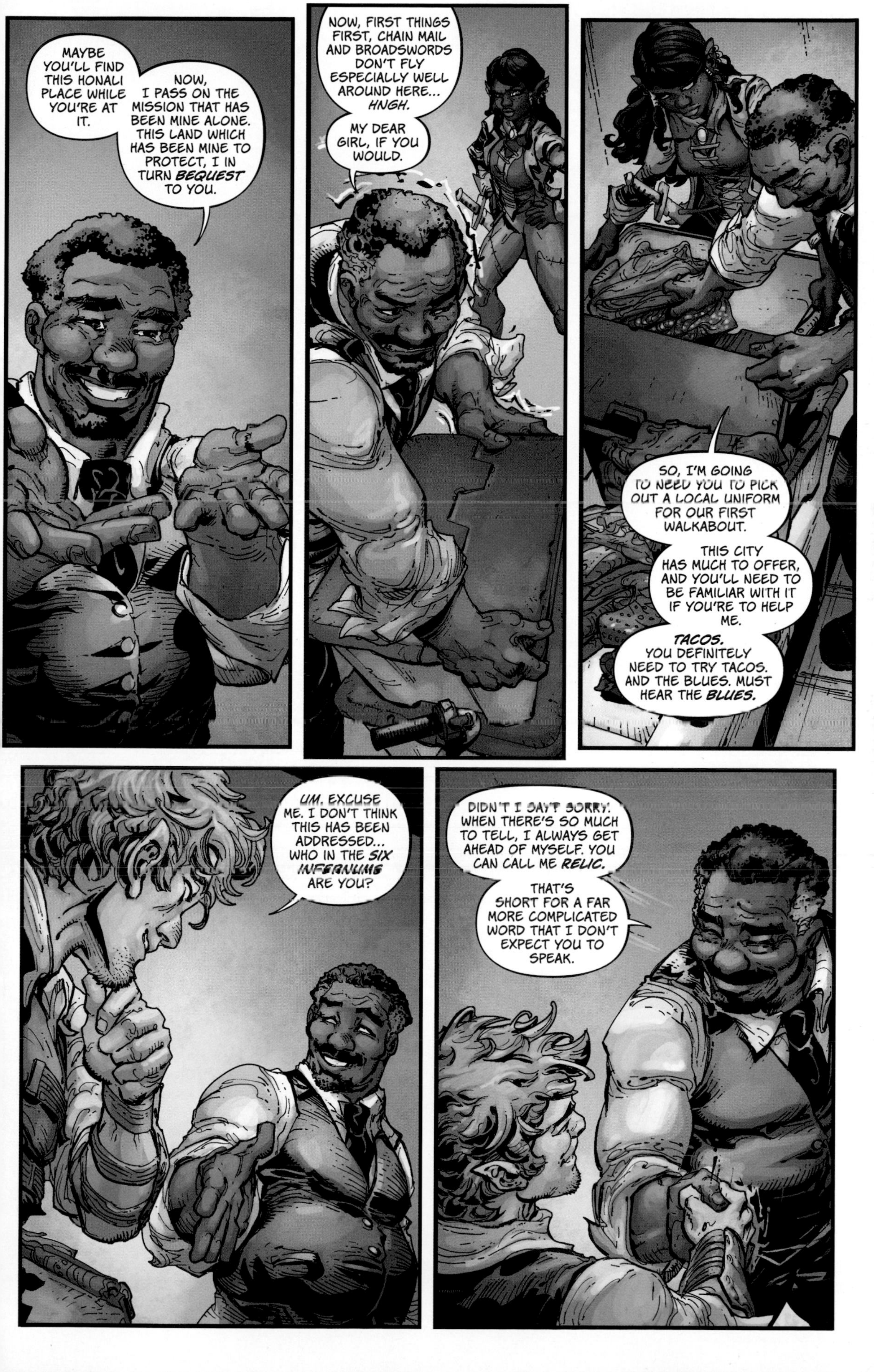
MAYBE YOU'LL FIND THIS HONALI PLACE WHILE YOU'RE AT IT.
NOW, I PASS ON THE MISSION THAT HAS BEEN MINE ALONE. THIS LAND WHICH HAS BEEN MINE TO PROTECT, I IN TURN BEQUEST TO YOU.
NOW, FIRST THINGS FIRST, CHAIN MAIL AND BROADSWORDS DON'T FLY ESPECIALLY WELL AROUND HERE... HNGH.
MY DEAR GIRL, IF YOU WOULD.
SO, I'M GOING TO NEED YOU TO PICK OUT A LOCAL UNIFORM FOR OUR FIRST WALKABOUT.
THIS CITY HAS MUCH TO OFFER, AND YOU'LL NEED TO BE FAMILIAR WITH IT IF YOU'RE TO HELP ME.
TACOS. YOU DEFINITELY NEED TO TRY TACOS. AND THE BLUES. MUST HEAR THE BLUES.
UM, EXCUSE ME. I DON'T THINK THIS HAS BEEN ADDRESSED... WHO IN THE SIX INFERNUMS ARE YOU?
DIDN'T I SAY? SORRY. WHEN THERE'S SO MUCH TO TELL, I ALWAYS GET AHEAD OF MYSELF. YOU CAN CALL ME RELIC.
THAT'S SHORT FOR A FAR MORE COMPLICATED WORD THAT I DON'T EXPECT YOU TO SPEAK.

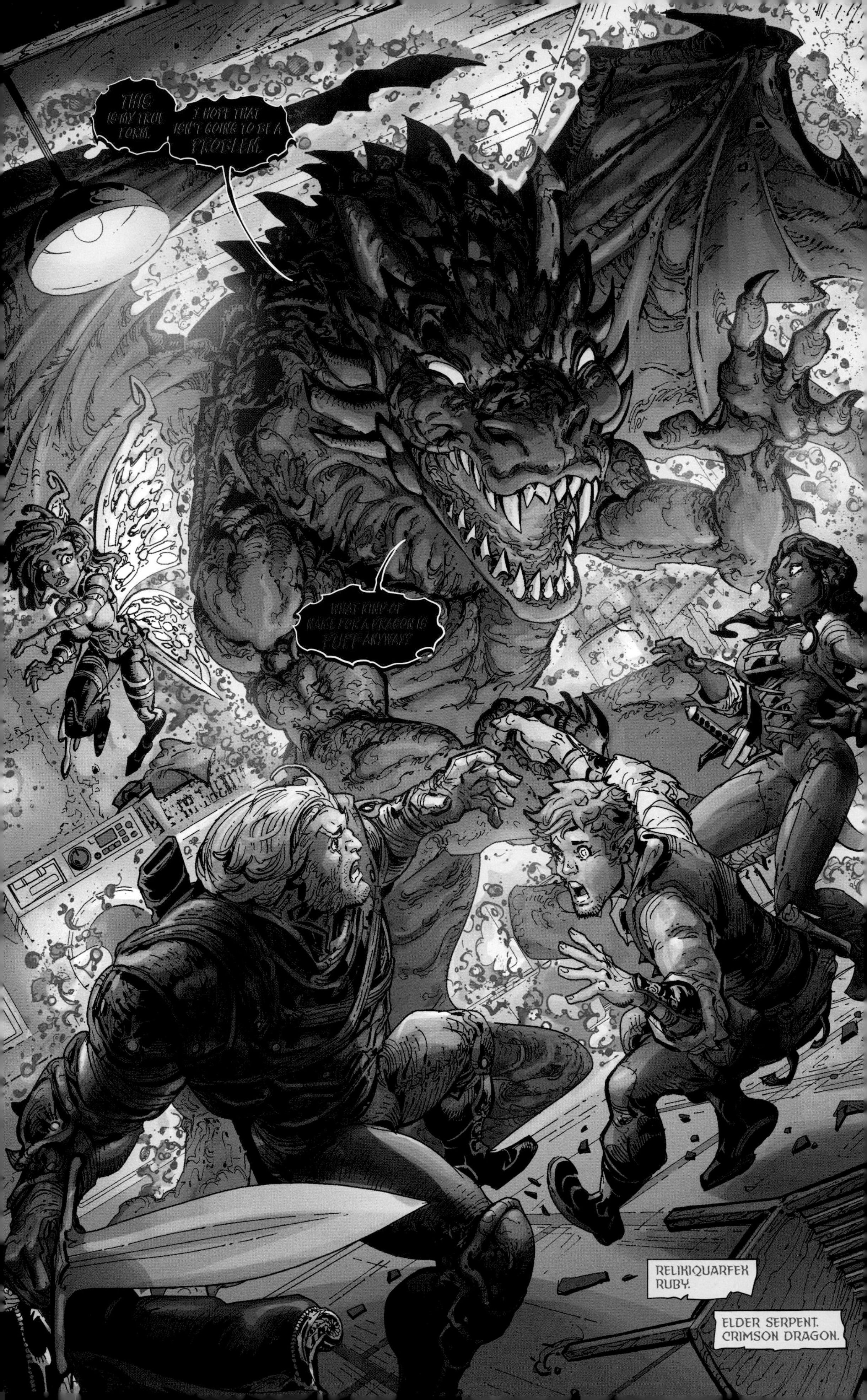
THIS IS MY TRUE FORM.
I HOPE THAT ISN'T GOING TO BE A PROBLEM.
WHAT KIND OF NAME FOR A DRAGON IS PUFF ANYWAY?
RELIKIQUARFEX RUBY.
ELDER SERPENT. CRIMSON DRAGON.

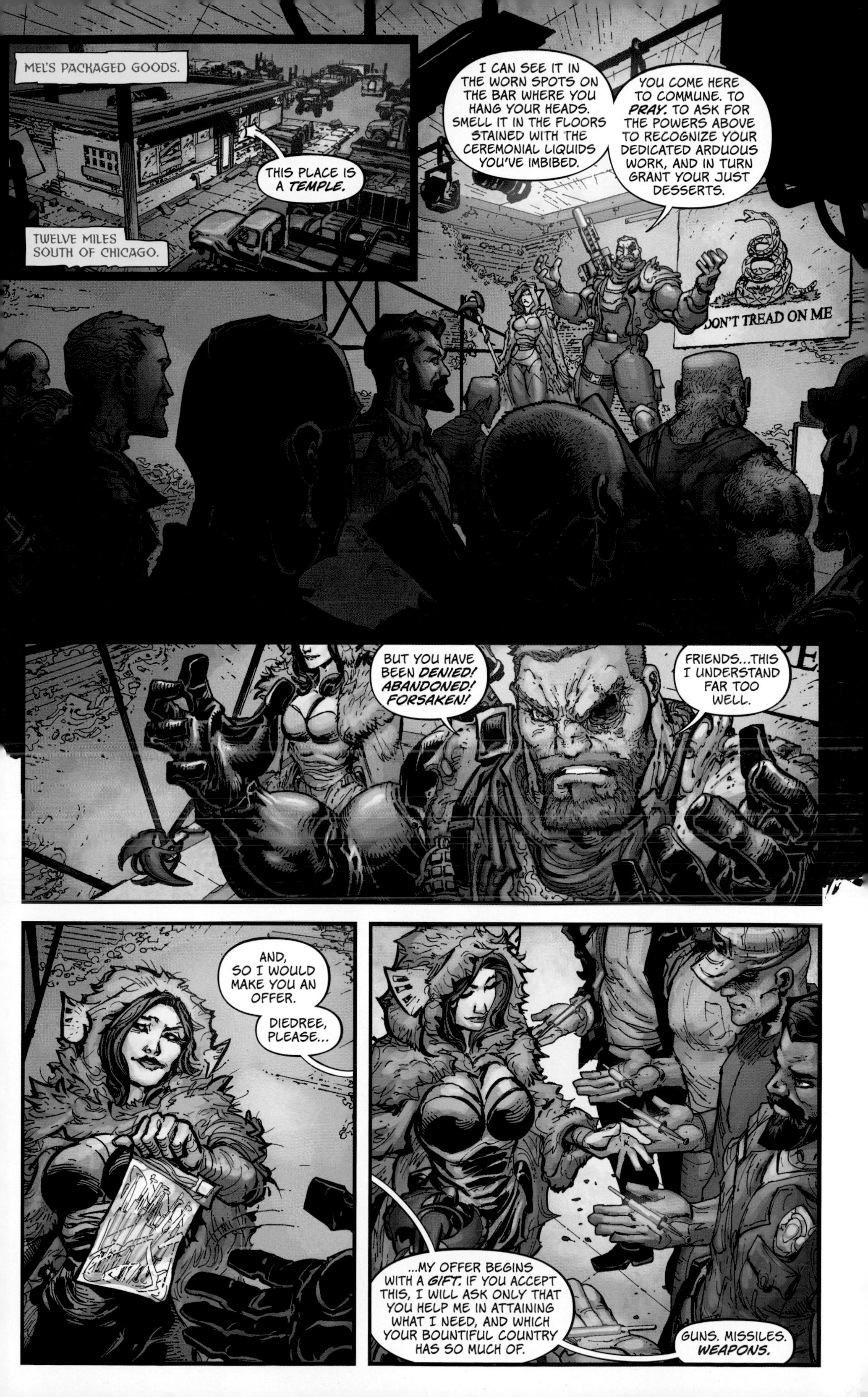
MEL'S PACKAGED GOODS.
TWELVE MILES SOUTH OF CHICAGO.
THIS PLACE IS A *TEMPLE.*
I CAN SEE IT IN THE WORN SPOTS ON THE BAR WHERE YOU HANG YOUR HEADS. SMELL IT IN THE FLOORS STAINED WITH THE CEREMONIAL LIQUIDS YOU'VE IMBIBED.
YOU COME HERE TO COMMUNE. TO *PRAY.* TO ASK FOR THE POWERS ABOVE TO RECOGNIZE YOUR DEDICATED ARDUOUS WORK, AND IN TURN GRANT YOUR JUST DESSERTS.
DON'T TREAD ON ME
BUT YOU HAVE BEEN *DENIED! ABANDONED! FORSAKEN!*
FRIENDS...THIS I UNDERSTAND FAR TOO WELL.
AND, SO I WOULD MAKE YOU AN OFFER.
DIEDREE, PLEASE...
...MY OFFER BEGINS WITH A *GIFT.* IF YOU ACCEPT THIS, I WILL ASK ONLY THAT YOU HELP ME IN ATTAINING WHAT I NEED, AND WHICH YOUR BOUNTIFUL COUNTRY HAS SO MUCH OF.
GUNS. MISSILES. *WEAPONS.*

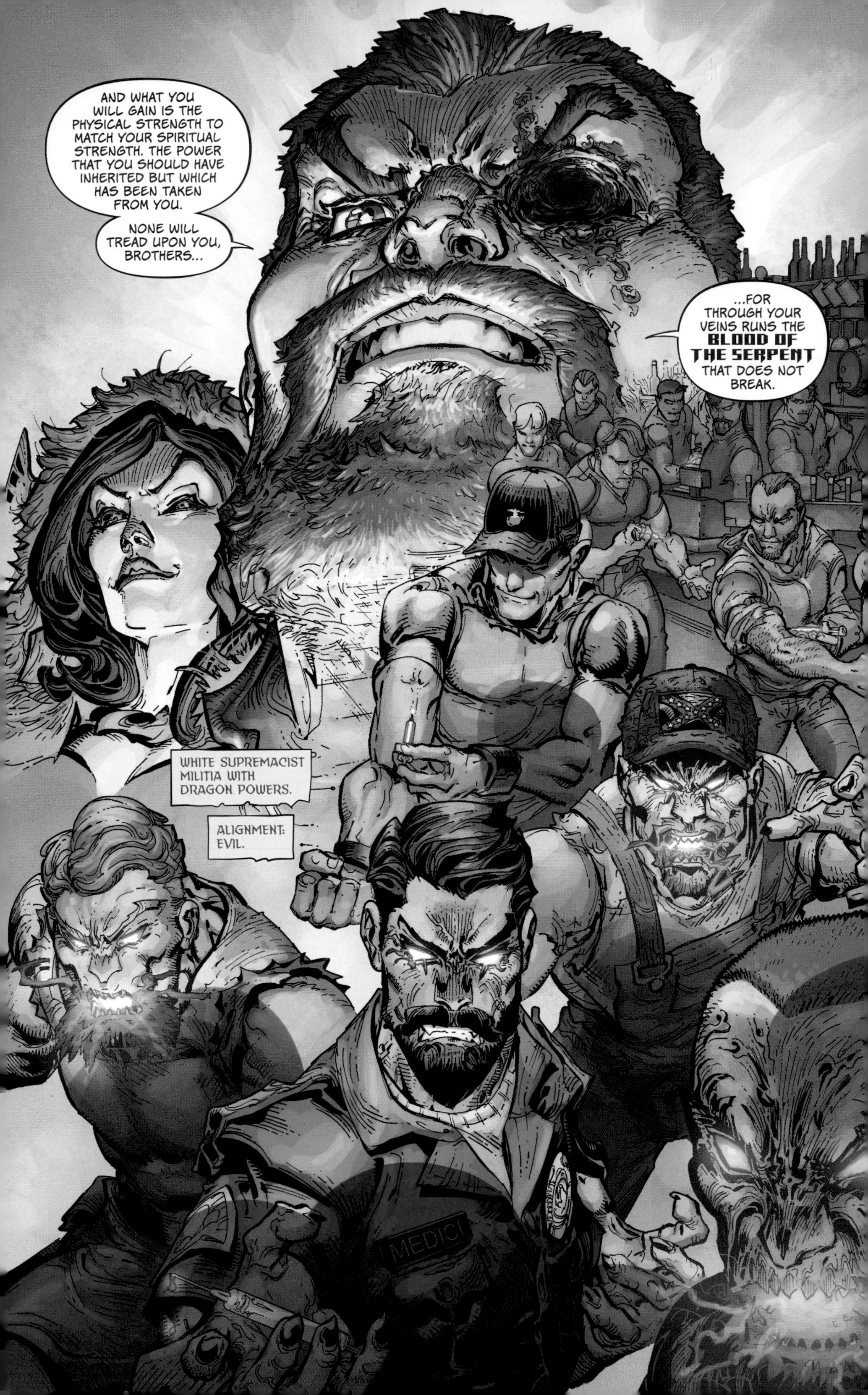
AND WHAT YOU WILL GAIN IS THE PHYSICAL STRENGTH TO MATCH YOUR SPIRITUAL STRENGTH. THE POWER THAT YOU SHOULD HAVE INHERITED BUT WHICH HAS BEEN TAKEN FROM YOU.
NONE WILL TREAD UPON YOU, BROTHERS...
...FOR THROUGH YOUR VEINS RUNS THE BLOOD OF THE SERPENT THAT DOES NOT BREAK.
WHITE SUPREMACIST MILITIA WITH DRAGON POWERS.
ALIGNMENT: EVIL.
MEDICI

2
LOWER WHACKER

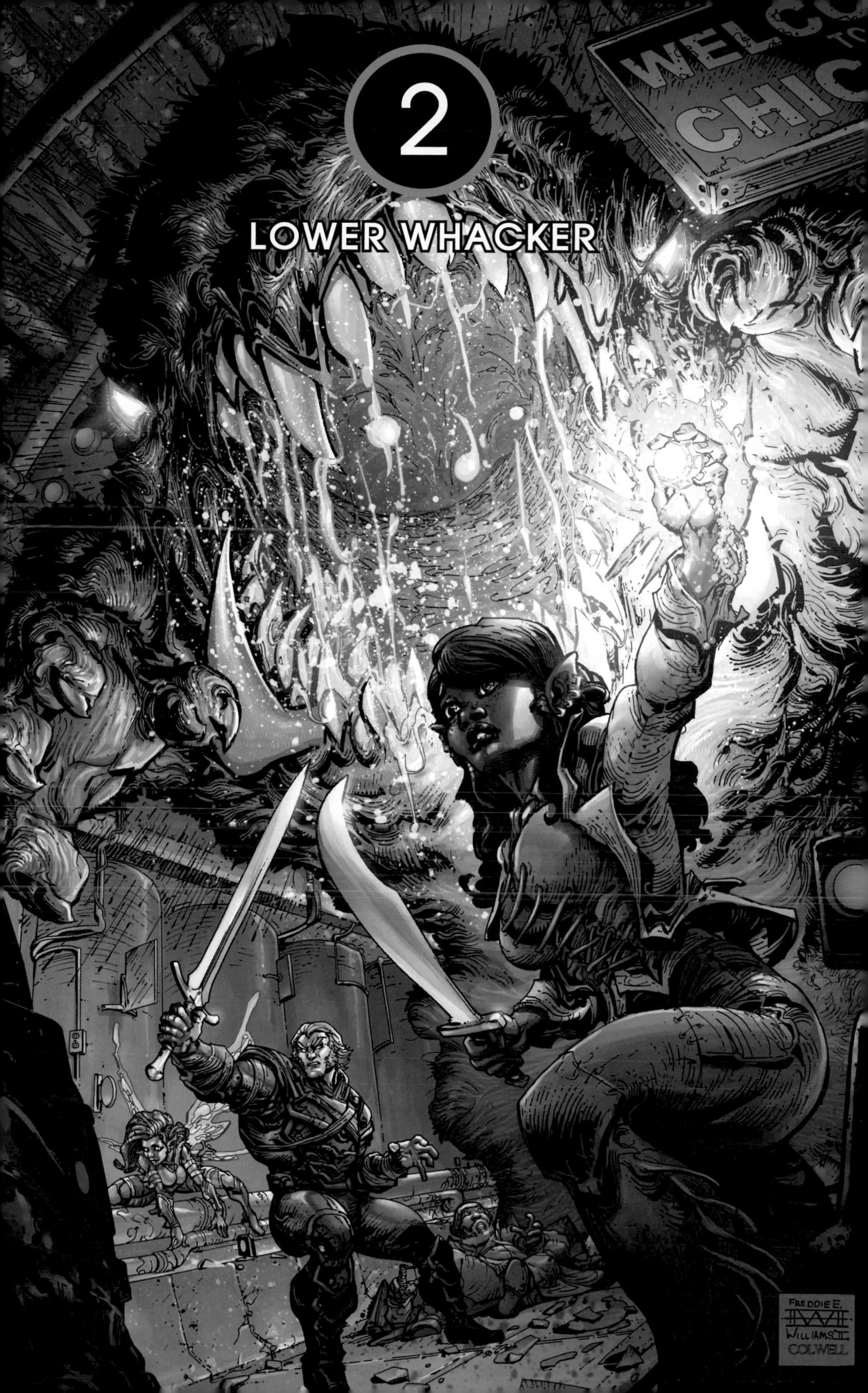
FREDDIE E. WILLIAMS II
COLWELL

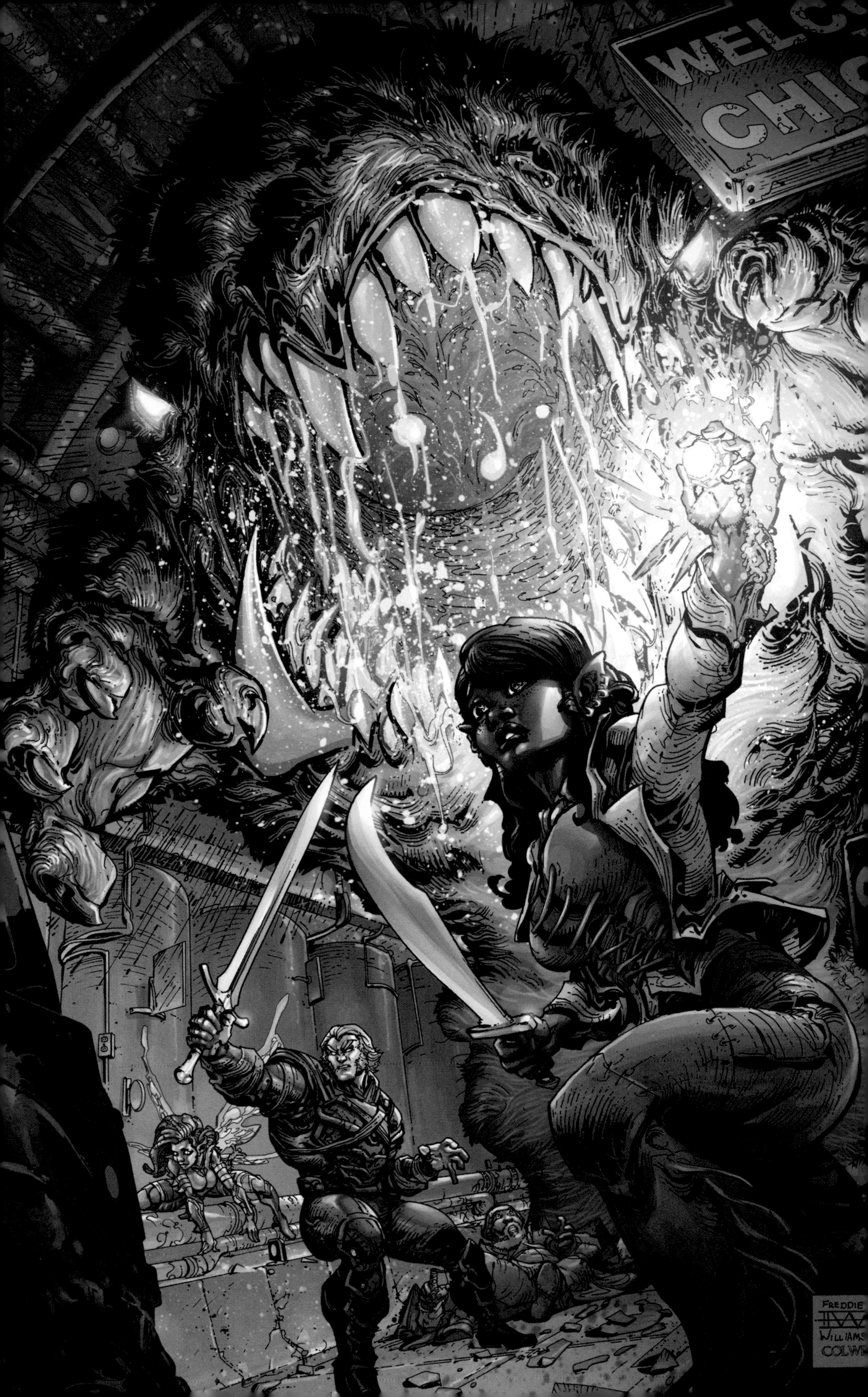
WELC
CHIC
FREDDIE
WILLIAMS

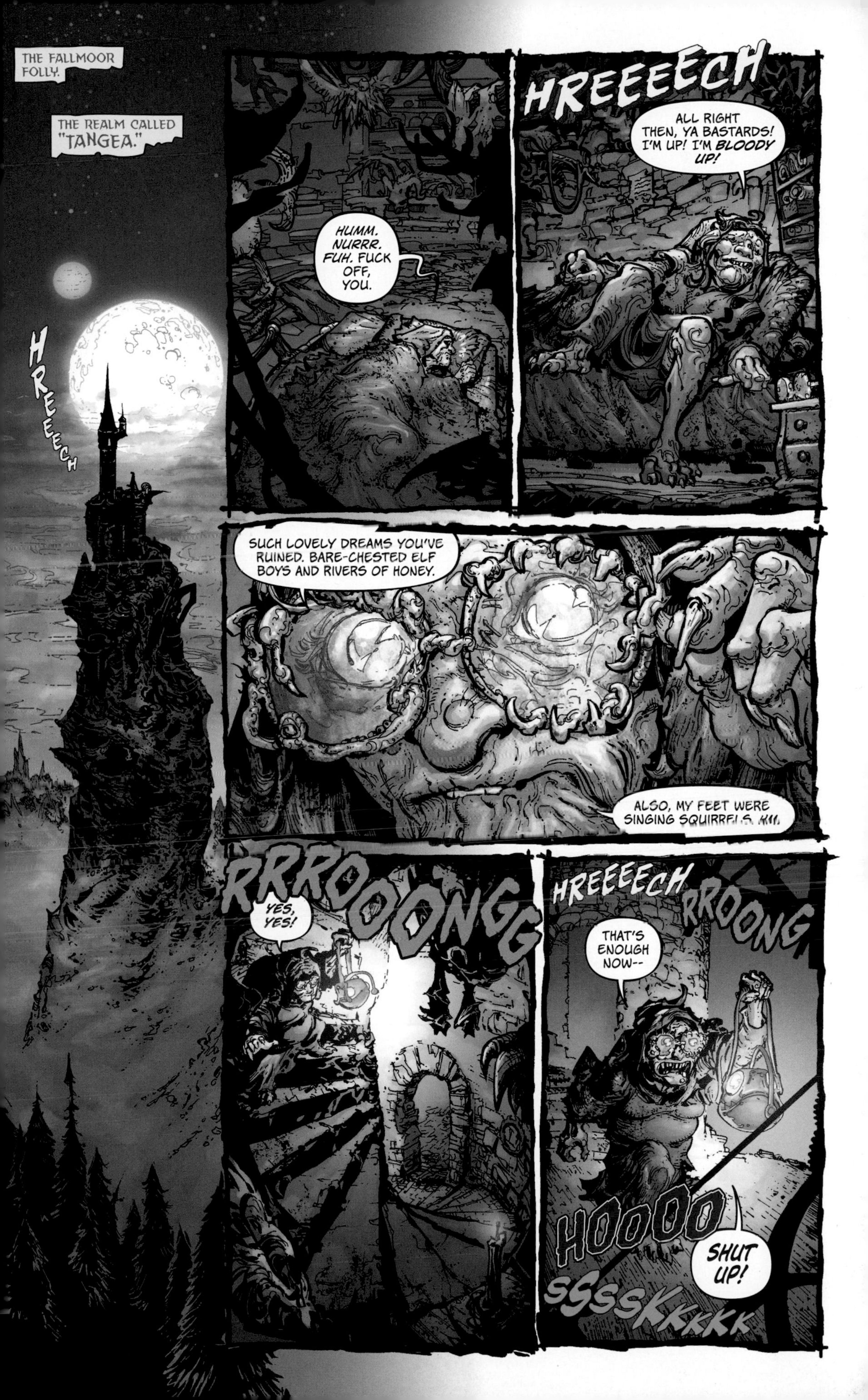
THE FALLMOOR FOLLY.
THE REALM CALLED "TANGEA."
HREEEECH
HUMM. NURRR. FUH. FUCK OFF, YOU.
HREEEECH
ALL RIGHT THEN, YA BASTARDS! I'M UP! I'M BLOODY UP!
SUCH LOVELY DREAMS YOU'VE RUINED. BARE-CHESTED ELF BOYS AND RIVERS OF HONEY.
ALSO, MY FEET WERE SINGING SQUIRRELS.
RRROOONGG
YES, YES!
HREEEECH
RROONG
THAT'S ENOUGH NOW--
HOOOO
SHUT UP!
SSSSKKKKKK

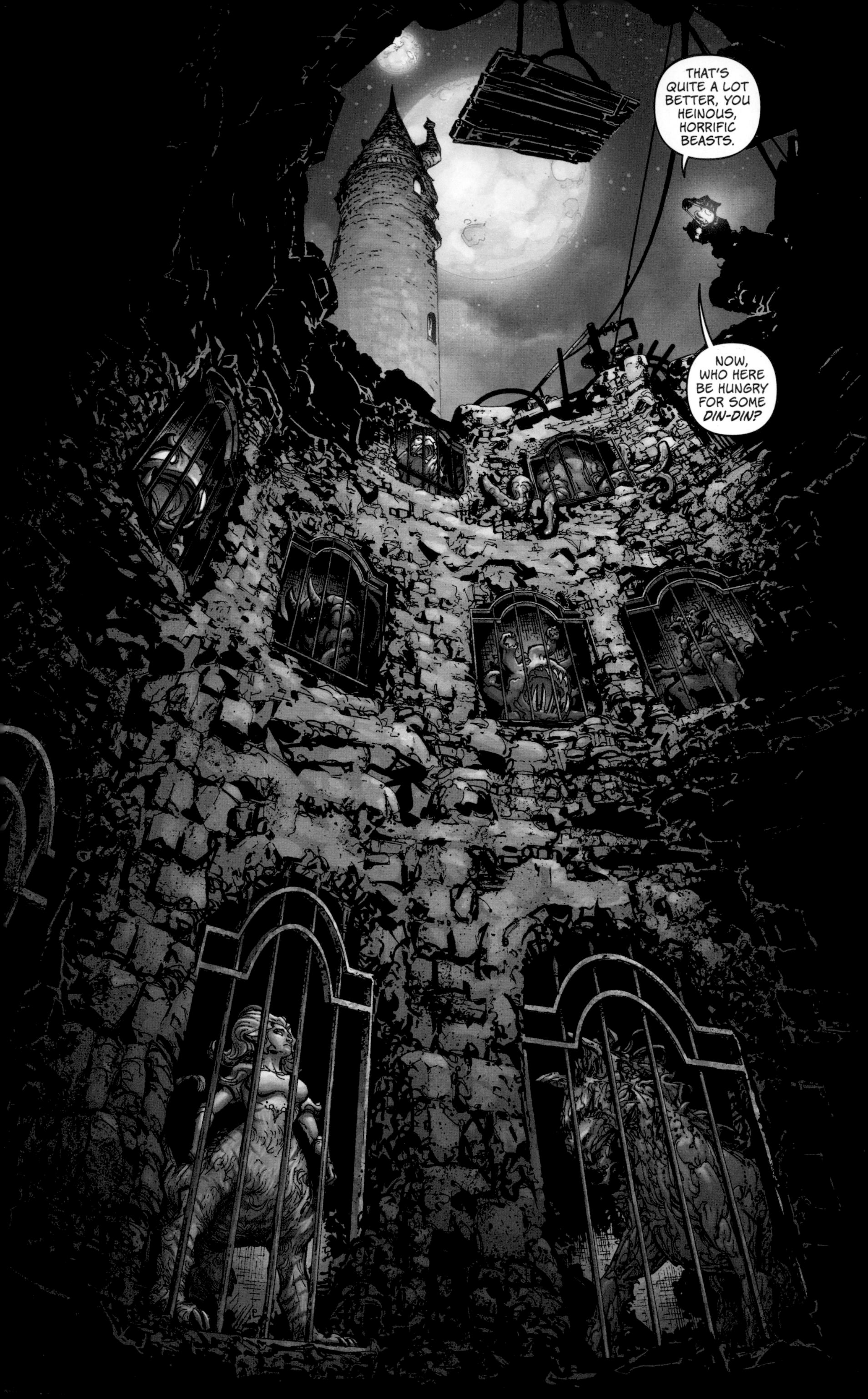
THAT'S QUITE A LOT BETTER, YOU HEINOUS, HORRIFIC BEASTS.
NOW, WHO HERE BE HUNGRY FOR SOME *DIN-DIN?*

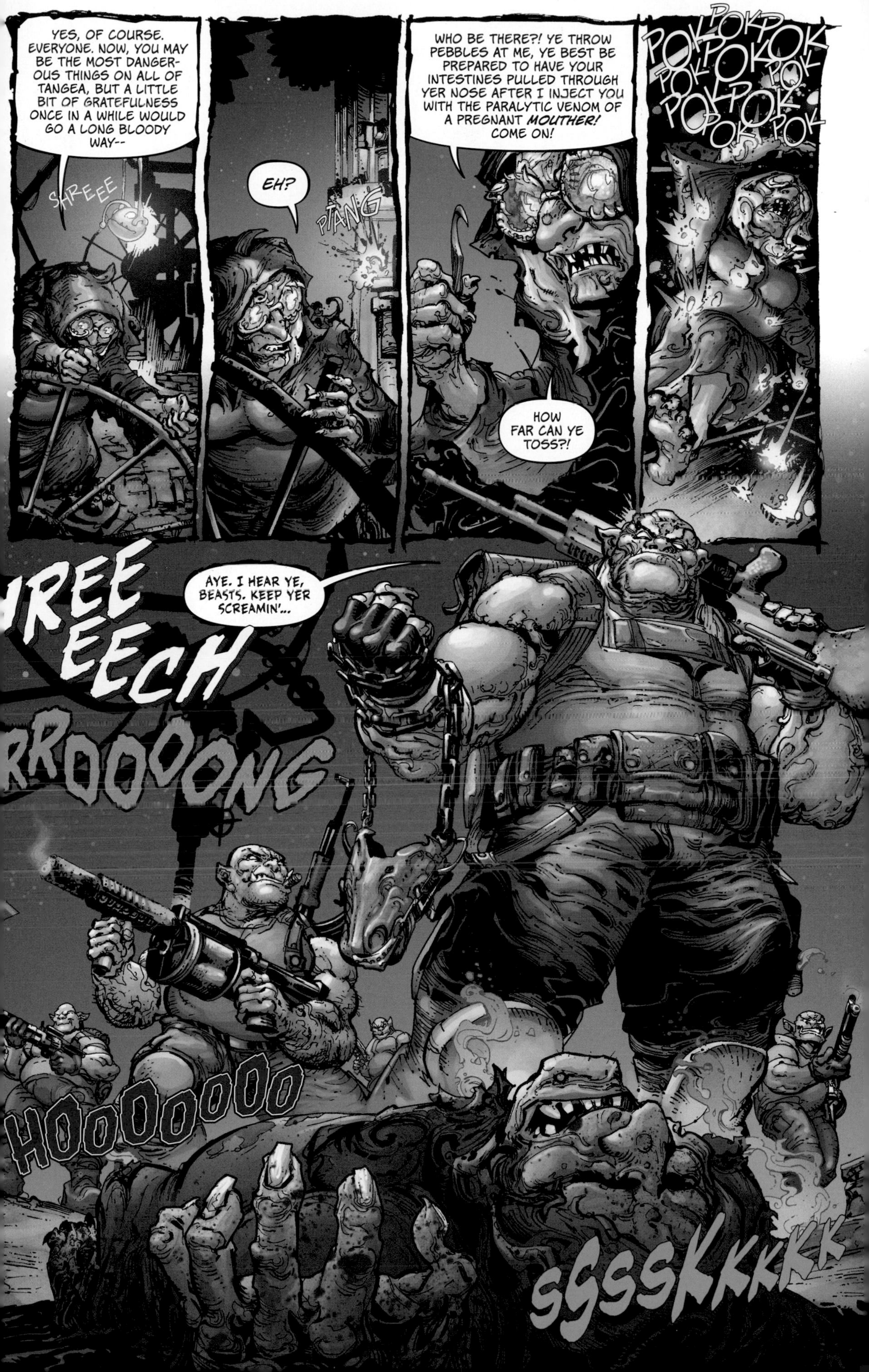
YES, OF COURSE. EVERYONE. NOW, YOU MAY BE THE MOST DANGER-OUS THINGS ON ALL OF TANGEA, BUT A LITTLE BIT OF GRATEFULNESS ONCE IN A WHILE WOULD GO A LONG BLOODY WAY--
SHREEEE
EH?
PTANG
WHO BE THERE?! YE THROW PEBBLES AT ME, YE BEST BE PREPARED TO HAVE YOUR INTESTINES PULLED THROUGH YER NOSE AFTER I INJECT YOU WITH THE PARALYTIC VENOM OF A PREGNANT MOUTHER! COME ON!
HOW FAR CAN YE TOSS?!
POKPOKPOK POKPOKPOK POKPOKPOK POKPOKPOK
AYE. I HEAR YE, BEASTS. KEEP YER SCREAMIN'...
REE EECH
RROOOONG
HOOOOOOO
SSSSKKKKK

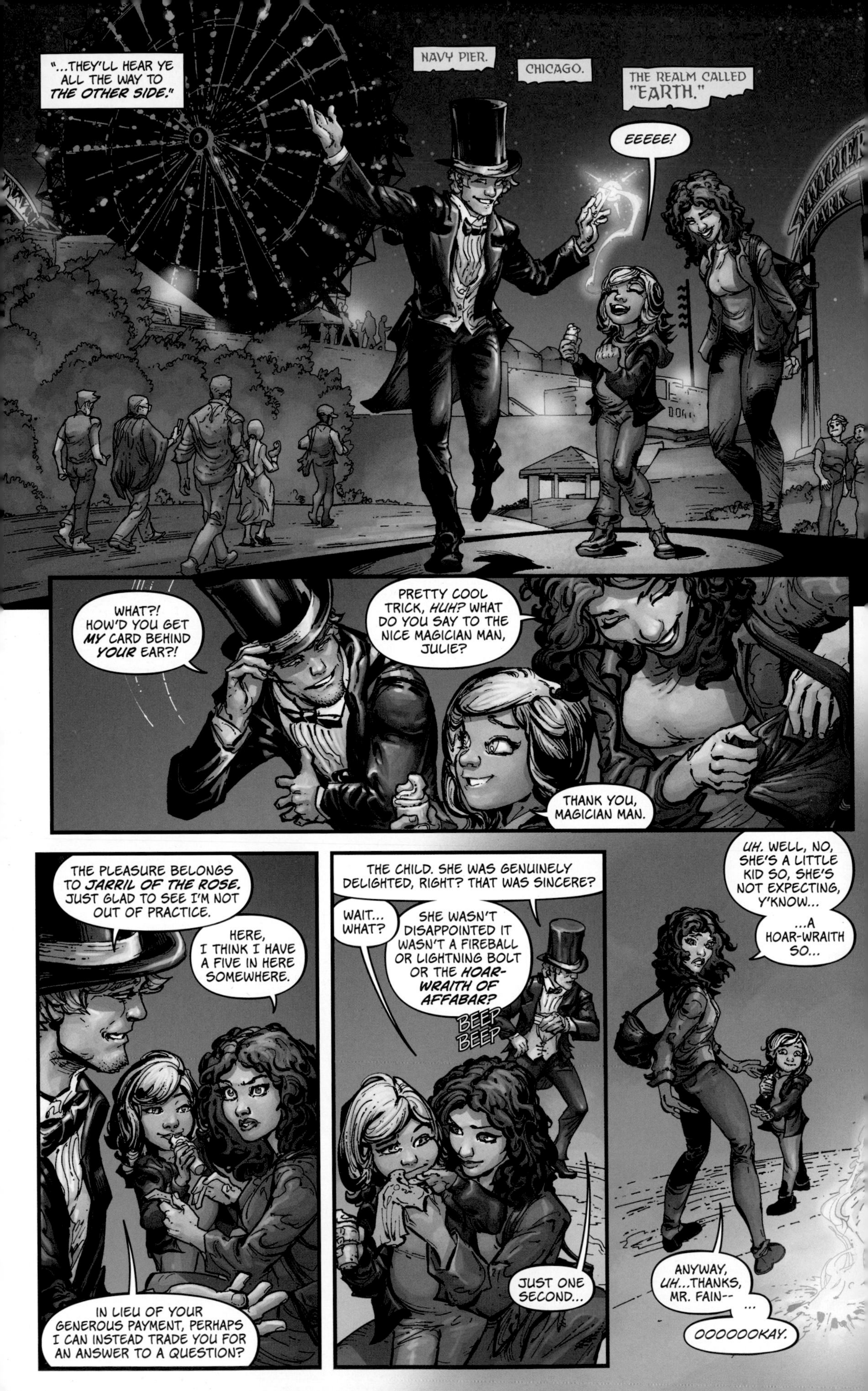

"...THEY'LL HEAR YE ALL THE WAY TO *THE OTHER SIDE.*"
NAVY PIER.
CHICAGO.
THE REALM CALLED "EARTH."
EEEEE!
WHAT?! HOW'D YOU GET *MY* CARD BEHIND *YOUR* EAR?!
PRETTY COOL TRICK, *HUH?* WHAT DO YOU SAY TO THE NICE MAGICIAN MAN, JULIE?
THANK YOU, MAGICIAN MAN.
THE PLEASURE BELONGS TO *JARRIL OF THE ROSE.* JUST GLAD TO SEE I'M NOT OUT OF PRACTICE.
HERE, I THINK I HAVE A FIVE IN HERE SOMEWHERE.
IN LIEU OF YOUR GENEROUS PAYMENT, PERHAPS I CAN INSTEAD TRADE YOU FOR AN ANSWER TO A QUESTION?
THE CHILD. SHE WAS GENUINELY DELIGHTED, RIGHT? THAT WAS SINCERE?
WAIT... WHAT?
SHE WASN'T DISAPPOINTED IT WASN'T A FIREBALL OR LIGHTNING BOLT OR THE *HOAR-WRAITH OF AFFABAR?*
BEEP BEEP
JUST ONE SECOND...
UH. WELL, NO, SHE'S A LITTLE KID SO, SHE'S NOT EXPECTING, Y'KNOW...
...A HOAR-WRAITH SO...
ANYWAY, *UH*...THANKS, MR. FAIN--
...
OOOOOOKAY.

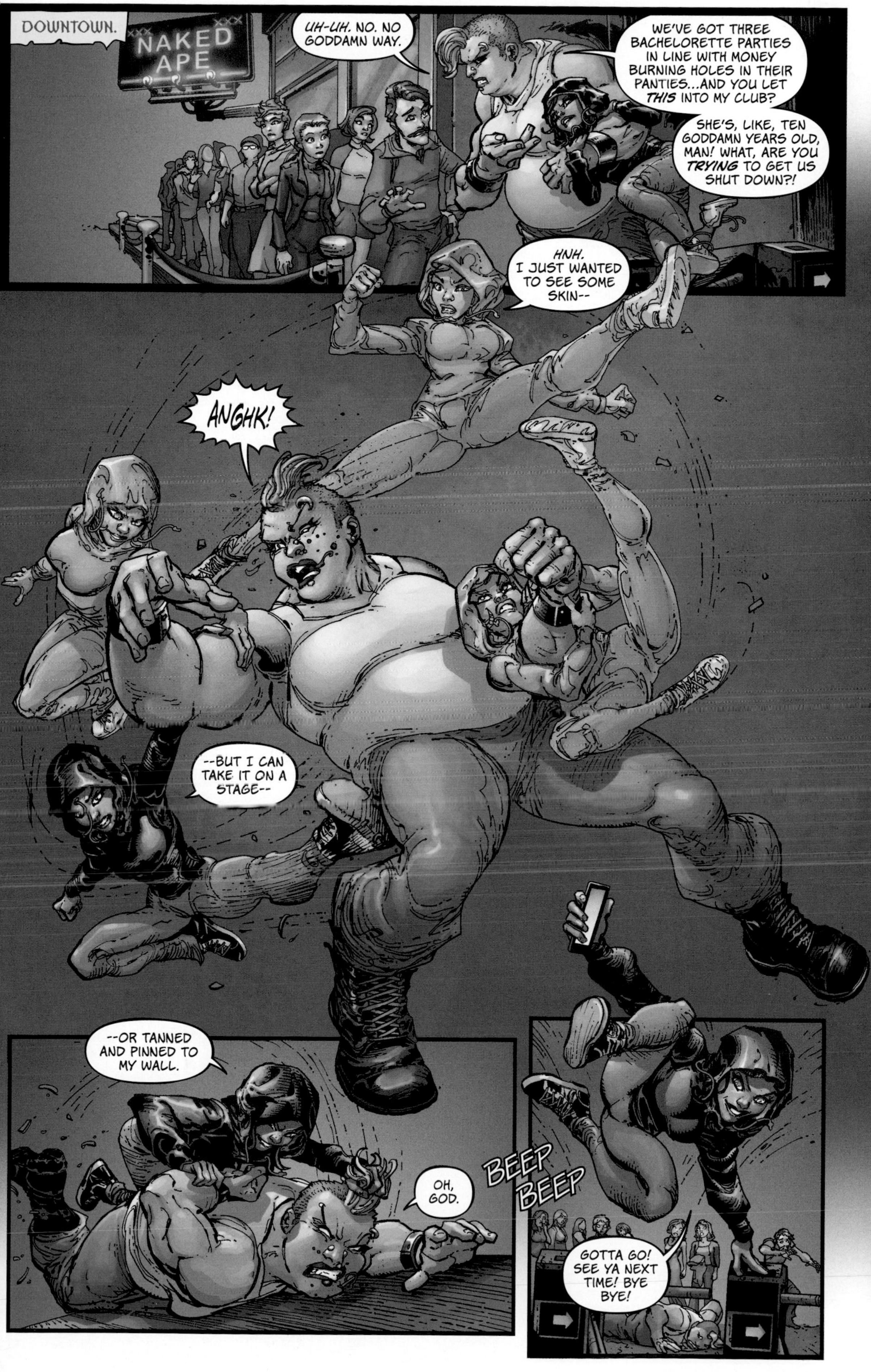

DOWNTOWN.
NAKED APE
UH-UH. NO. NO GODDAMN WAY.
WE'VE GOT THREE BACHELORETTE PARTIES IN LINE WITH MONEY BURNING HOLES IN THEIR PANTIES...AND YOU LET *THIS* INTO MY CLUB?
SHE'S, LIKE, TEN GODDAMN YEARS OLD, MAN! WHAT, ARE YOU *TRYING* TO GET US SHUT DOWN?!
HNH. I JUST WANTED TO SEE SOME SKIN--
ANGHK!
--BUT I CAN TAKE IT ON A STAGE--
--OR TANNED AND PINNED TO MY WALL.
OH, GOD.
BEEP BEEP
GOTTA GO! SEE YA NEXT TIME! BYE BYE!

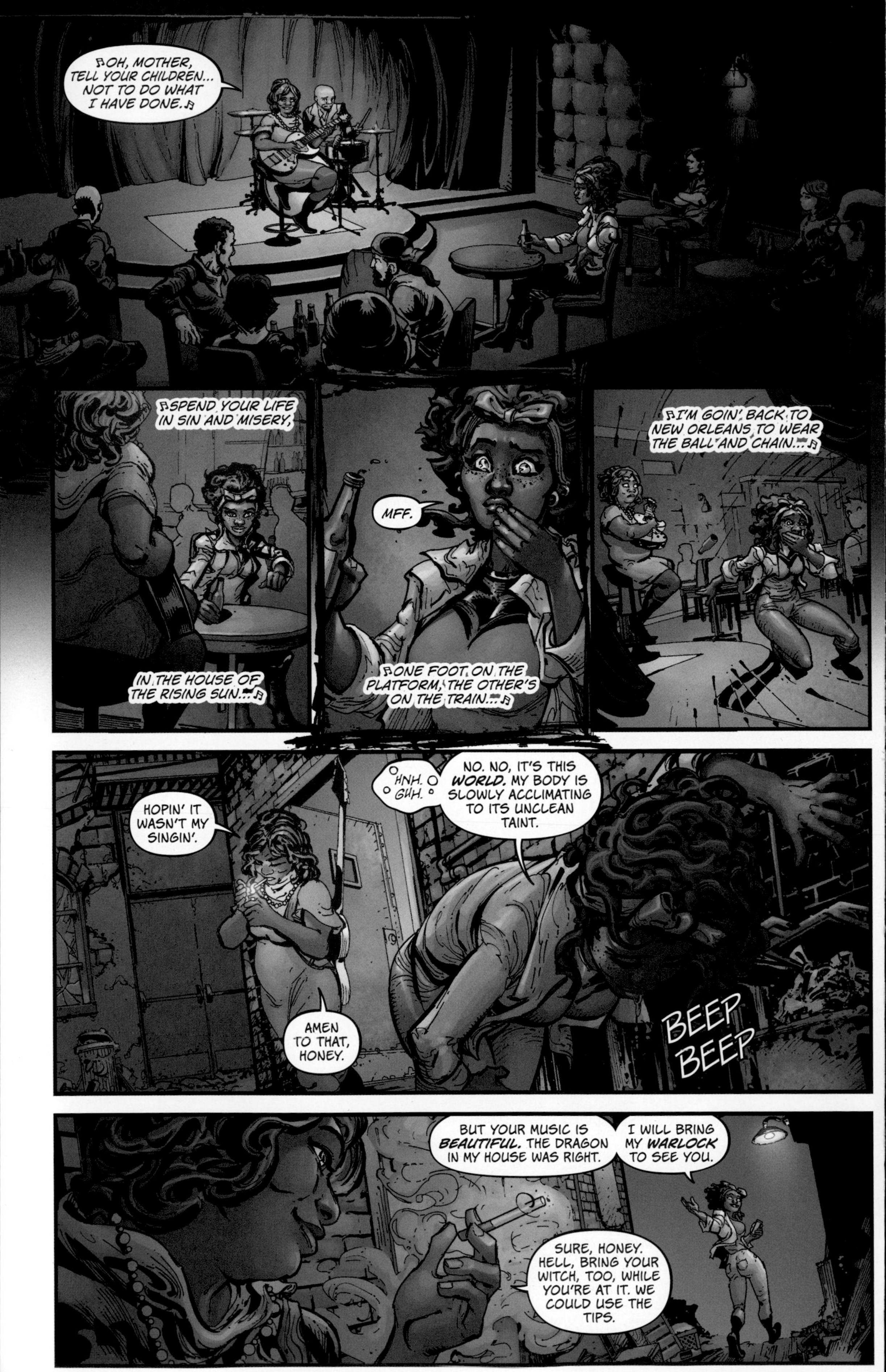
♫OH, MOTHER, TELL YOUR CHILDREN... NOT TO DO WHAT I HAVE DONE.♫
♫SPEND YOUR LIFE IN SIN AND MISERY,
IN THE HOUSE OF THE RISING SUN...♫
MFF.
♫ONE FOOT ON THE PLATFORM, THE OTHER'S ON THE TRAIN...♫
♫I'M GOIN' BACK TO NEW ORLEANS TO WEAR THE BALL AND CHAIN...♫
HOPIN' IT WASN'T MY SINGIN'.
HNH. GUH.
NO. NO, IT'S THIS WORLD. MY BODY IS SLOWLY ACCLIMATING TO ITS UNCLEAN TAINT.
AMEN TO THAT, HONEY.
BEEP BEEP
BUT YOUR MUSIC IS BEAUTIFUL. THE DRAGON IN MY HOUSE WAS RIGHT.
I WILL BRING MY WARLOCK TO SEE YOU.
SURE, HONEY. HELL, BRING YOUR WITCH, TOO, WHILE YOU'RE AT IT. WE COULD USE THE TIPS.

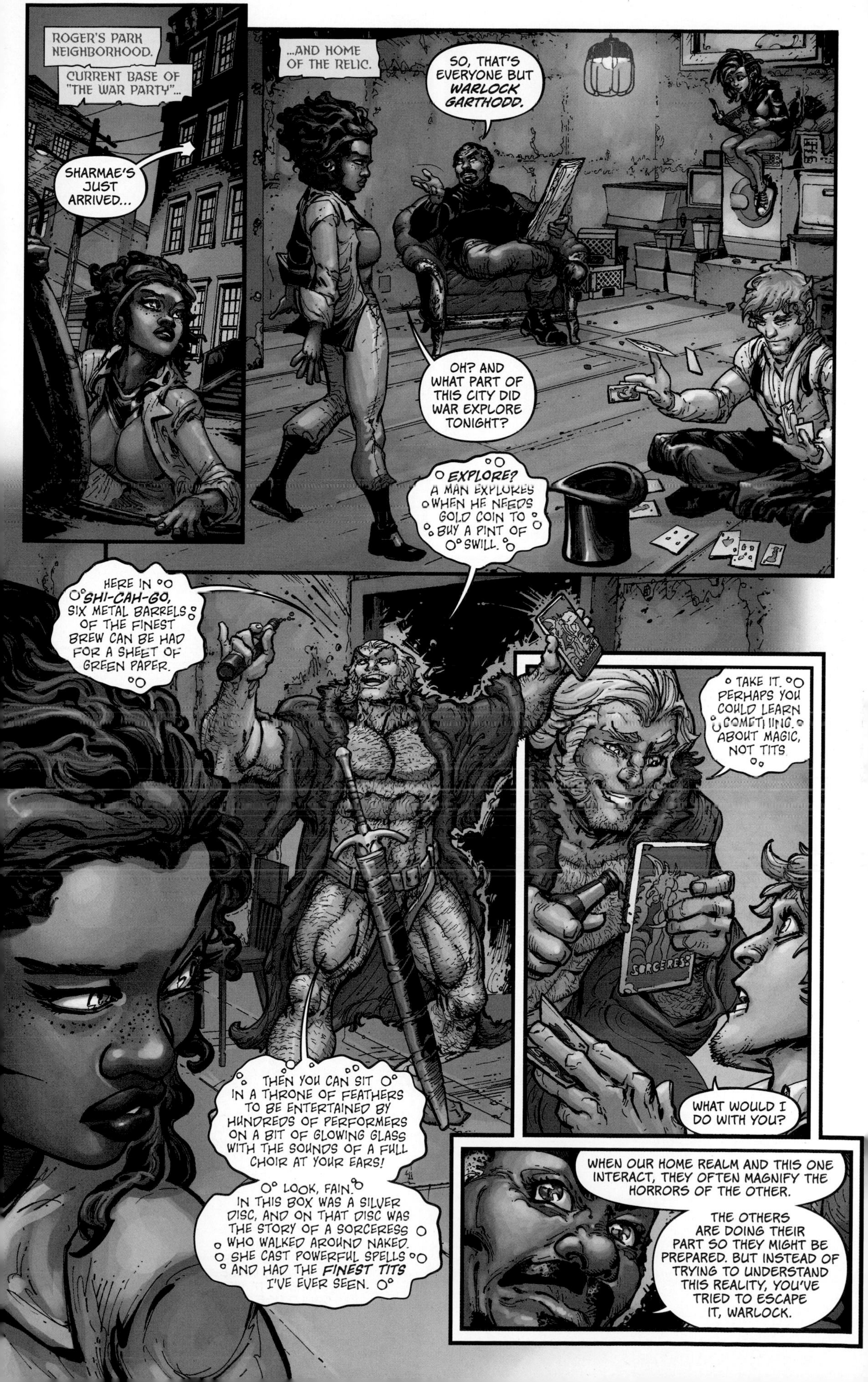
ROGER'S PARK NEIGHBORHOOD.
CURRENT BASE OF "THE WAR PARTY"...
SHARMAE'S JUST ARRIVED...
...AND HOME OF THE RELIC.
SO, THAT'S EVERYONE BUT *WARLOCK GARTHODD.*
OH? AND WHAT PART OF THIS CITY DID WAR EXPLORE TONIGHT?
EXPLORE? A MAN EXPLORES WHEN HE NEEDS GOLD COIN TO BUY A PINT OF SWILL.
HERE IN *SHI-CAH-GO,* SIX METAL BARRELS OF THE FINEST BREW CAN BE HAD FOR A SHEET OF GREEN PAPER.
THEN YOU CAN SIT IN A THRONE OF FEATHERS TO BE ENTERTAINED BY HUNDREDS OF PERFORMERS ON A BIT OF GLOWING GLASS WITH THE SOUNDS OF A FULL CHOIR AT YOUR EARS!
LOOK, FAIN. IN THIS BOX WAS A SILVER DISC, AND ON THAT DISC WAS THE STORY OF A SORCERESS WHO WALKED AROUND NAKED. SHE CAST POWERFUL SPELLS AND HAD THE *FINEST TITS* I'VE EVER SEEN.
TAKE IT. PERHAPS YOU COULD LEARN SOMETHING. ABOUT MAGIC, NOT TITS.
SORCERESS
WHAT WOULD I DO WITH YOU?
WHEN OUR HOME REALM AND THIS ONE INTERACT, THEY OFTEN MAGNIFY THE HORRORS OF THE OTHER.
THE OTHERS ARE DOING THEIR PART SO THEY MIGHT BE PREPARED. BUT INSTEAD OF TRYING TO UNDERSTAND THIS REALITY, YOU'VE TRIED TO ESCAPE IT, WARLOCK.

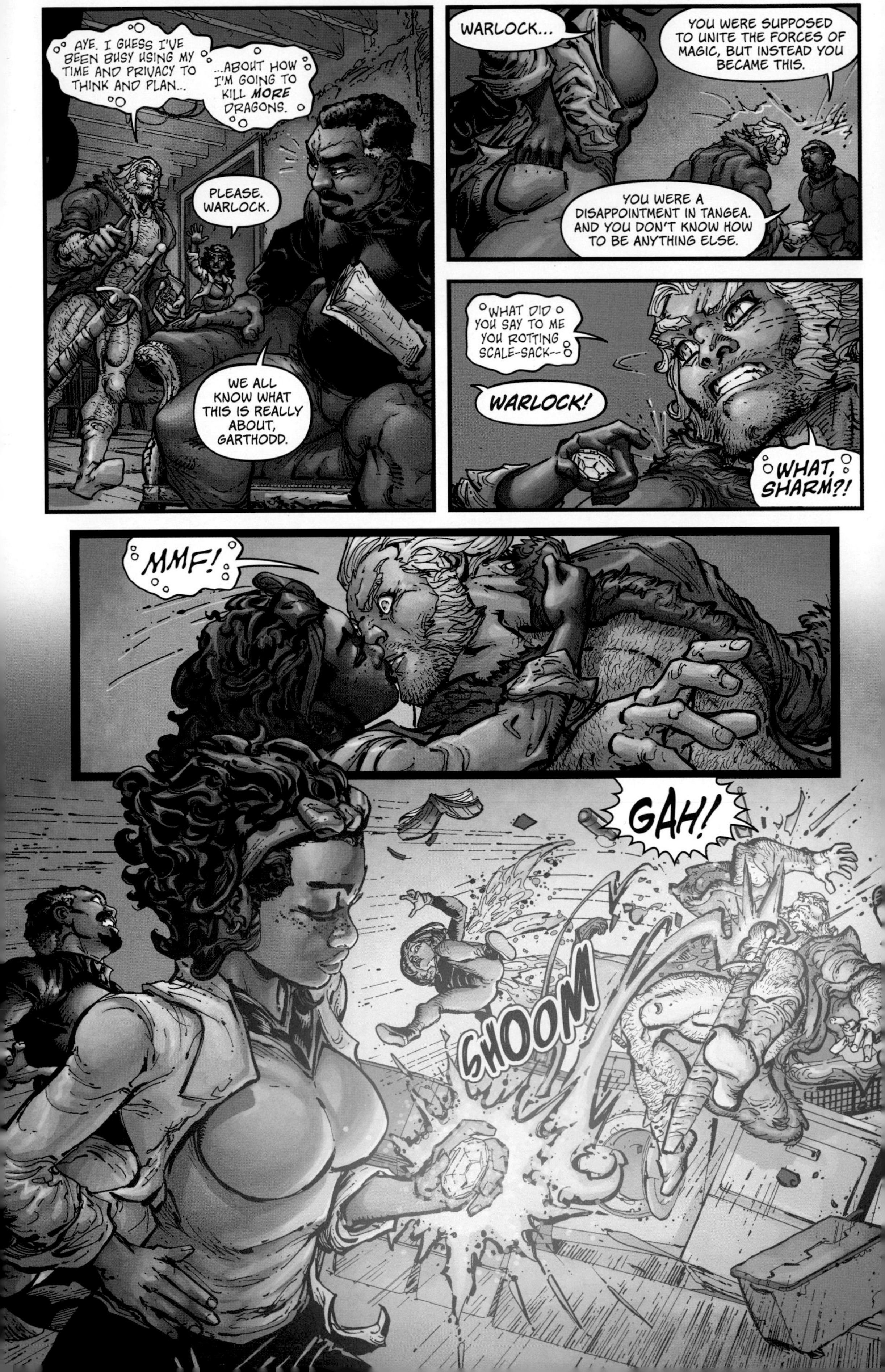
AYE. I GUESS I'VE BEEN BUSY USING MY TIME AND PRIVACY TO THINK AND PLAN...
...ABOUT HOW I'M GOING TO KILL MORE DRAGONS.
PLEASE. WARLOCK.
WE ALL KNOW WHAT THIS IS REALLY ABOUT, GARTHODD.
WARLOCK...
YOU WERE SUPPOSED TO UNITE THE FORCES OF MAGIC, BUT INSTEAD YOU BECAME THIS.
YOU WERE A DISAPPOINTMENT IN TANGEA. AND YOU DON'T KNOW HOW TO BE ANYTHING ELSE.
WHAT DID YOU SAY TO ME YOU ROTTING SCALE-SACK--
WARLOCK!
WHAT, SHARM?!
MMF!
GAH!
SHOOM

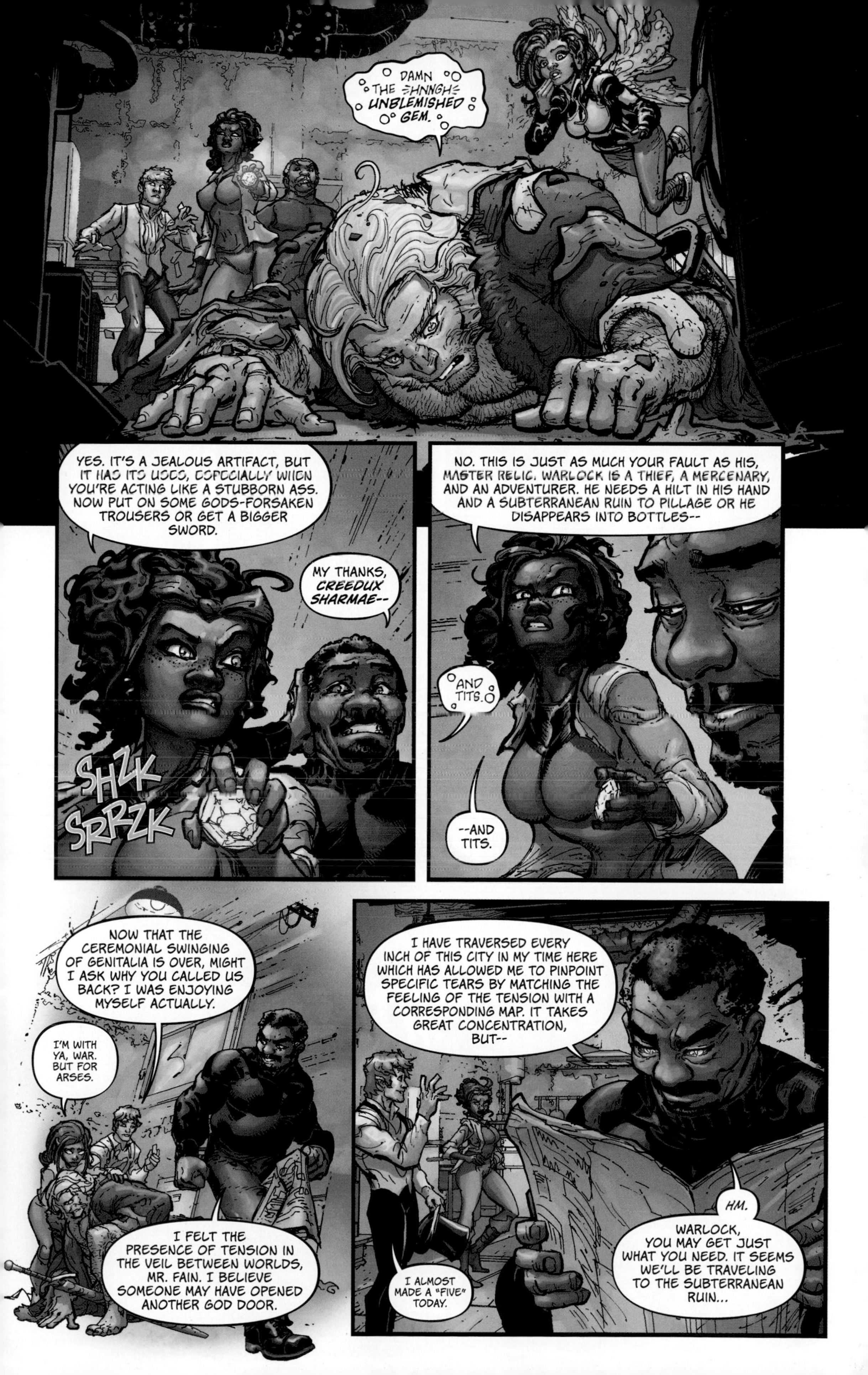
DAMN THE ≡HNNGH≡ UNBLEMISHED GEM.
YES. IT'S A JEALOUS ARTIFACT, BUT IT HAS ITS USES, ESPECIALLY WHEN YOU'RE ACTING LIKE A STUBBORN ASS. NOW PUT ON SOME GODS-FORSAKEN TROUSERS OR GET A BIGGER SWORD.
MY THANKS, CREEDUX SHARMAE--
SHZK SRRZK
NO. THIS IS JUST AS MUCH YOUR FAULT AS HIS, MASTER RELIC. WARLOCK IS A THIEF, A MERCENARY, AND AN ADVENTURER. HE NEEDS A HILT IN HIS HAND AND A SUBTERRANEAN RUIN TO PILLAGE OR HE DISAPPEARS INTO BOTTLES--
AND TITS.
--AND TITS.
NOW THAT THE CEREMONIAL SWINGING OF GENITALIA IS OVER, MIGHT I ASK WHY YOU CALLED US BACK? I WAS ENJOYING MYSELF ACTUALLY.
I'M WITH YA, WAR. BUT FOR ARSES.
I FELT THE PRESENCE OF TENSION IN THE VEIL BETWEEN WORLDS, MR. FAIN. I BELIEVE SOMEONE MAY HAVE OPENED ANOTHER GOD DOOR.
I HAVE TRAVERSED EVERY INCH OF THIS CITY IN MY TIME HERE WHICH HAS ALLOWED ME TO PINPOINT SPECIFIC TEARS BY MATCHING THE FEELING OF THE TENSION WITH A CORRESPONDING MAP. IT TAKES GREAT CONCENTRATION, BUT--
I ALMOST MADE A "FIVE" TODAY.
HM.
WARLOCK, YOU MAY GET JUST WHAT YOU NEED. IT SEEMS WE'LL BE TRAVELING TO THE SUBTERRANEAN RUIN...

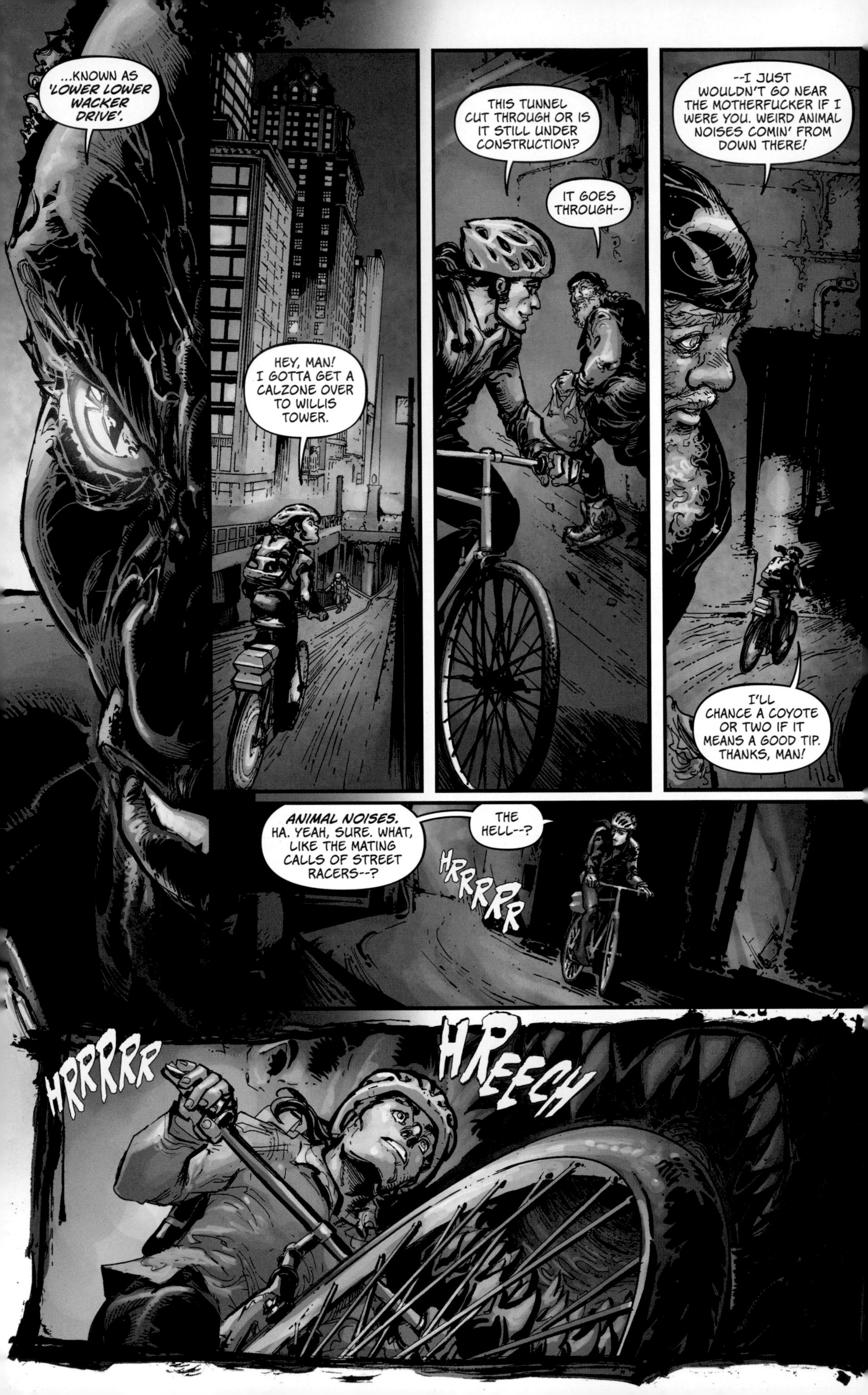
...KNOWN AS 'LOWER LOWER WACKER DRIVE'.
HEY, MAN! I GOTTA GET A CALZONE OVER TO WILLIS TOWER.
THIS TUNNEL CUT THROUGH OR IS IT STILL UNDER CONSTRUCTION?
IT GOES THROUGH--
--I JUST WOULDN'T GO NEAR THE MOTHERFUCKER IF I WERE YOU. WEIRD ANIMAL NOISES COMIN' FROM DOWN THERE!
I'LL CHANCE A COYOTE OR TWO IF IT MEANS A GOOD TIP. THANKS, MAN!
ANIMAL NOISES. HA. YEAH, SURE. WHAT, LIKE THE MATING CALLS OF STREET RACERS--?
THE HELL--?
HRRRRR
HRRRRR
HREECH

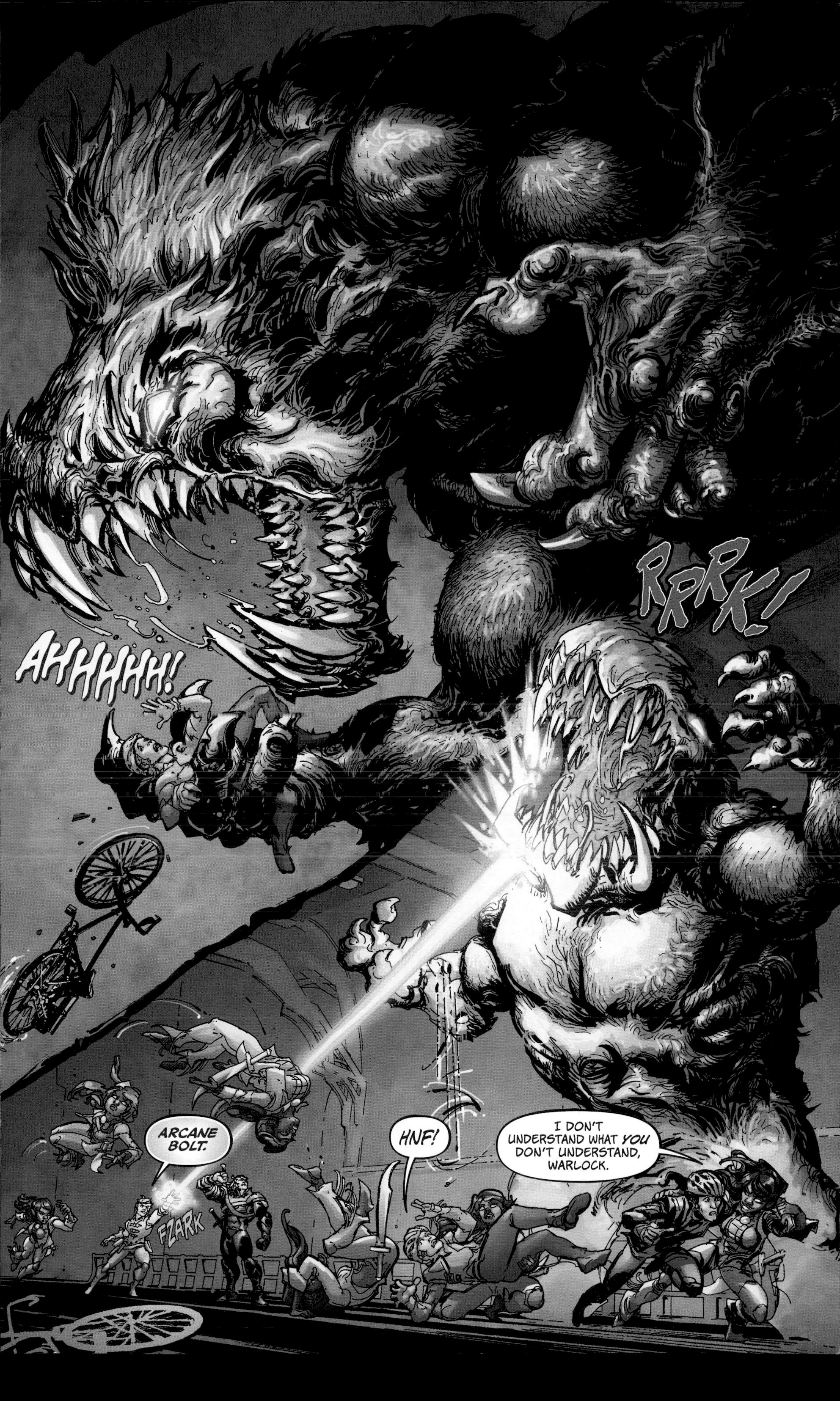
RRRK!
AHHHHH!
ARCANE BOLT.
FZARK
HNF!
I DON'T UNDERSTAND WHAT YOU DON'T UNDERSTAND, WARLOCK.

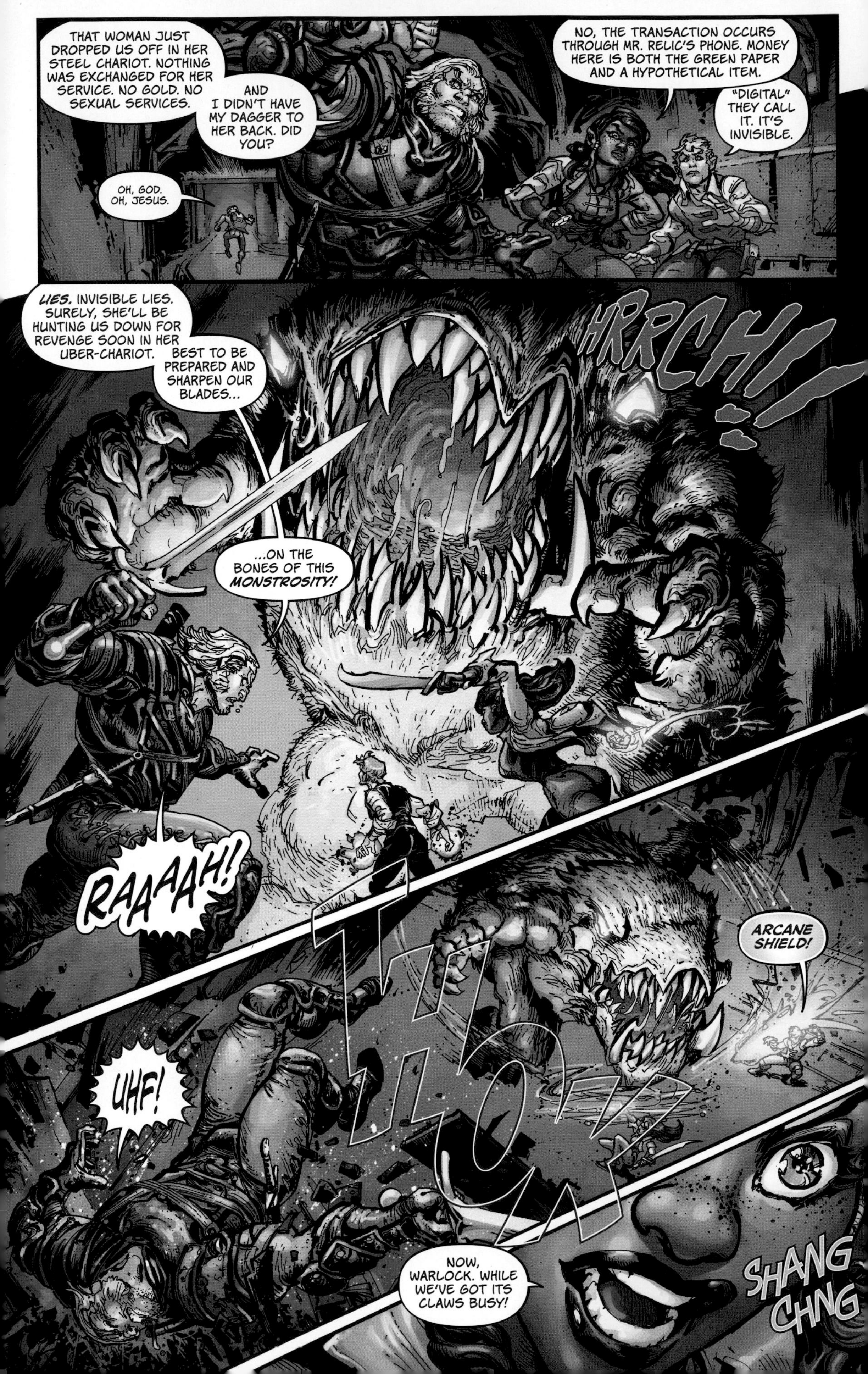
THAT WOMAN JUST DROPPED US OFF IN HER STEEL CHARIOT. NOTHING WAS EXCHANGED FOR HER SERVICE. NO GOLD. NO SEXUAL SERVICES.
AND I DIDN'T HAVE MY DAGGER TO HER BACK. DID YOU?
NO, THE TRANSACTION OCCURS THROUGH MR. RELIC'S PHONE. MONEY HERE IS BOTH THE GREEN PAPER AND A HYPOTHETICAL ITEM.
"DIGITAL" THEY CALL IT. IT'S INVISIBLE.
OH, GOD. OH, JESUS.
LIES. INVISIBLE LIES. SURELY, SHE'LL BE HUNTING US DOWN FOR REVENGE SOON IN HER UBER-CHARIOT.
BEST TO BE PREPARED AND SHARPEN OUR BLADES...
HRRCH!!
...ON THE BONES OF THIS MONSTROSITY!
RAAAAH!
ARCANE SHIELD!
UHF!
THOOM
NOW, WARLOCK. WHILE WE'VE GOT ITS CLAWS BUSY!
SHANG CHNG

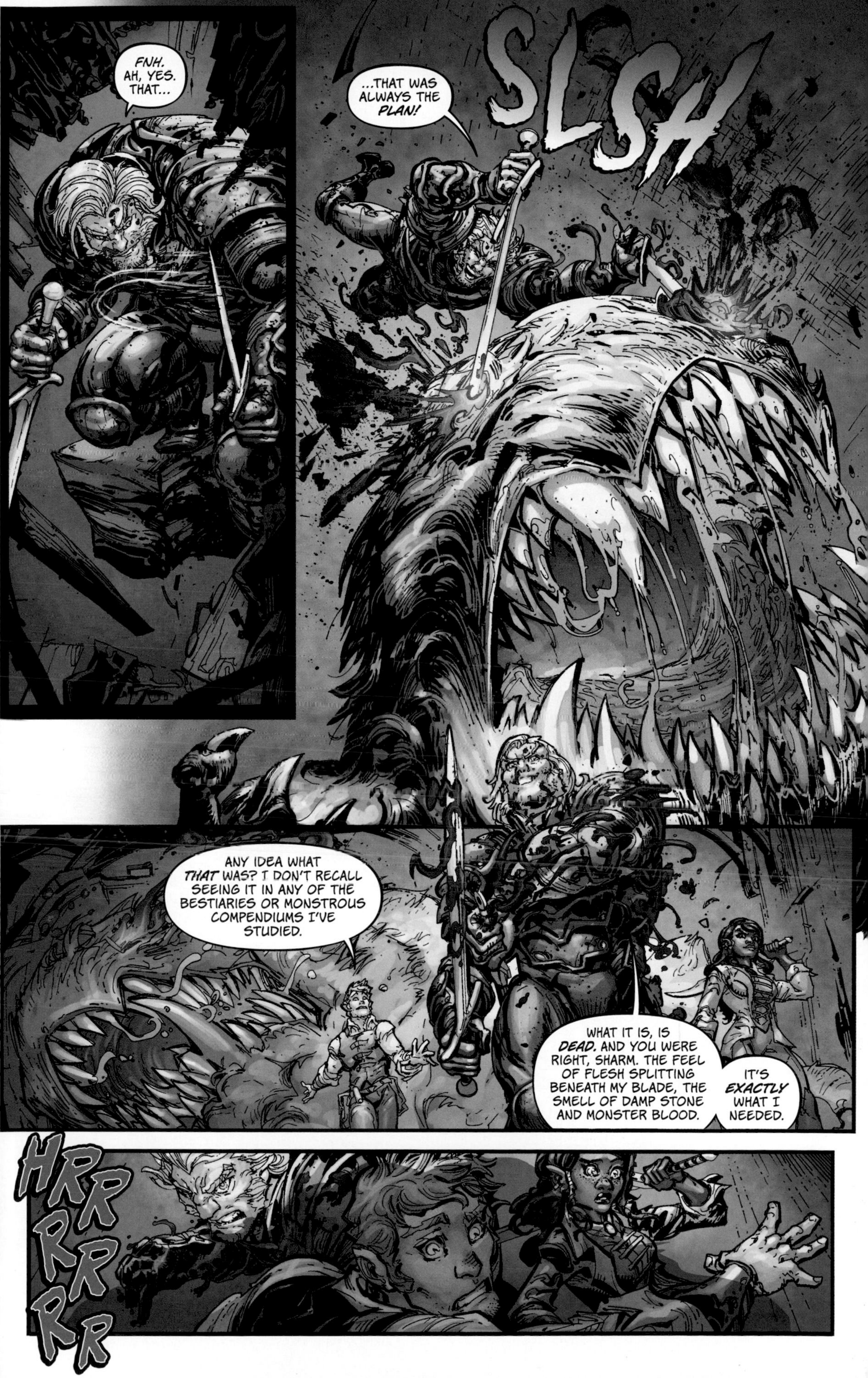
FNH. AH, YES. THAT...
...THAT WAS ALWAYS THE PLAN!
SLSH
ANY IDEA WHAT THAT WAS? I DON'T RECALL SEEING IT IN ANY OF THE BESTIARIES OR MONSTROUS COMPENDIUMS I'VE STUDIED.
WHAT IT IS, IS DEAD. AND YOU WERE RIGHT, SHARM. THE FEEL OF FLESH SPLITTING BENEATH MY BLADE, THE SMELL OF DAMP STONE AND MONSTER BLOOD.
IT'S EXACTLY WHAT I NEEDED.
HRRRRRRR

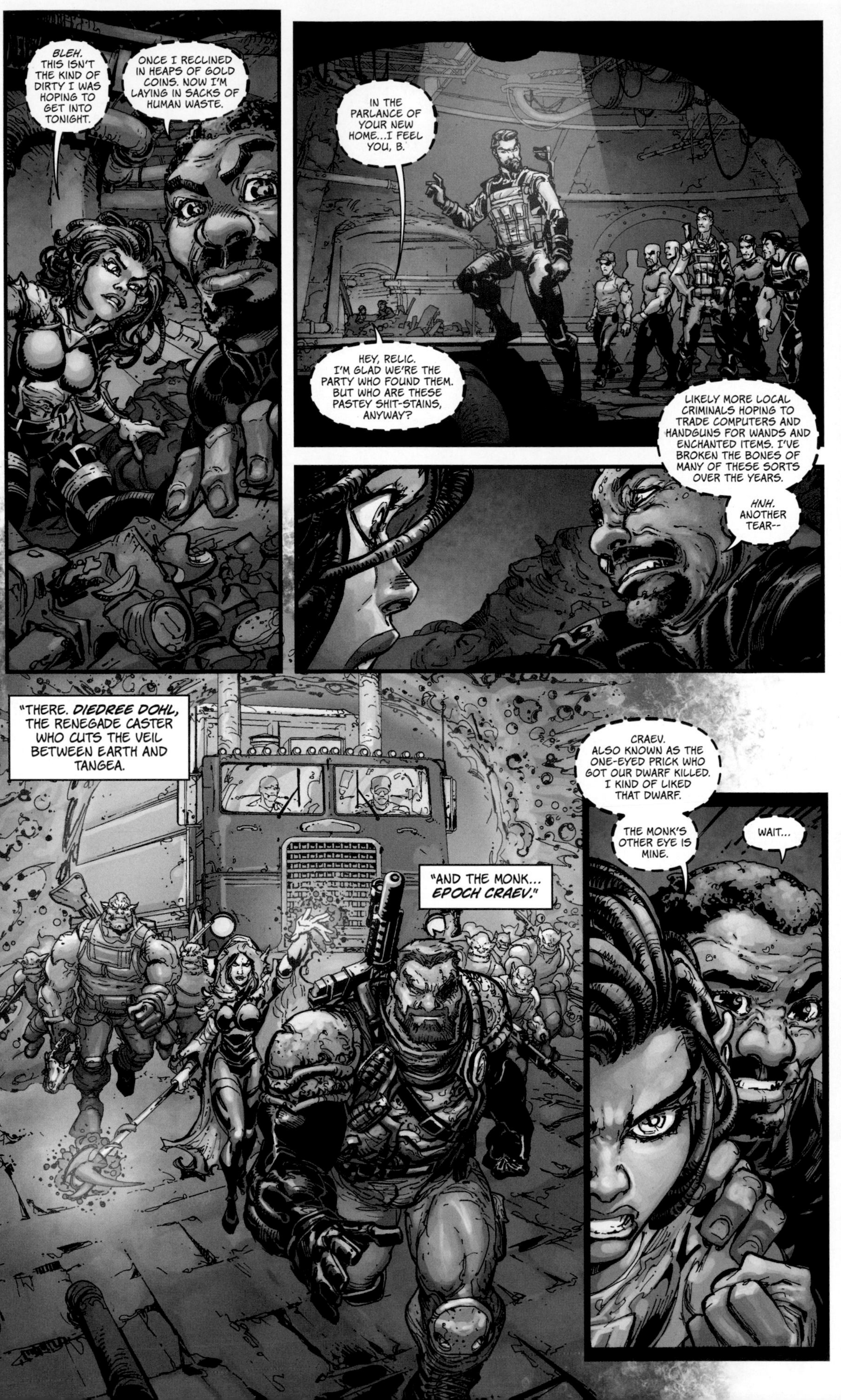
BLEH. THIS ISN'T THE KIND OF DIRTY I WAS HOPING TO GET INTO TONIGHT.
ONCE I RECLINED IN HEAPS OF GOLD COINS. NOW I'M LAYING IN SACKS OF HUMAN WASTE.
IN THE PARLANCE OF YOUR NEW HOME...I FEEL YOU, B.
HEY, RELIC. I'M GLAD WE'RE THE PARTY WHO FOUND THEM. BUT WHO ARE THESE PASTEY SHIT-STAINS, ANYWAY?
LIKELY MORE LOCAL CRIMINALS HOPING TO TRADE COMPUTERS AND HANDGUNS FOR WANDS AND ENCHANTED ITEMS. I'VE BROKEN THE BONES OF MANY OF THESE SORTS OVER THE YEARS.
HNH. ANOTHER TEAR--
"THERE. DIEDREE DOHL, THE RENEGADE CASTER WHO CUTS THE VEIL BETWEEN EARTH AND TANGEA.
"AND THE MONK... EPOCH CRAEV."
CRAEV. ALSO KNOWN AS THE ONE-EYED PRICK WHO GOT OUR DWARF KILLED. I KIND OF LIKED THAT DWARF.
THE MONK'S OTHER EYE IS MINE.
WAIT...

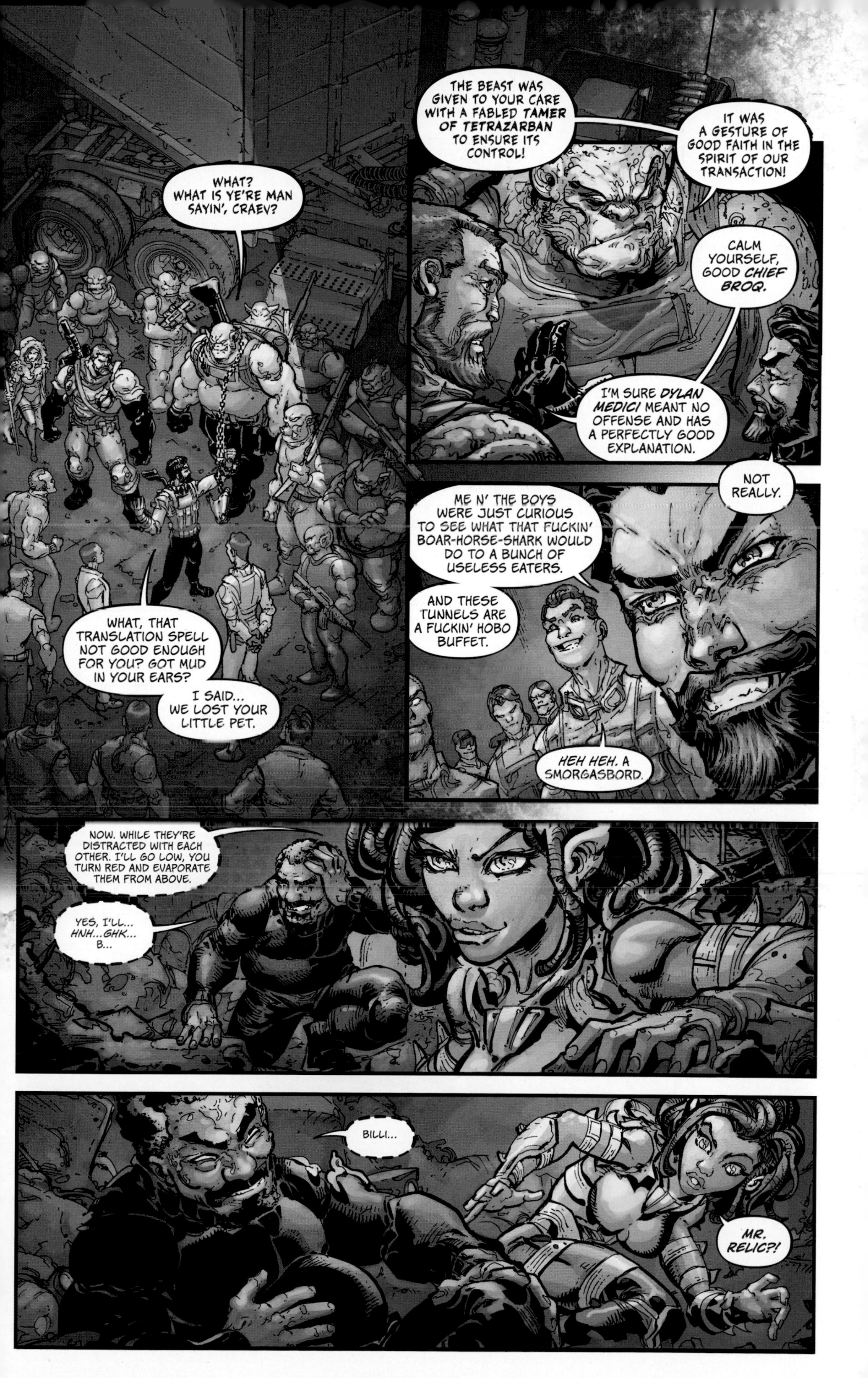
WHAT? WHAT IS YE'RE MAN SAYIN', CRAEV?
THE BEAST WAS GIVEN TO YOUR CARE WITH A FABLED TAMER OF TETRAZARBAN TO ENSURE ITS CONTROL!
IT WAS A GESTURE OF GOOD FAITH IN THE SPIRIT OF OUR TRANSACTION!
CALM YOURSELF, GOOD CHIEF BROQ.
I'M SURE DYLAN MEDICI MEANT NO OFFENSE AND HAS A PERFECTLY GOOD EXPLANATION.
NOT REALLY.
ME N' THE BOYS WERE JUST CURIOUS TO SEE WHAT THAT FUCKIN' BOAR-HORSE-SHARK WOULD DO TO A BUNCH OF USELESS EATERS.
AND THESE TUNNELS ARE A FUCKIN' HOBO BUFFET.
HEH HEH. A SMORGASBORD.
WHAT, THAT TRANSLATION SPELL NOT GOOD ENOUGH FOR YOU? GOT MUD IN YOUR EARS?
I SAID... WE LOST YOUR LITTLE PET.
NOW. WHILE THEY'RE DISTRACTED WITH EACH OTHER. I'LL GO LOW, YOU TURN RED AND EVAPORATE THEM FROM ABOVE.
YES, I'LL... HNH...GHK... B...
BILLI...
MR. RELIC?!

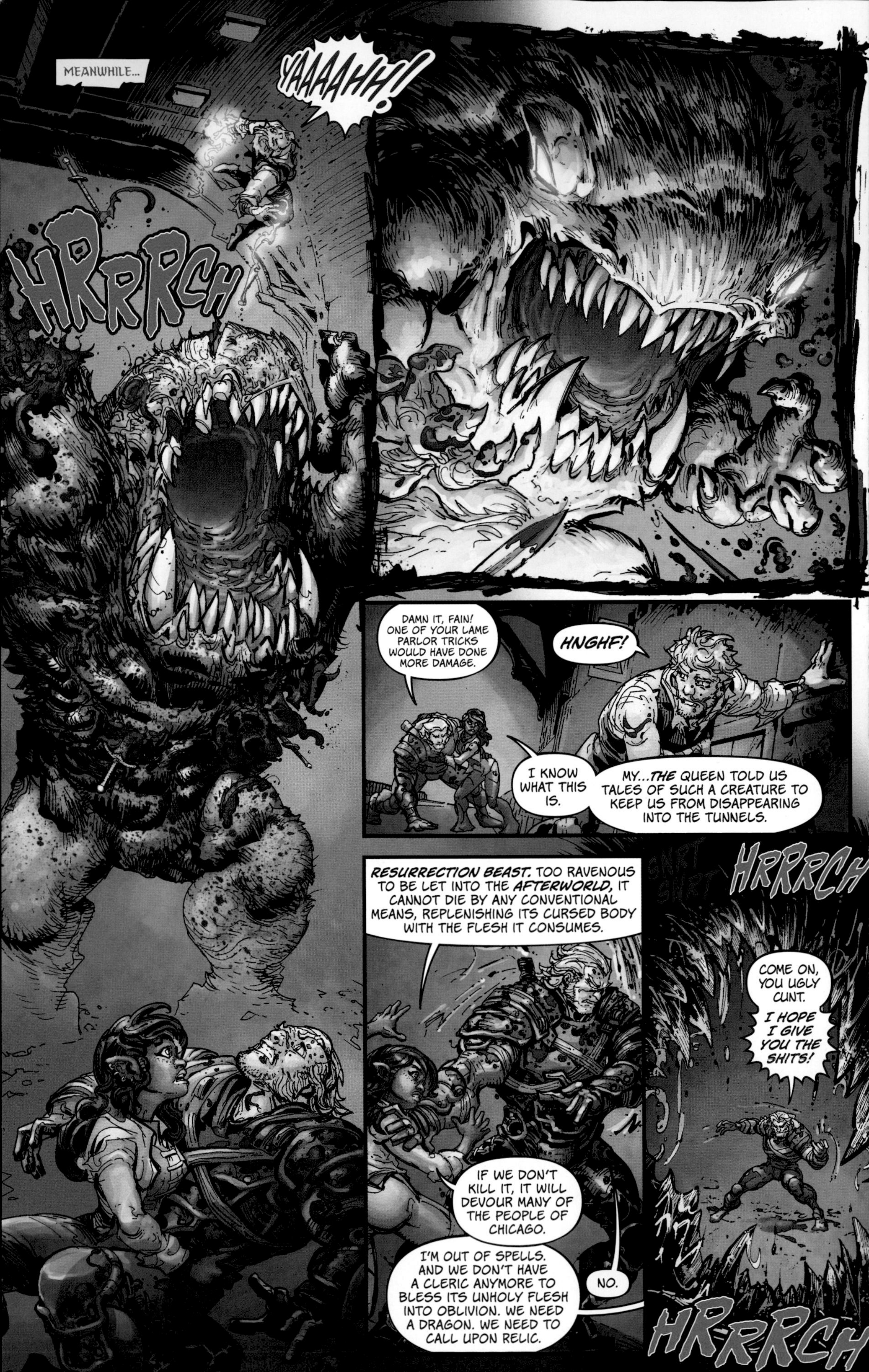
MEANWHILE...
YAAAAAHH!
HRRRCH
DAMN IT, FAIN! ONE OF YOUR LAME PARLOR TRICKS WOULD HAVE DONE MORE DAMAGE.
HNGHF!
I KNOW WHAT THIS IS.
MY...THE QUEEN TOLD US TALES OF SUCH A CREATURE TO KEEP US FROM DISAPPEARING INTO THE TUNNELS.
RESURRECTION BEAST. TOO RAVENOUS TO BE LET INTO THE AFTERWORLD, IT CANNOT DIE BY ANY CONVENTIONAL MEANS, REPLENISHING ITS CURSED BODY WITH THE FLESH IT CONSUMES.
IF WE DON'T KILL IT, IT WILL DEVOUR MANY OF THE PEOPLE OF CHICAGO.
I'M OUT OF SPELLS. AND WE DON'T HAVE A CLERIC ANYMORE TO BLESS ITS UNHOLY FLESH INTO OBLIVION. WE NEED A DRAGON. WE NEED TO CALL UPON RELIC.
NO.
SHRT SHRT
HRRRCH
COME ON, YOU UGLY CUNT. I HOPE I GIVE YOU THE SHITS!
HRRRCH

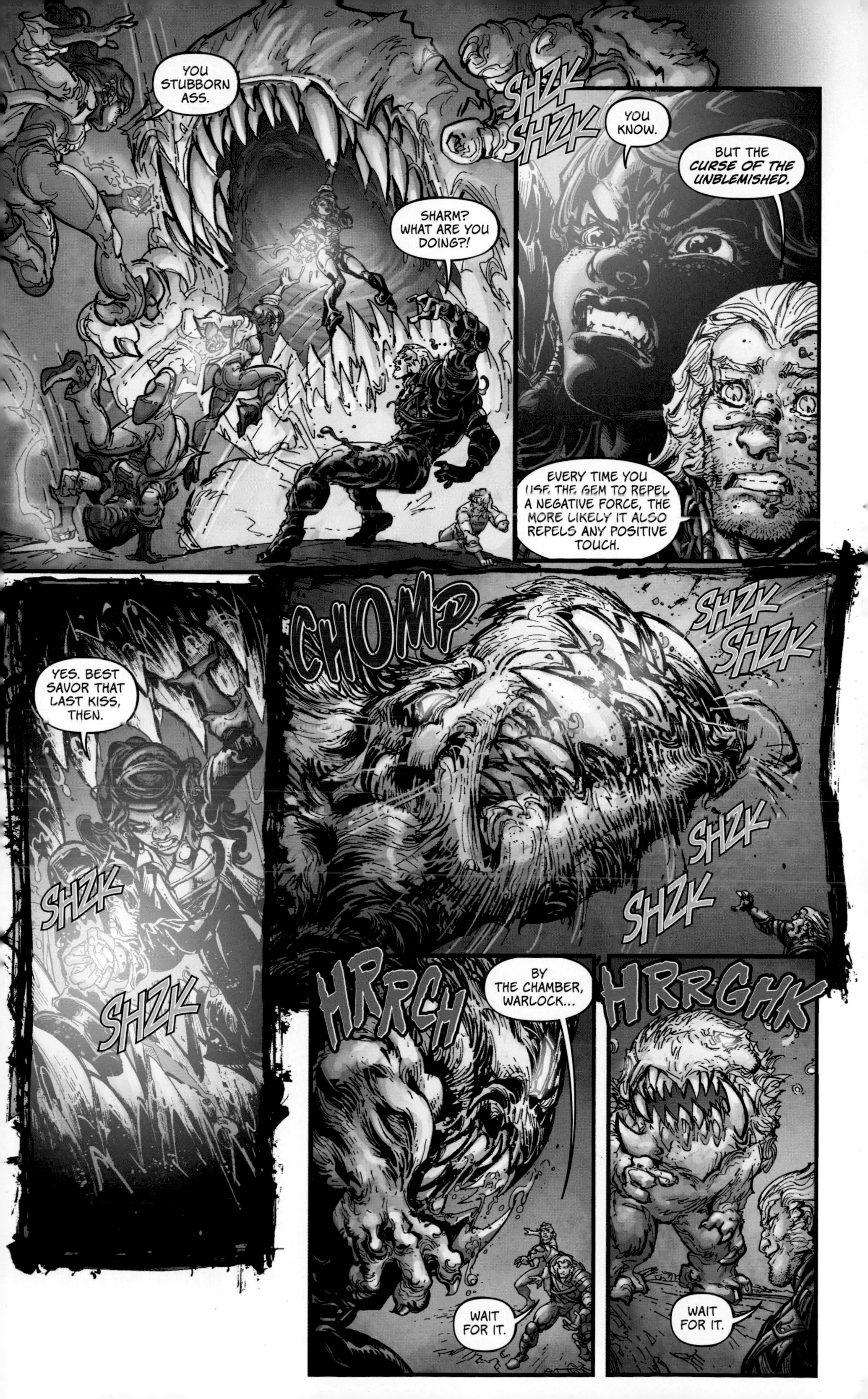
YOU STUBBORN ASS.
SHZK SHZK
YOU KNOW.
BUT THE CURSE OF THE UNBLEMISHED.
SHARM? WHAT ARE YOU DOING?!
EVERY TIME YOU USE THE GEM TO REPEL A NEGATIVE FORCE, THE MORE LIKELY IT ALSO REPELS ANY POSITIVE TOUCH.
YES. BEST SAVOR THAT LAST KISS, THEN.
SHZK
SHZK
CHOMP
SHZK SHZK
SHZK
SHZK
HRRCH
BY THE CHAMBER, WARLOCK...
WAIT FOR IT.
HRRGHK
WAIT FOR IT.

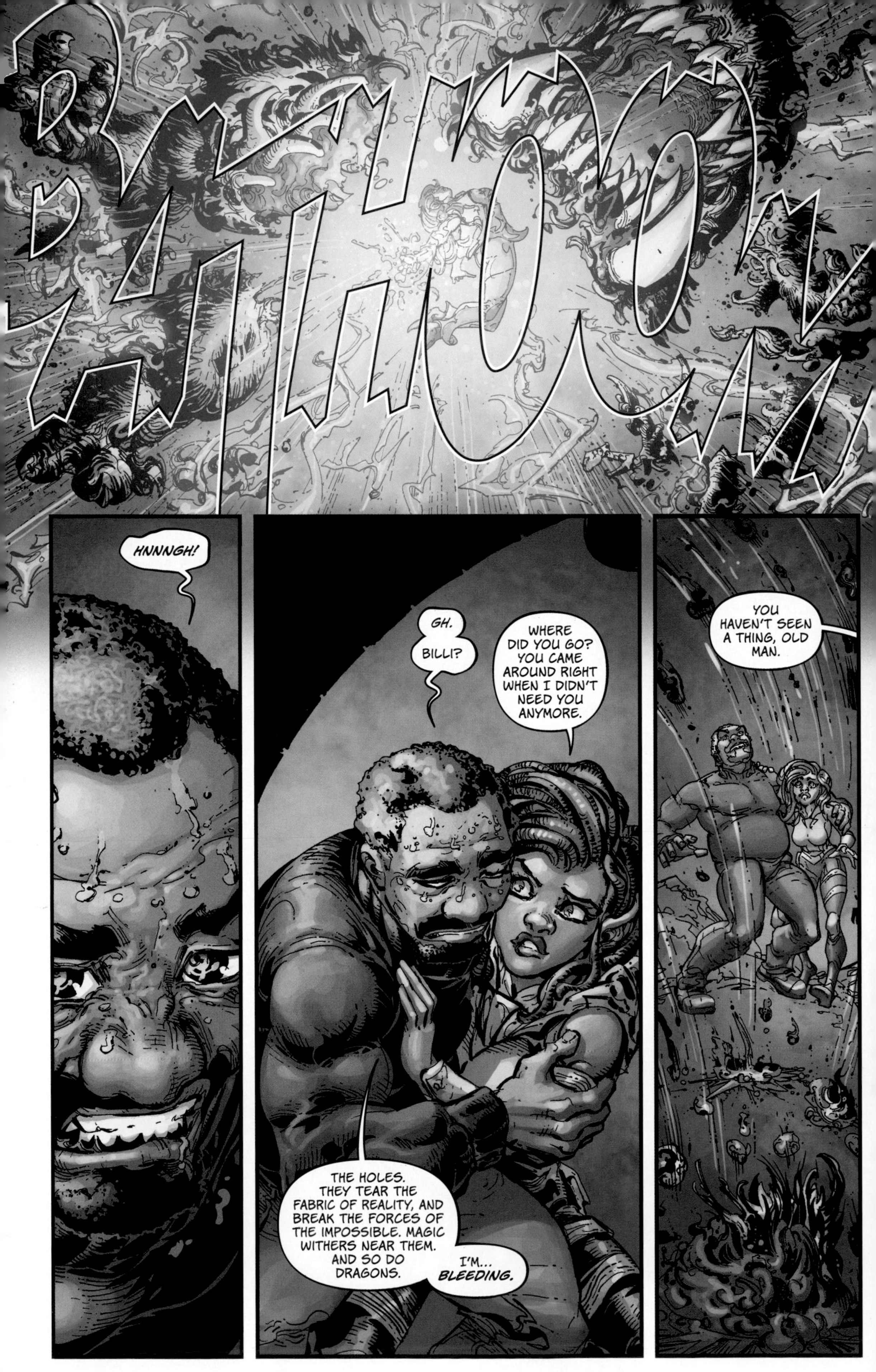

HNNNGH!
GH.
BILLI?
WHERE DID YOU GO? YOU CAME AROUND RIGHT WHEN I DIDN'T NEED YOU ANYMORE.
THE HOLES. THEY TEAR THE FABRIC OF REALITY, AND BREAK THE FORCES OF THE IMPOSSIBLE. MAGIC WITHERS NEAR THEM. AND SO DO DRAGONS.
I'M... BLEEDING.
YOU HAVEN'T SEEN A THING, OLD MAN.

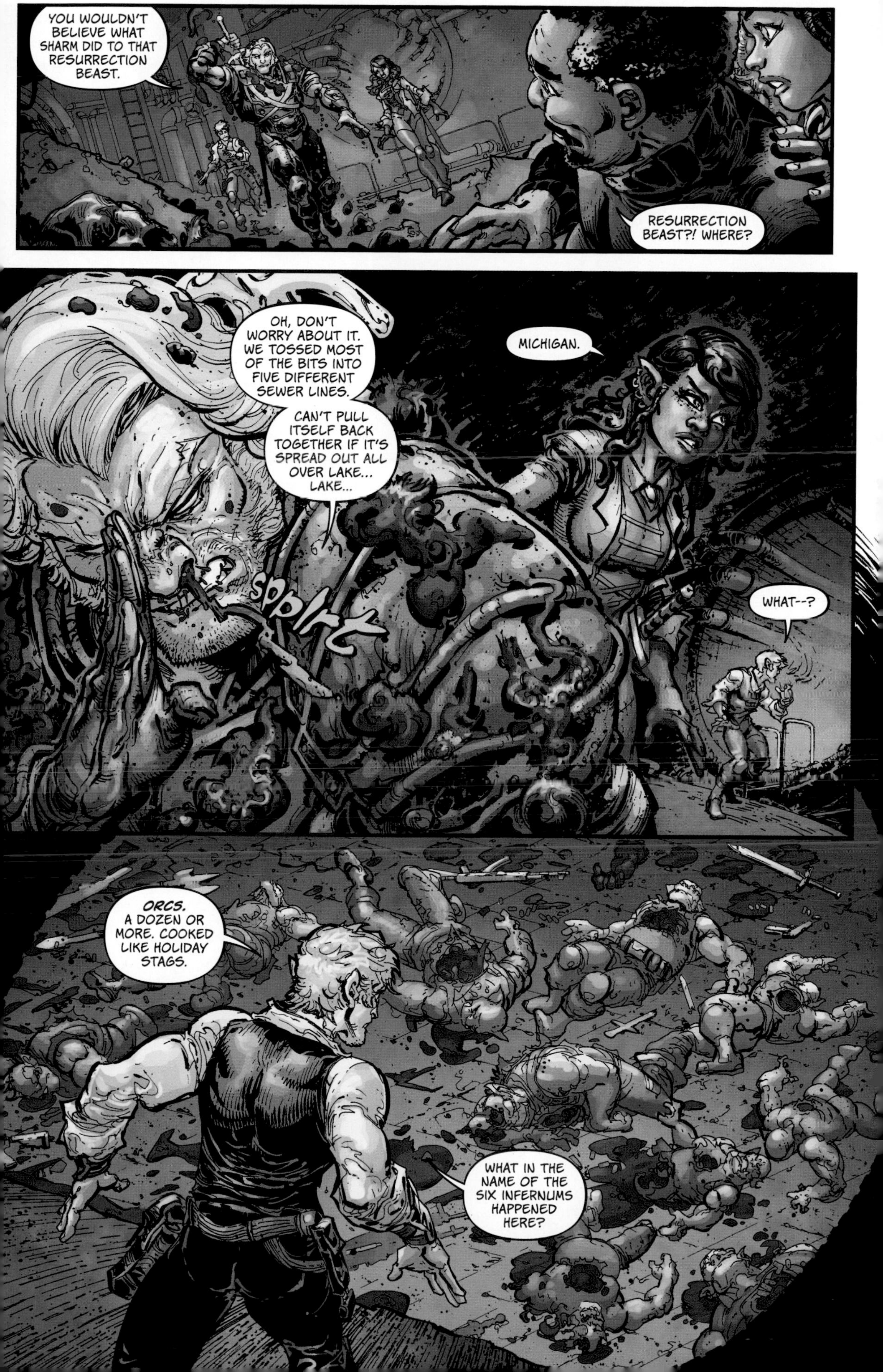
YOU WOULDN'T BELIEVE WHAT SHARM DID TO THAT RESURRECTION BEAST.
RESURRECTION BEAST?! WHERE?
OH, DON'T WORRY ABOUT IT. WE TOSSED MOST OF THE BITS INTO FIVE DIFFERENT SEWER LINES.
CAN'T PULL ITSELF BACK TOGETHER IF IT'S SPREAD OUT ALL OVER LAKE... LAKE...
MICHIGAN.
SPPLRT
WHAT--?
ORCS. A DOZEN OR MORE. COOKED LIKE HOLIDAY STAGS.
WHAT IN THE NAME OF THE SIX INFERNUMS HAPPENED HERE?

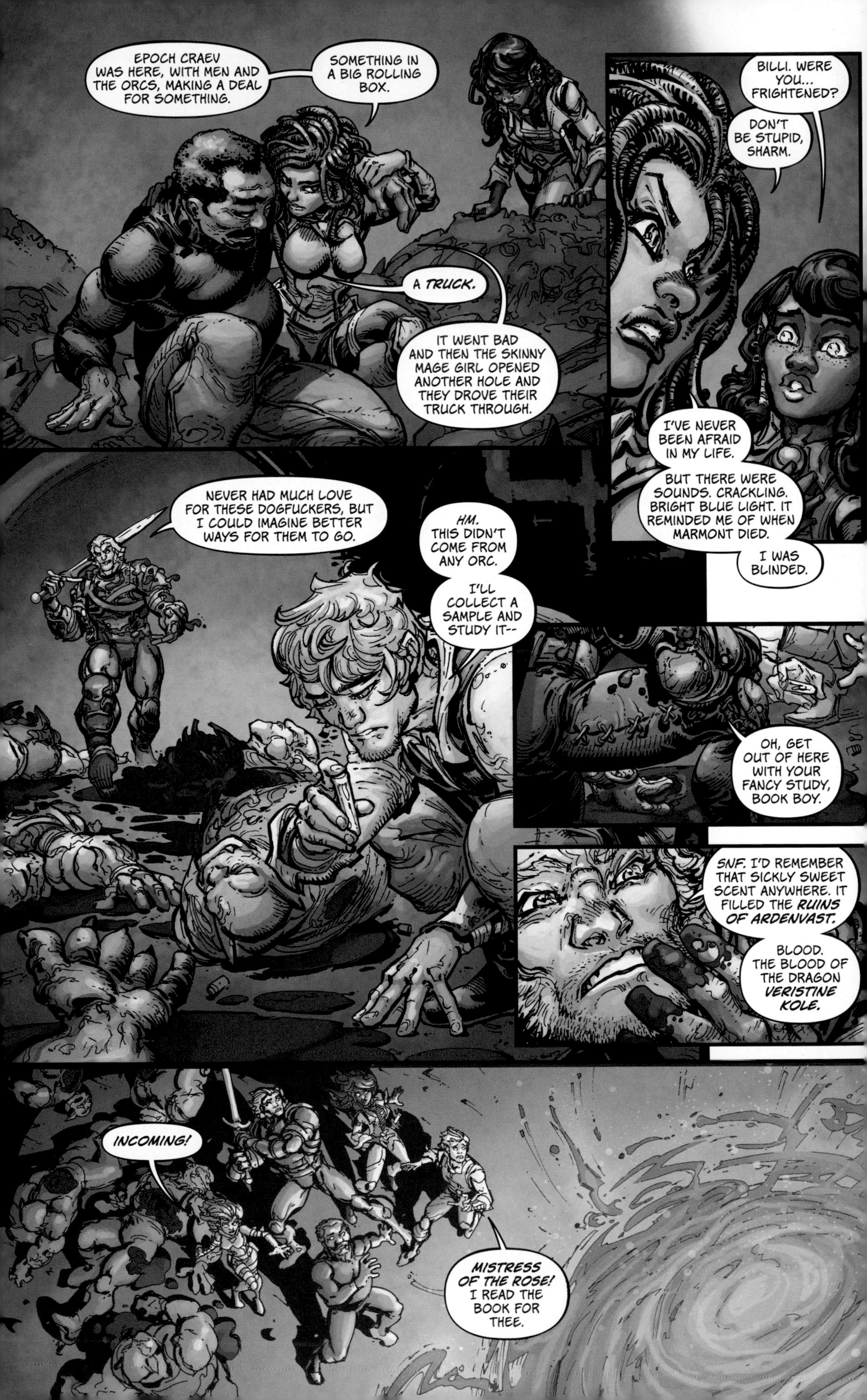

EPOCH CRAEV WAS HERE, WITH MEN AND THE ORCS, MAKING A DEAL FOR SOMETHING.
SOMETHING IN A BIG ROLLING BOX.
A *TRUCK.*
IT WENT BAD AND THEN THE SKINNY MAGE GIRL OPENED ANOTHER HOLE AND THEY DROVE THEIR TRUCK THROUGH.
BILLI. WERE YOU... FRIGHTENED?
DON'T BE STUPID, SHARM.
I'VE NEVER BEEN AFRAID IN MY LIFE.
BUT THERE WERE SOUNDS. CRACKLING. BRIGHT BLUE LIGHT. IT REMINDED ME OF WHEN MARMONT DIED.
I WAS BLINDED.
NEVER HAD MUCH LOVE FOR THESE DOGFUCKERS, BUT I COULD IMAGINE BETTER WAYS FOR THEM TO GO.
HM. THIS DIDN'T COME FROM ANY ORC.
I'LL COLLECT A SAMPLE AND STUDY IT--
OH, GET OUT OF HERE WITH YOUR FANCY STUDY, BOOK BOY.
SNF. I'D REMEMBER THAT SICKLY SWEET SCENT ANYWHERE. IT FILLED THE *RUINS OF ARDENVAST.*
BLOOD. THE BLOOD OF THE DRAGON *VERISTINE KOLE.*
INCOMING!
MISTRESS OF THE ROSE! I READ THE BOOK FOR THEE.

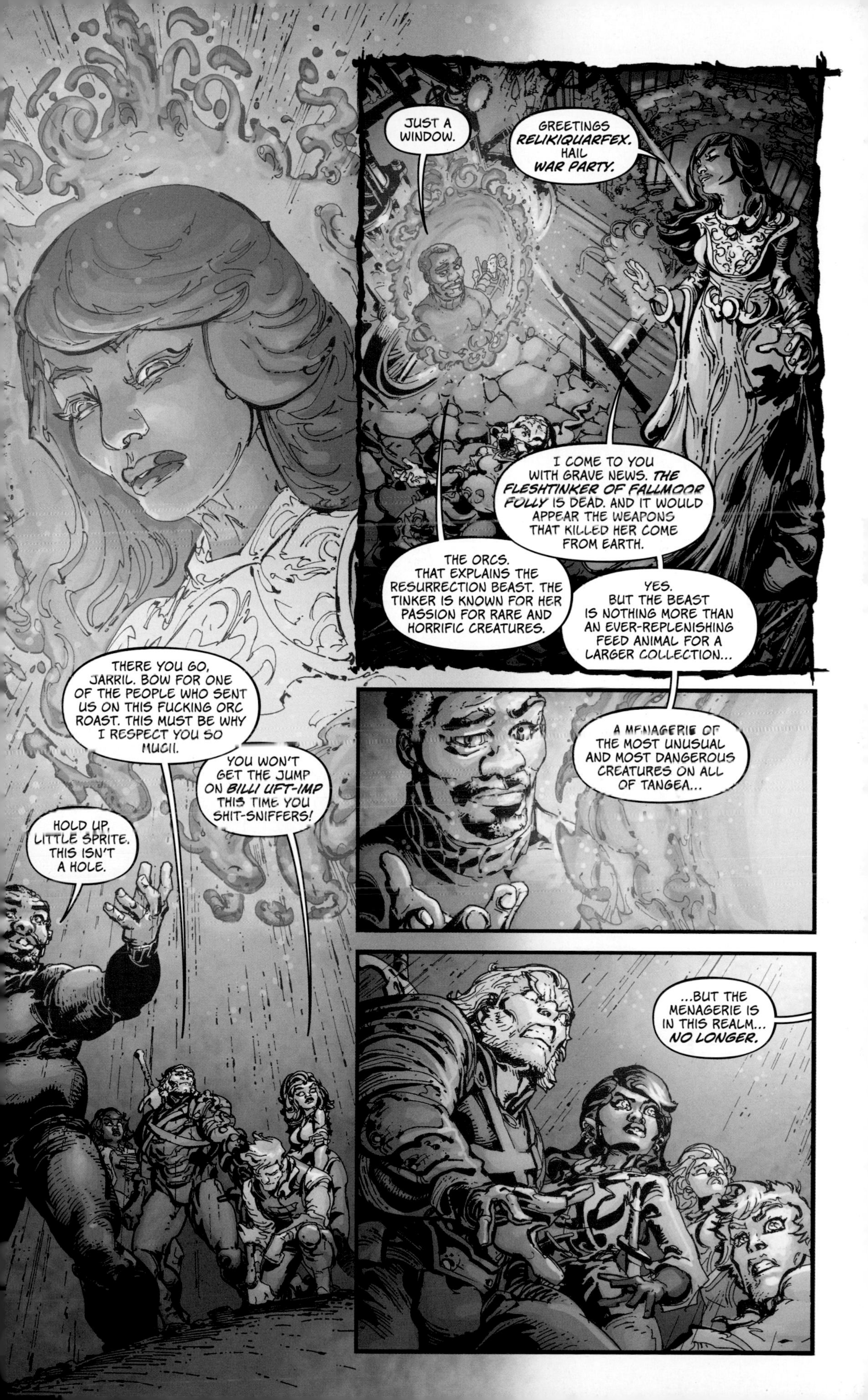
THERE YOU GO, JARRIL. BOW FOR ONE OF THE PEOPLE WHO SENT US ON THIS FUCKING ORC ROAST. THIS MUST BE WHY I RESPECT YOU SO MUCH.
YOU WON'T GET THE JUMP ON *BILLI UFT-IMP* THIS TIME YOU SHIT-SNIFFERS!
HOLD UP, LITTLE SPRITE. THIS ISN'T A HOLE.
JUST A WINDOW.
GREETINGS *RELIKIQUARFEX.* HAIL *WAR PARTY.*
I COME TO YOU WITH GRAVE NEWS. *THE FLESHTINKER OF FALLMOOR FOLLY* IS DEAD. AND IT WOULD APPEAR THE WEAPONS THAT KILLED HER COME FROM EARTH.
THE ORCS. THAT EXPLAINS THE RESURRECTION BEAST. THE TINKER IS KNOWN FOR HER PASSION FOR RARE AND HORRIFIC CREATURES.
YES. BUT THE BEAST IS NOTHING MORE THAN AN EVER-REPLENISHING FEED ANIMAL FOR A LARGER COLLECTION...
A MENAGERIE OF THE MOST UNUSUAL AND MOST DANGEROUS CREATURES ON ALL OF TANGEA...
...BUT THE MENAGERIE IS IN THIS REALM... *NO LONGER.*

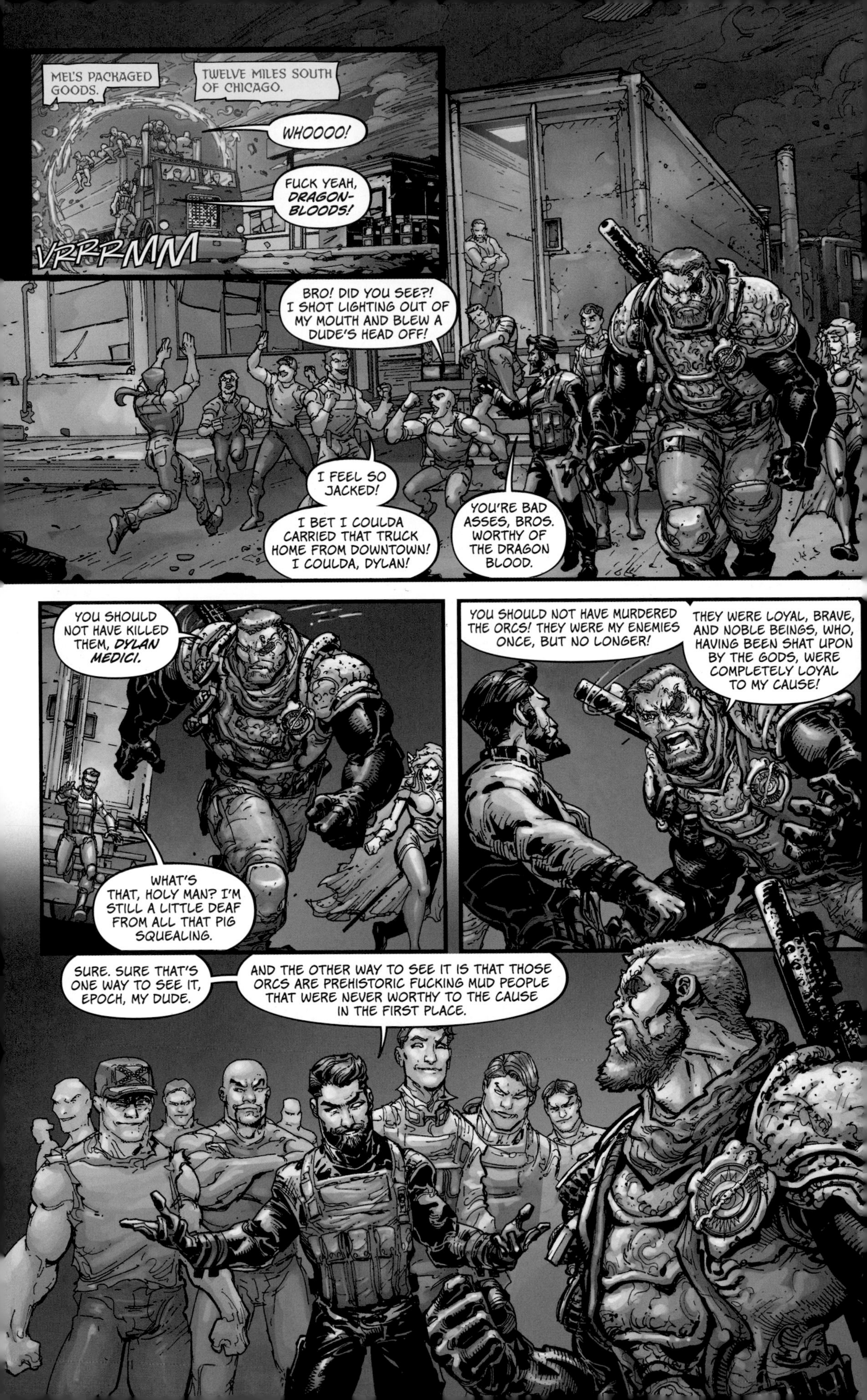

MEL'S PACKAGED GOODS.
TWELVE MILES SOUTH OF CHICAGO.
WHOOOO!
FUCK YEAH, DRAGON-BLOODS!
VRRRMMM
BRO! DID YOU SEE?! I SHOT LIGHTING OUT OF MY MOUTH AND BLEW A DUDE'S HEAD OFF!
I FEEL SO JACKED!
I BET I COULDA CARRIED THAT TRUCK HOME FROM DOWNTOWN! I COULDA, DYLAN!
YOU'RE BAD ASSES, BROS. WORTHY OF THE DRAGON BLOOD.
YOU SHOULD NOT HAVE KILLED THEM, DYLAN MEDICI.
WHAT'S THAT, HOLY MAN? I'M STILL A LITTLE DEAF FROM ALL THAT PIG SQUEALING.
YOU SHOULD NOT HAVE MURDERED THE ORCS! THEY WERE MY ENEMIES ONCE, BUT NO LONGER!
THEY WERE LOYAL, BRAVE, AND NOBLE BEINGS, WHO, HAVING BEEN SHAT UPON BY THE GODS, WERE COMPLETELY LOYAL TO MY CAUSE!
SURE. SURE THAT'S ONE WAY TO SEE IT, EPOCH, MY DUDE.
AND THE OTHER WAY TO SEE IT IS THAT THOSE ORCS ARE PREHISTORIC FUCKING MUD PEOPLE THAT WERE NEVER WORTHY TO THE CAUSE IN THE FIRST PLACE.

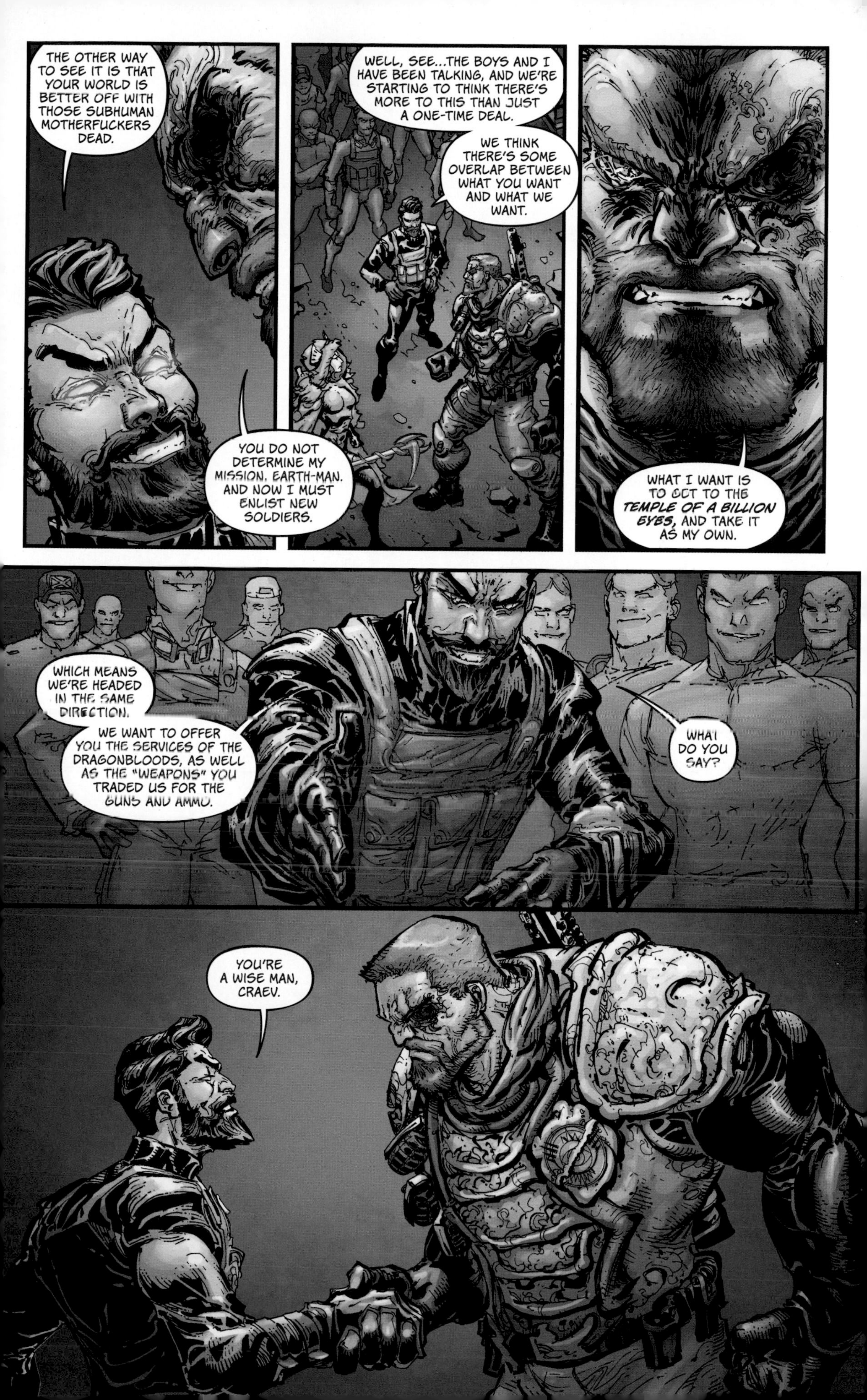
THE OTHER WAY TO SEE IT IS THAT YOUR WORLD IS BETTER OFF WITH THOSE SUBHUMAN MOTHERFUCKERS DEAD.
YOU DO NOT DETERMINE MY MISSION, EARTH-MAN. AND NOW I MUST ENLIST NEW SOLDIERS.
WELL, SEE...THE BOYS AND I HAVE BEEN TALKING, AND WE'RE STARTING TO THINK THERE'S MORE TO THIS THAN JUST A ONE-TIME DEAL.
WE THINK THERE'S SOME OVERLAP BETWEEN WHAT YOU WANT AND WHAT WE WANT.
WHAT I WANT IS TO GET TO THE *TEMPLE OF A BILLION EYES*, AND TAKE IT AS MY OWN.
WHICH MEANS WE'RE HEADED IN THE SAME DIRECTION.
WE WANT TO OFFER YOU THE SERVICES OF THE DRAGONBLOODS, AS WELL AS THE "WEAPONS" YOU TRADED US FOR THE GUNS AND AMMO.
WHAT DO YOU SAY?
YOU'RE A WISE MAN, CRAEV.

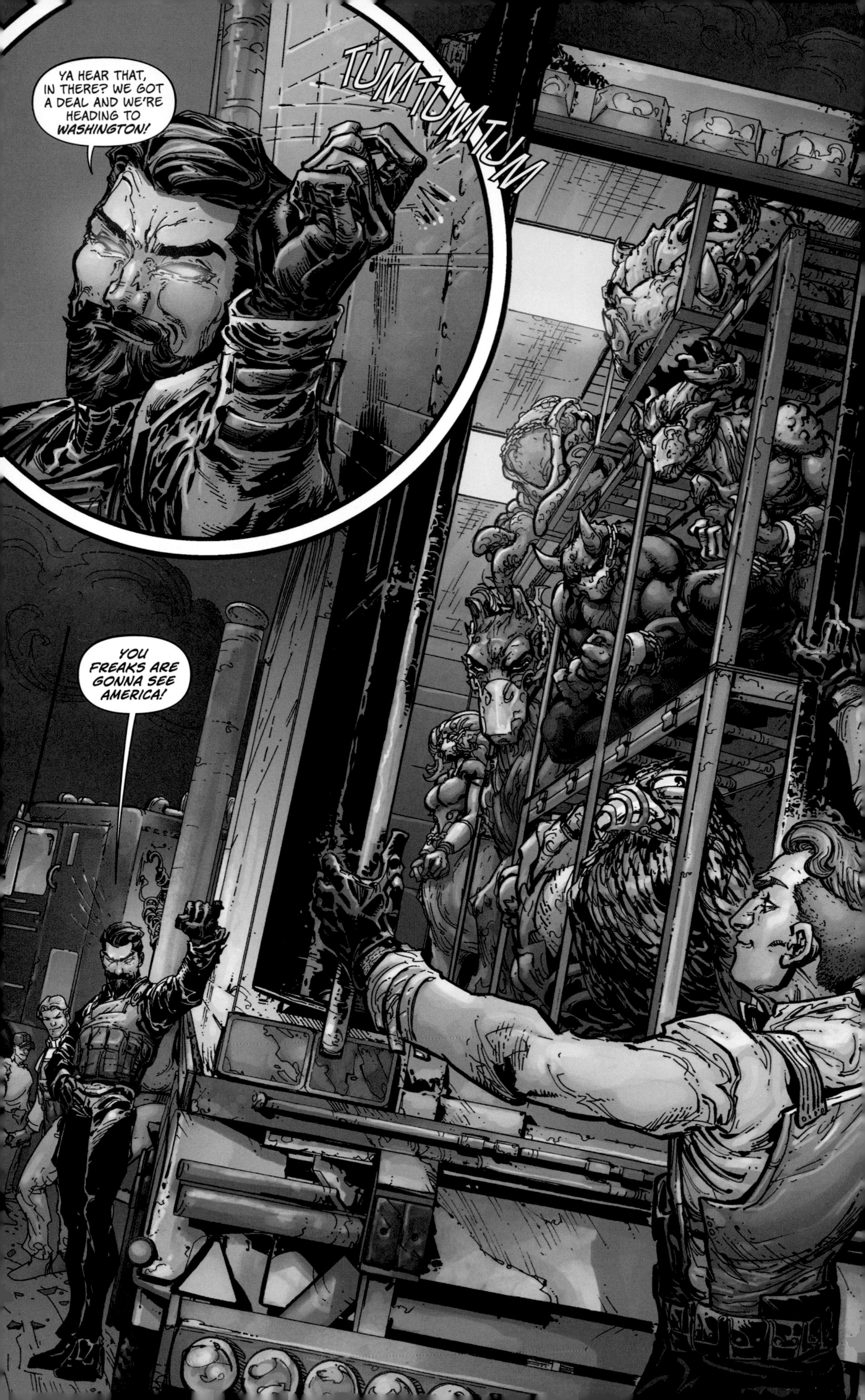
YA HEAR THAT, IN THERE? WE GOT A DEAL AND WE'RE HEADING TO WASHINGTON!
TUMTUMTUMTUM
YOU FREAKS ARE GONNA SEE AMERICA!

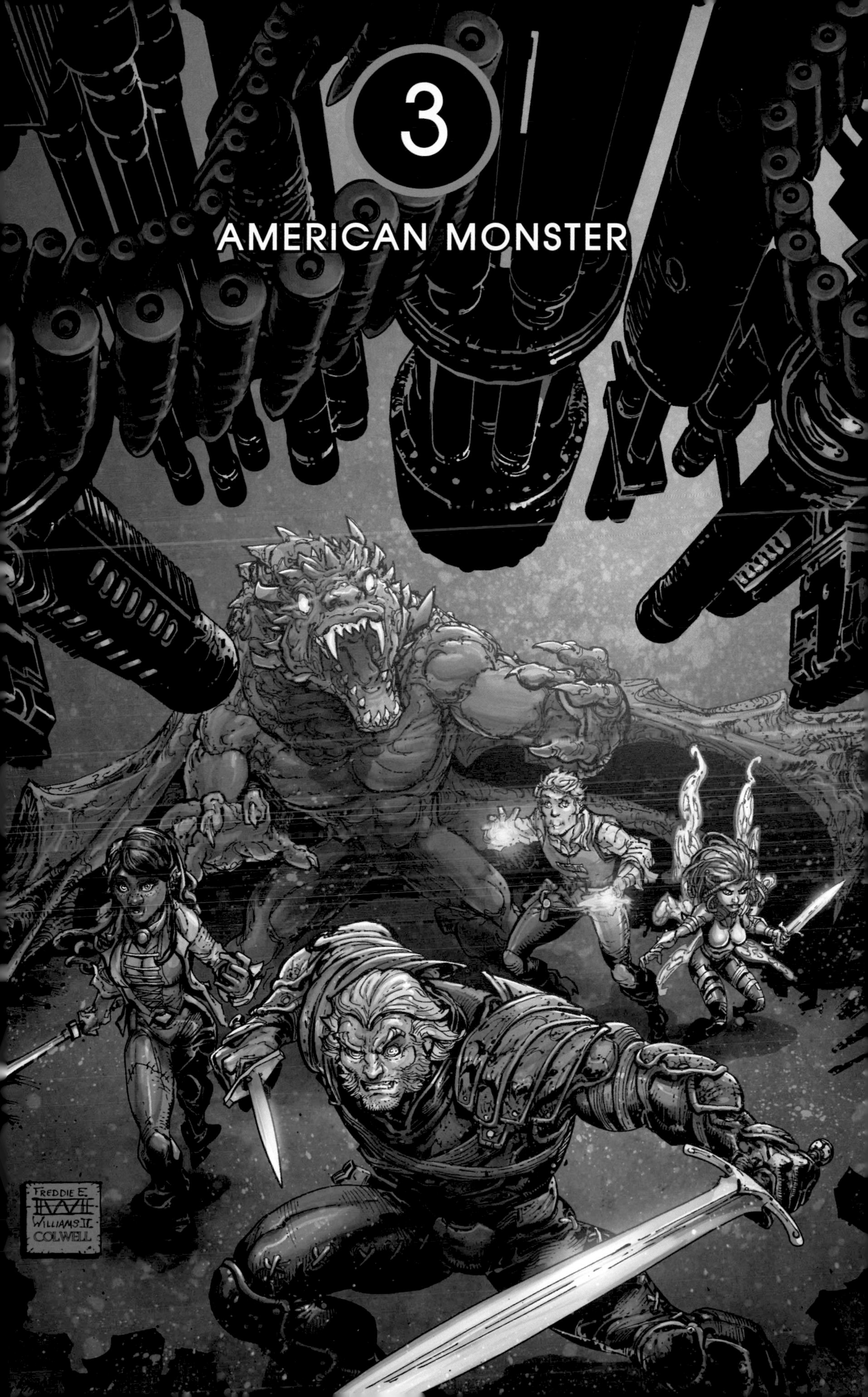
3
AMERICAN MONSTER
FREDDIE E. WILLIAMS II
COLWELL

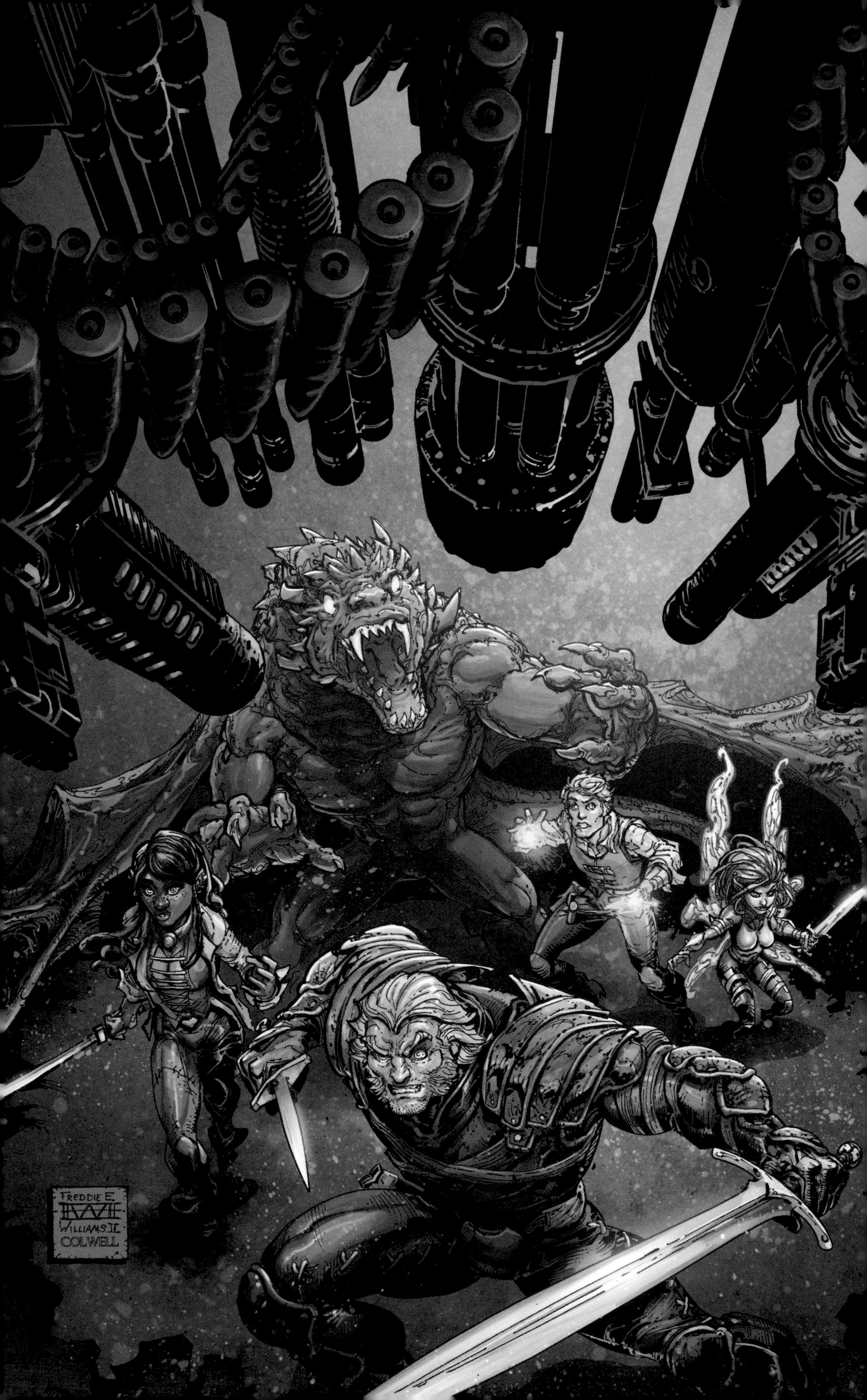
FREDDIE E.
WILLIAMS II
COLWELL

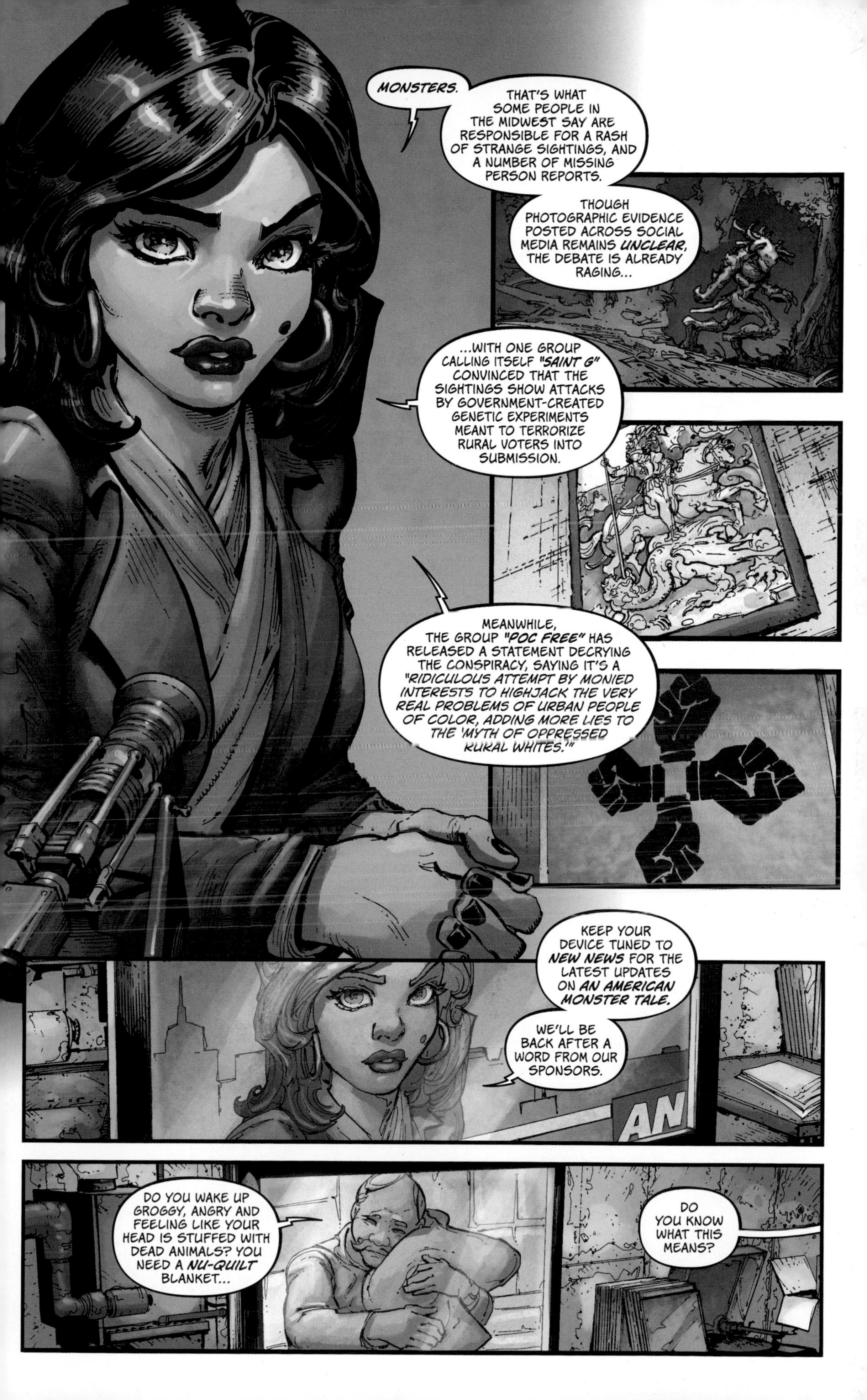
MONSTERS.
THAT'S WHAT SOME PEOPLE IN THE MIDWEST SAY ARE RESPONSIBLE FOR A RASH OF STRANGE SIGHTINGS, AND A NUMBER OF MISSING PERSON REPORTS.
THOUGH PHOTOGRAPHIC EVIDENCE POSTED ACROSS SOCIAL MEDIA REMAINS UNCLEAR, THE DEBATE IS ALREADY RAGING...
...WITH ONE GROUP CALLING ITSELF "SAINT G" CONVINCED THAT THE SIGHTINGS SHOW ATTACKS BY GOVERNMENT-CREATED GENETIC EXPERIMENTS MEANT TO TERRORIZE RURAL VOTERS INTO SUBMISSION.
MEANWHILE, THE GROUP "POC FREE" HAS RELEASED A STATEMENT DECRYING THE CONSPIRACY, SAYING IT'S A "RIDICULOUS ATTEMPT BY MONIED INTERESTS TO HIGHJACK THE VERY REAL PROBLEMS OF URBAN PEOPLE OF COLOR, ADDING MORE LIES TO THE 'MYTH OF OPPRESSED RURAL WHITES.'"
KEEP YOUR DEVICE TUNED TO NEW NEWS FOR THE LATEST UPDATES ON AN AMERICAN MONSTER TALE.
WE'LL BE BACK AFTER A WORD FROM OUR SPONSORS.
AN
DO YOU WAKE UP GROGGY, ANGRY AND FEELING LIKE YOUR HEAD IS STUFFED WITH DEAD ANIMALS? YOU NEED A NU-QUILT BLANKET...
DO YOU KNOW WHAT THIS MEANS?

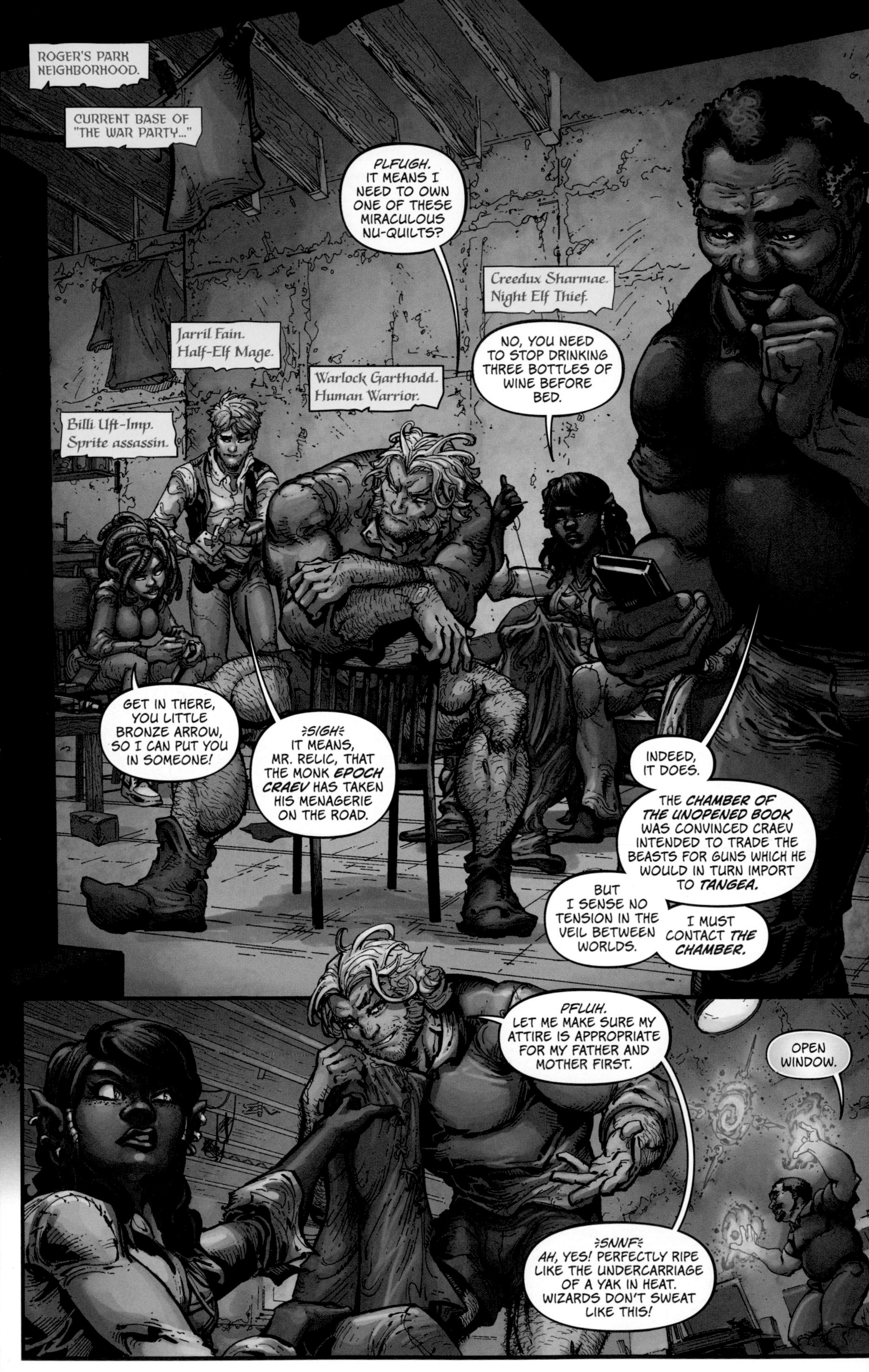
ROGER'S PARK NEIGHBORHOOD.
CURRENT BASE OF "THE WAR PARTY..."
PLFUGH. IT MEANS I NEED TO OWN ONE OF THESE MIRACULOUS NU-QUILTS?
Creedux Sharmae. Night Elf Thief.
Jarril Fain. Half-Elf Mage.
Warlock Garthodd. Human Warrior.
NO, YOU NEED TO STOP DRINKING THREE BOTTLES OF WINE BEFORE BED.
Billi Uft-Imp. Sprite assassin.
GET IN THERE, YOU LITTLE BRONZE ARROW, SO I CAN PUT YOU IN SOMEONE!
SIGH IT MEANS, MR. RELIC, THAT THE MONK EPOCH CRAEV HAS TAKEN HIS MENAGERIE ON THE ROAD.
INDEED, IT DOES.
THE CHAMBER OF THE UNOPENED BOOK WAS CONVINCED CRAEV INTENDED TO TRADE THE BEASTS FOR GUNS WHICH HE WOULD IN TURN IMPORT TO TANGEA.
BUT I SENSE NO TENSION IN THE VEIL BETWEEN WORLDS.
I MUST CONTACT THE CHAMBER.
PFLUH. LET ME MAKE SURE MY ATTIRE IS APPROPRIATE FOR MY FATHER AND MOTHER FIRST.
OPEN WINDOW.
SNNF AH, YES! PERFECTLY RIPE LIKE THE UNDERCARRIAGE OF A YAK IN HEAT. WIZARDS DON'T SWEAT LIKE THIS!

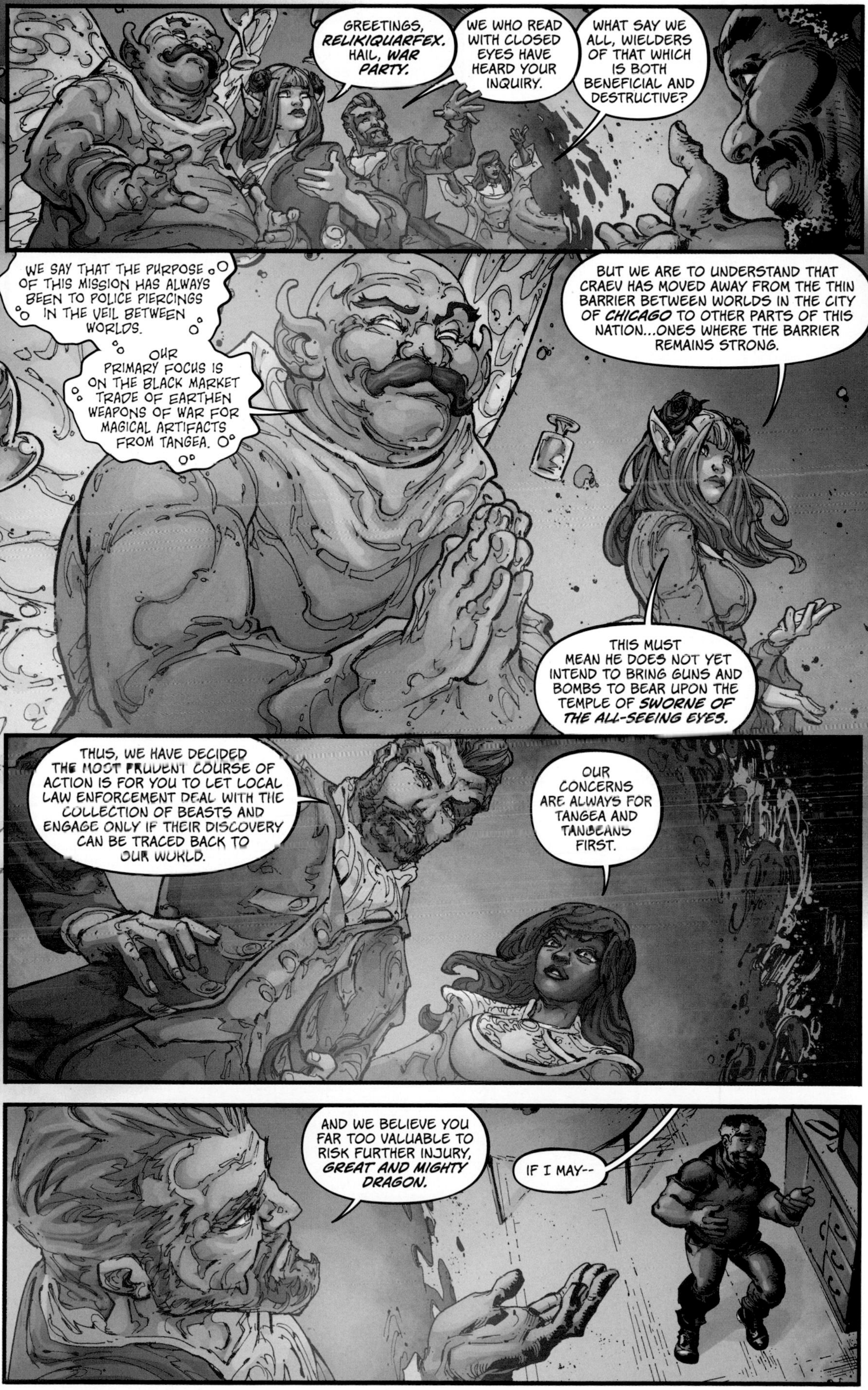
GREETINGS, **RELIKIQUARFEX.** HAIL, **WAR PARTY.**
WE WHO READ WITH CLOSED EYES HAVE HEARD YOUR INQUIRY.
WHAT SAY WE ALL, WIELDERS OF THAT WHICH IS BOTH BENEFICIAL AND DESTRUCTIVE?
WE SAY THAT THE PURPOSE OF THIS MISSION HAS ALWAYS BEEN TO POLICE PIERCINGS IN THE VEIL BETWEEN WORLDS.
OUR PRIMARY FOCUS IS ON THE BLACK MARKET TRADE OF EARTHEN WEAPONS OF WAR FOR MAGICAL ARTIFACTS FROM TANGEA.
BUT WE ARE TO UNDERSTAND THAT CRAEV HAS MOVED AWAY FROM THE THIN BARRIER BETWEEN WORLDS IN THE CITY OF **CHICAGO** TO OTHER PARTS OF THIS NATION...ONES WHERE THE BARRIER REMAINS STRONG.
THIS MUST MEAN HE DOES NOT YET INTEND TO BRING GUNS AND BOMBS TO BEAR UPON THE TEMPLE OF **SWORNE OF THE ALL-SEEING EYES.**
THUS, WE HAVE DECIDED THE MOST PRUDENT COURSE OF ACTION IS FOR YOU TO LET LOCAL LAW ENFORCEMENT DEAL WITH THE COLLECTION OF BEASTS AND ENGAGE ONLY IF THEIR DISCOVERY CAN BE TRACED BACK TO OUR WORLD.
OUR CONCERNS ARE ALWAYS FOR TANGEA AND TANGEANS FIRST.
AND WE BELIEVE YOU FAR TOO VALUABLE TO RISK FURTHER INJURY, **GREAT AND MIGHTY DRAGON.**
IF I MAY--

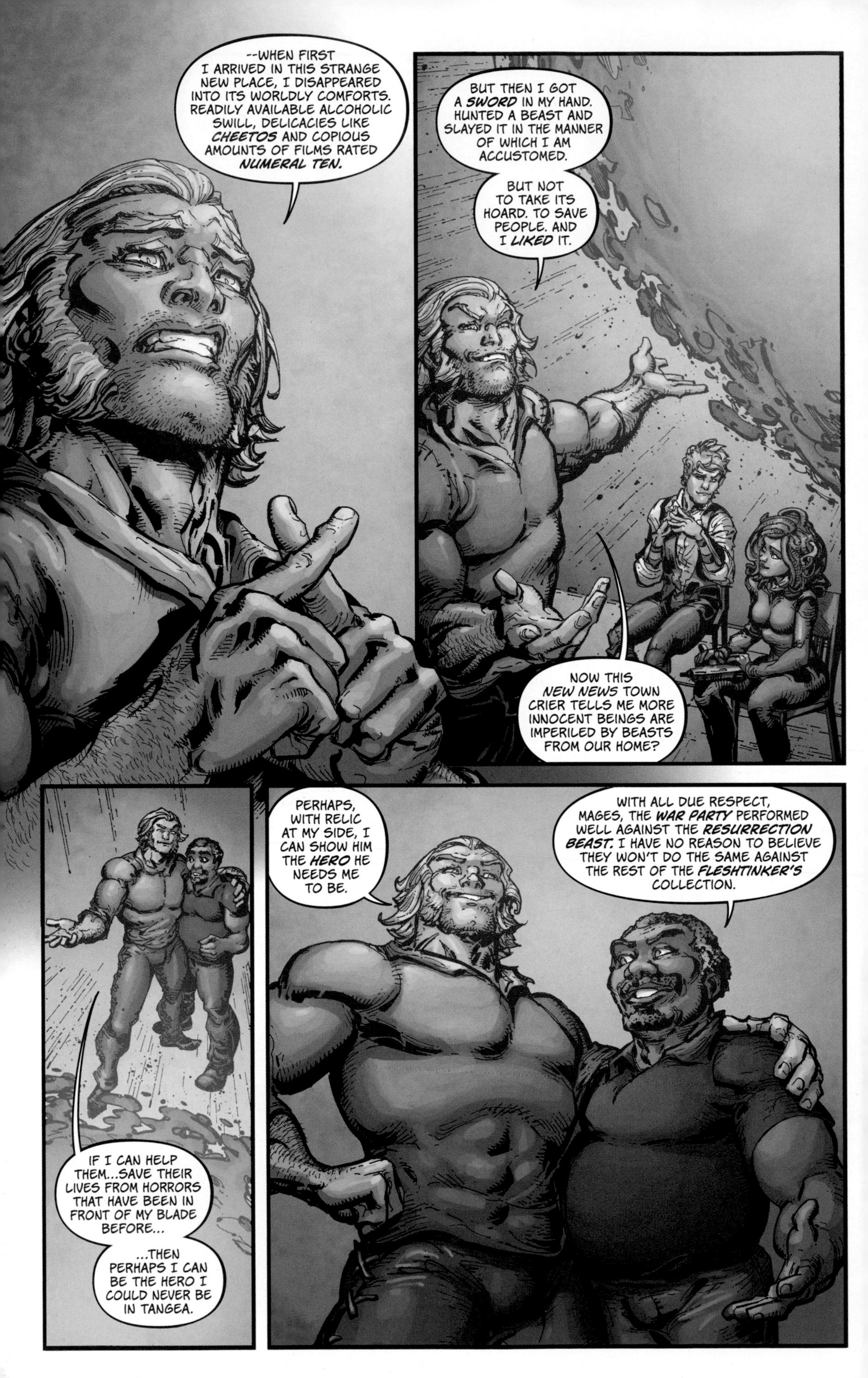

--WHEN FIRST I ARRIVED IN THIS STRANGE NEW PLACE, I DISAPPEARED INTO ITS WORLDLY COMFORTS. READILY AVAILABLE ALCOHOLIC SWILL, DELICACIES LIKE *CHEETOS* AND COPIOUS AMOUNTS OF FILMS RATED *NUMERAL TEN.*
BUT THEN I GOT A *SWORD* IN MY HAND. HUNTED A BEAST AND SLAYED IT IN THE MANNER OF WHICH I AM ACCUSTOMED.
BUT NOT TO TAKE ITS HOARD. TO SAVE PEOPLE. AND I *LIKED* IT.
NOW THIS *NEW NEWS* TOWN CRIER TELLS ME MORE INNOCENT BEINGS ARE IMPERILED BY BEASTS FROM OUR HOME?
IF I CAN HELP THEM...SAVE THEIR LIVES FROM HORRORS THAT HAVE BEEN IN FRONT OF MY BLADE BEFORE...
...THEN PERHAPS I CAN BE THE HERO I COULD NEVER BE IN TANGEA.
PERHAPS, WITH RELIC AT MY SIDE, I CAN SHOW HIM THE *HERO* HE NEEDS ME TO BE.
WITH ALL DUE RESPECT, MAGES, THE *WAR PARTY* PERFORMED WELL AGAINST THE *RESURRECTION BEAST.* I HAVE NO REASON TO BELIEVE THEY WON'T DO THE SAME AGAINST THE REST OF THE *FLESHTINKER'S* COLLECTION.

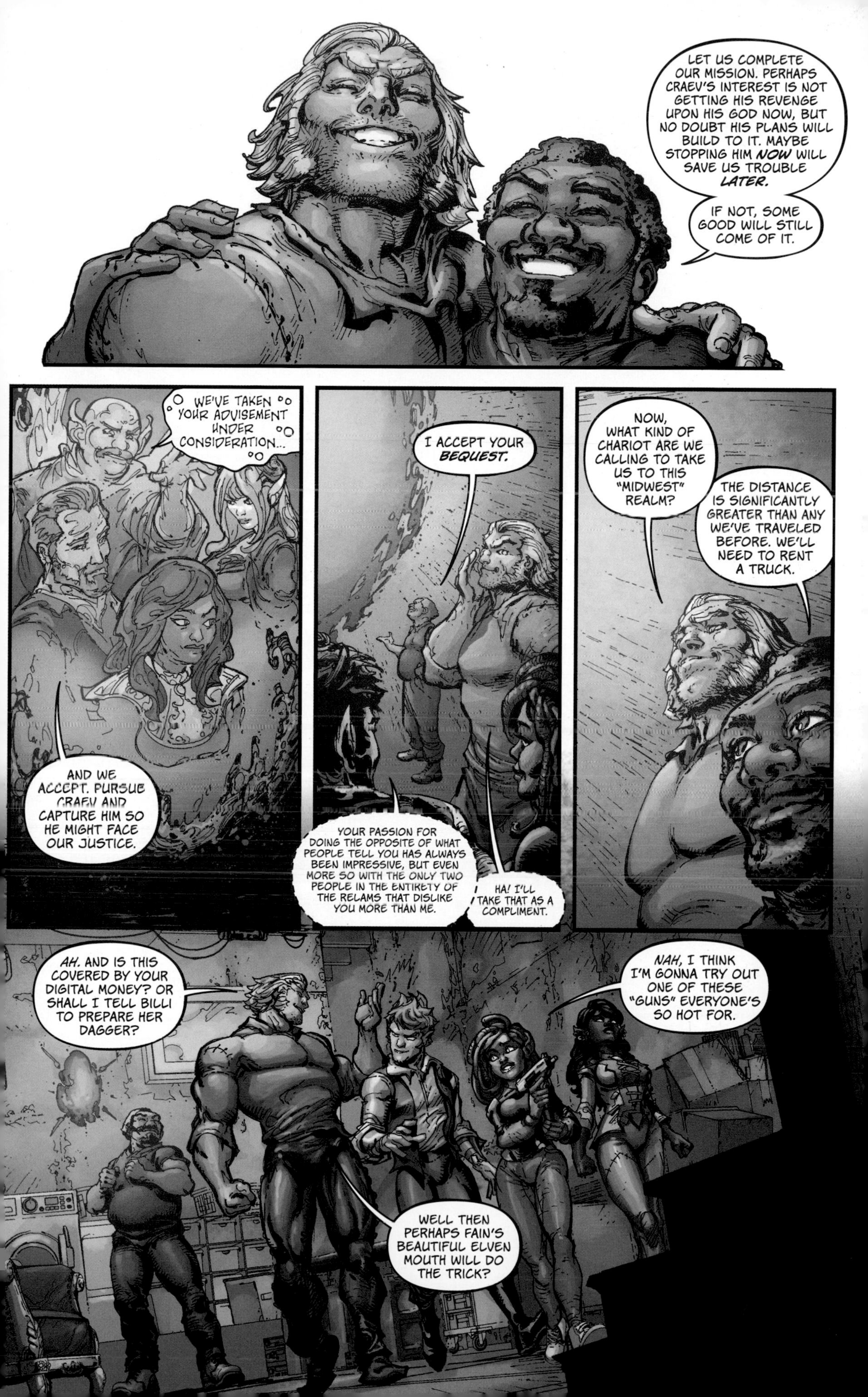
LET US COMPLETE OUR MISSION. PERHAPS CRAEV'S INTEREST IS NOT GETTING HIS REVENGE UPON HIS GOD NOW, BUT NO DOUBT HIS PLANS WILL BUILD TO IT. MAYBE STOPPING HIM *NOW* WILL SAVE US TROUBLE *LATER.*
IF NOT, SOME GOOD WILL STILL COME OF IT.
WE'VE TAKEN YOUR ADVISEMENT UNDER CONSIDERATION...
AND WE ACCEPT. PURSUE CRAEV AND CAPTURE HIM SO HE MIGHT FACE OUR JUSTICE.
I ACCEPT YOUR *BEQUEST.*
YOUR PASSION FOR DOING THE OPPOSITE OF WHAT PEOPLE TELL YOU HAS ALWAYS BEEN IMPRESSIVE, BUT EVEN MORE SO WITH THE ONLY TWO PEOPLE IN THE ENTIRETY OF THE RELAMS THAT DISLIKE YOU MORE THAN ME.
HA! I'LL TAKE THAT AS A COMPLIMENT.
NOW, WHAT KIND OF CHARIOT ARE WE CALLING TO TAKE US TO THIS "MIDWEST" REALM?
THE DISTANCE IS SIGNIFICANTLY GREATER THAN ANY WE'VE TRAVELED BEFORE. WE'LL NEED TO RENT A TRUCK.
AH. AND IS THIS COVERED BY YOUR DIGITAL MONEY? OR SHALL I TELL BILLI TO PREPARE HER DAGGER?
NAH, I THINK I'M GONNA TRY OUT ONE OF THESE "GUNS" EVERYONE'S SO HOT FOR.
WELL THEN PERHAPS FAIN'S BEAUTIFUL ELVEN MOUTH WILL DO THE TRICK?

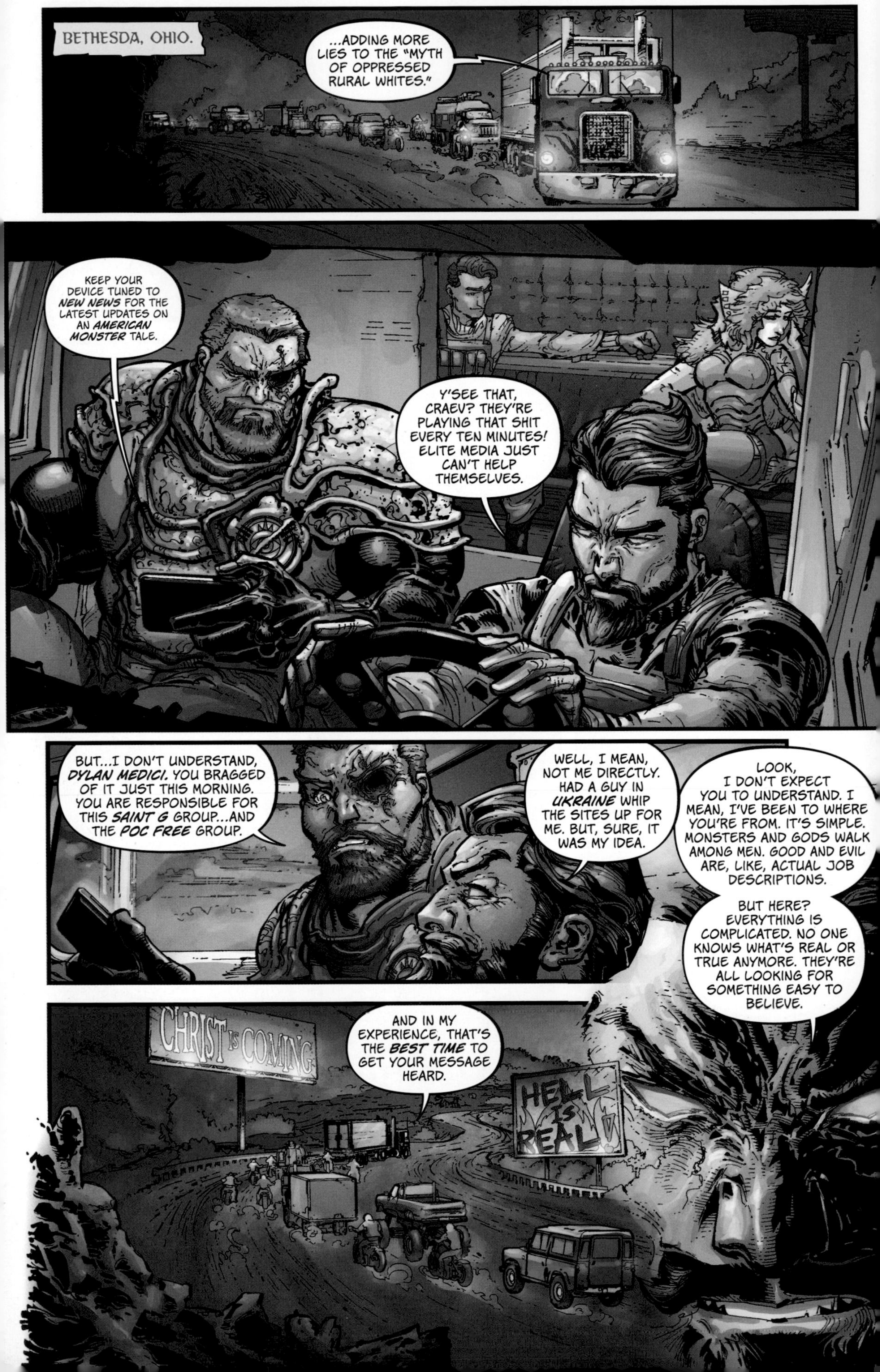
BETHESDA, OHIO.
...ADDING MORE LIES TO THE "MYTH OF OPPRESSED RURAL WHITES."
KEEP YOUR DEVICE TUNED TO NEW NEWS FOR THE LATEST UPDATES ON AN AMERICAN MONSTER TALE.
Y'SEE THAT, CRAEV? THEY'RE PLAYING THAT SHIT EVERY TEN MINUTES! ELITE MEDIA JUST CAN'T HELP THEMSELVES.
BUT...I DON'T UNDERSTAND, DYLAN MEDICI. YOU BRAGGED OF IT JUST THIS MORNING. YOU ARE RESPONSIBLE FOR THIS SAINT G GROUP...AND THE POC FREE GROUP.
WELL, I MEAN, NOT ME DIRECTLY. HAD A GUY IN UKRAINE WHIP THE SITES UP FOR ME. BUT, SURE, IT WAS MY IDEA.
LOOK, I DON'T EXPECT YOU TO UNDERSTAND. I MEAN, I'VE BEEN TO WHERE YOU'RE FROM. IT'S SIMPLE. MONSTERS AND GODS WALK AMONG MEN. GOOD AND EVIL ARE, LIKE, ACTUAL JOB DESCRIPTIONS.
BUT HERE? EVERYTHING IS COMPLICATED. NO ONE KNOWS WHAT'S REAL OR TRUE ANYMORE. THEY'RE ALL LOOKING FOR SOMETHING EASY TO BELIEVE.
CHRIST IS COMING
AND IN MY EXPERIENCE, THAT'S THE BEST TIME TO GET YOUR MESSAGE HEARD.
HELL IS REAL

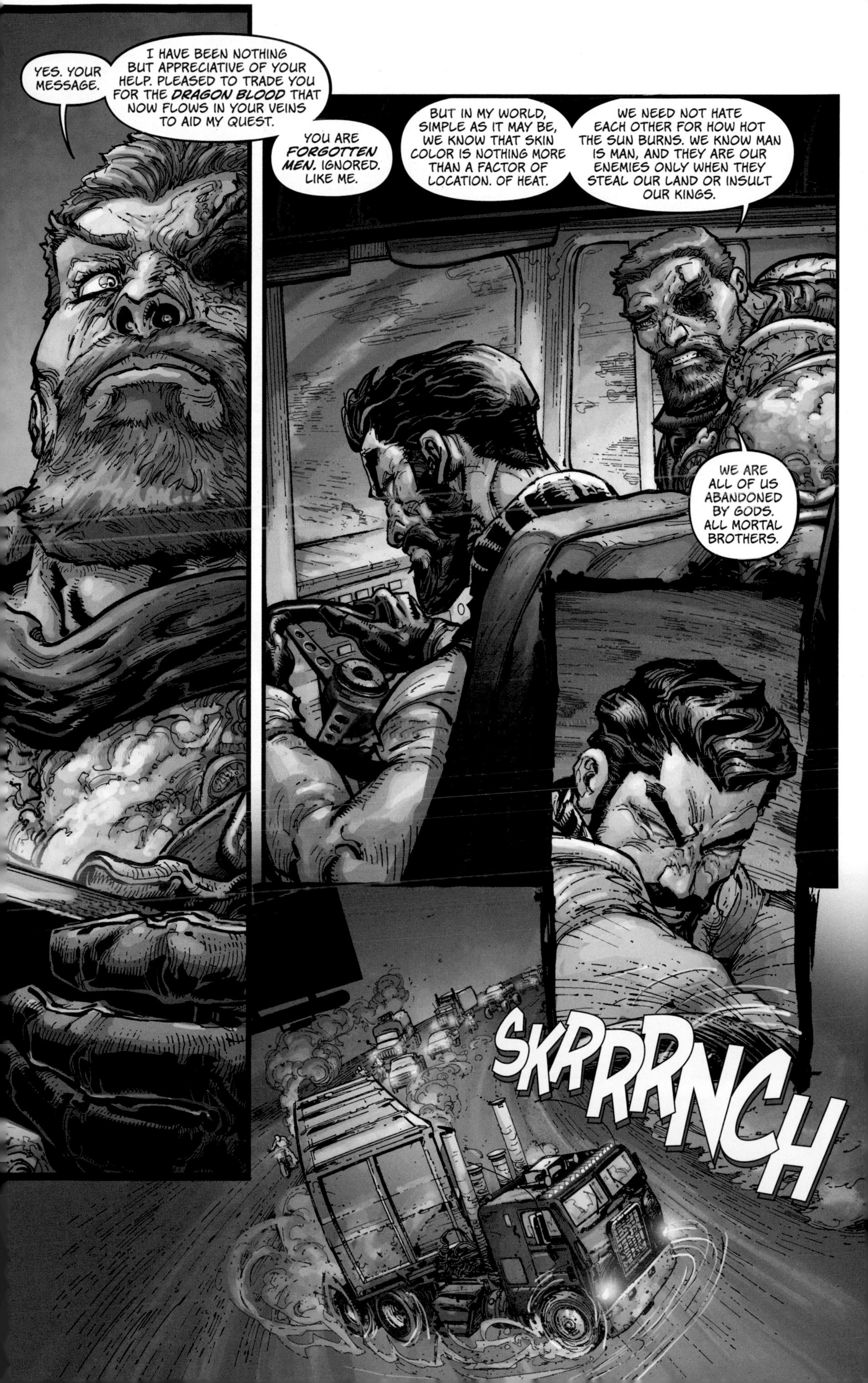
YES. YOUR MESSAGE.
I HAVE BEEN NOTHING BUT APPRECIATIVE OF YOUR HELP. PLEASED TO TRADE YOU FOR THE DRAGON BLOOD THAT NOW FLOWS IN YOUR VEINS TO AID MY QUEST.
YOU ARE FORGOTTEN MEN. IGNORED. LIKE ME.
BUT IN MY WORLD, SIMPLE AS IT MAY BE, WE KNOW THAT SKIN COLOR IS NOTHING MORE THAN A FACTOR OF LOCATION. OF HEAT.
WE NEED NOT HATE EACH OTHER FOR HOW HOT THE SUN BURNS. WE KNOW MAN IS MAN, AND THEY ARE OUR ENEMIES ONLY WHEN THEY STEAL OUR LAND OR INSULT OUR KINGS.
WE ARE ALL OF US ABANDONED BY GODS. ALL MORTAL BROTHERS.
SKRRRNCH

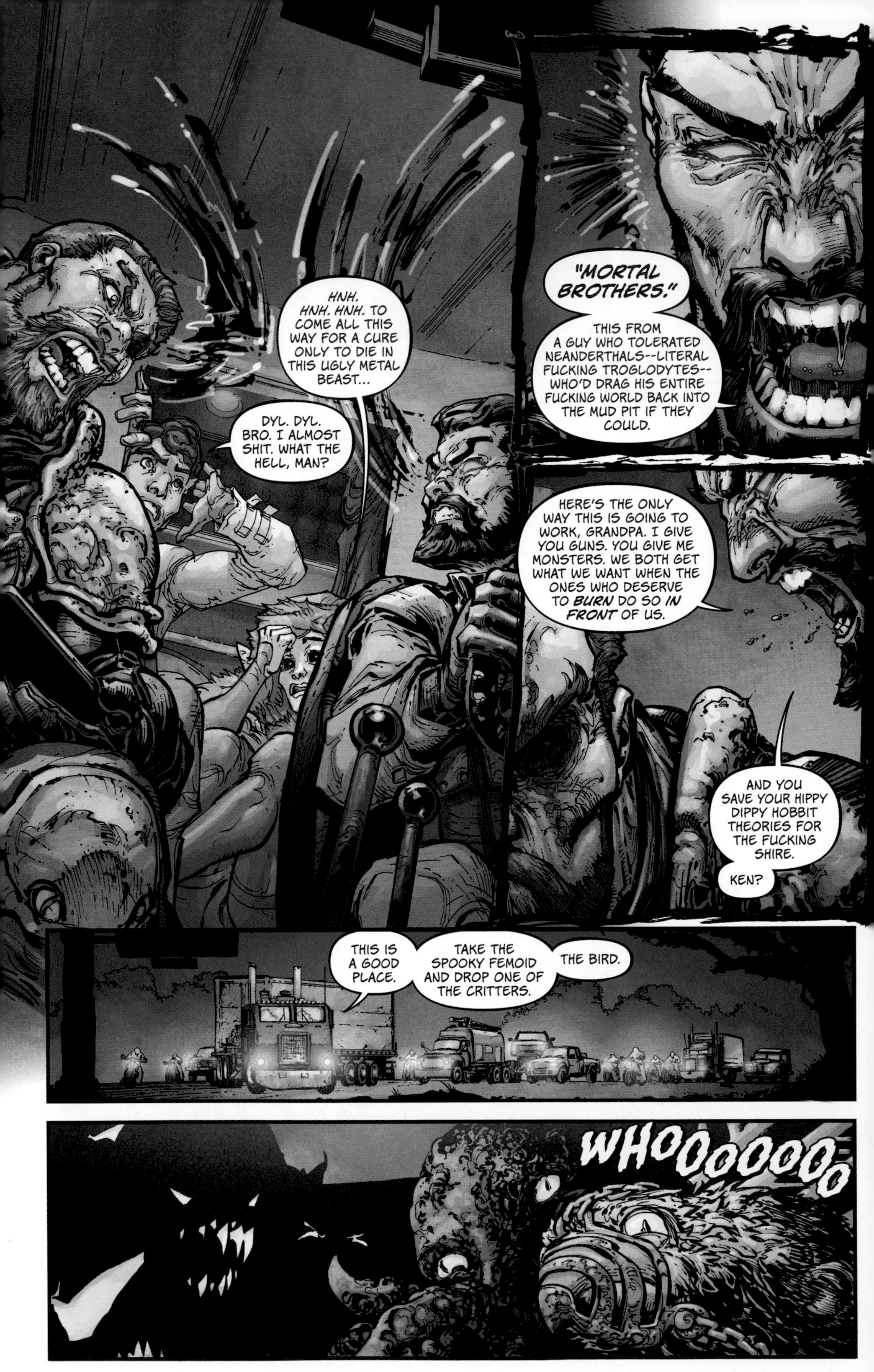

HNH. HNH. HNH. TO COME ALL THIS WAY FOR A CURE ONLY TO DIE IN THIS UGLY METAL BEAST...
DYL. DYL. BRO. I ALMOST SHIT. WHAT THE HELL, MAN?
"MORTAL BROTHERS."
THIS FROM A GUY WHO TOLERATED NEANDERTHALS--LITERAL FUCKING TROGLODYTES--WHO'D DRAG HIS ENTIRE FUCKING WORLD BACK INTO THE MUD PIT IF THEY COULD.
HERE'S THE ONLY WAY THIS IS GOING TO WORK, GRANDPA. I GIVE YOU GUNS. YOU GIVE ME MONSTERS. WE BOTH GET WHAT WE WANT WHEN THE ONES WHO DESERVE TO BURN DO SO IN FRONT OF US.
AND YOU SAVE YOUR HIPPY DIPPY HOBBIT THEORIES FOR THE FUCKING SHIRE.
KEN?
THIS IS A GOOD PLACE.
TAKE THE SPOOKY FEMOID AND DROP ONE OF THE CRITTERS.
THE BIRD.
WHOOOOOOOO

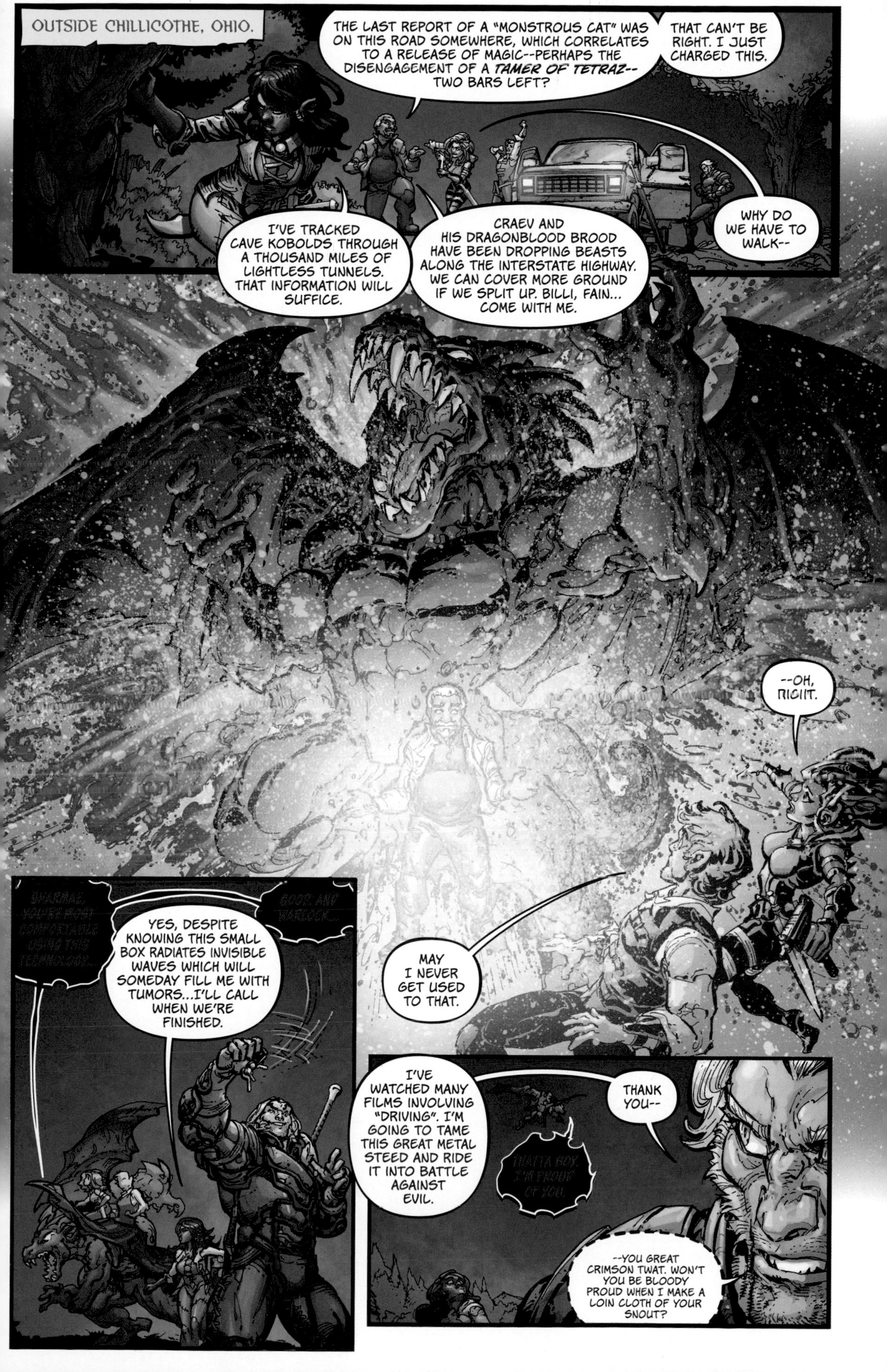
OUTSIDE CHILLICOTHE, OHIO.
THE LAST REPORT OF A "MONSTROUS CAT" WAS ON THIS ROAD SOMEWHERE, WHICH CORRELATES TO A RELEASE OF MAGIC--PERHAPS THE DISENGAGEMENT OF A *TAMER OF TETRAZ*-- TWO BARS LEFT?
THAT CAN'T BE RIGHT. I JUST CHARGED THIS.
I'VE TRACKED CAVE KOBOLDS THROUGH A THOUSAND MILES OF LIGHTLESS TUNNELS. THAT INFORMATION WILL SUFFICE.
CRAEV AND HIS DRAGONBLOOD BROOD HAVE BEEN DROPPING BEASTS ALONG THE INTERSTATE HIGHWAY. WE CAN COVER MORE GROUND IF WE SPLIT UP. BILLI, FAIN... COME WITH ME.
WHY DO WE HAVE TO WALK--
--OH, RIGHT.
MAY I NEVER GET USED TO THAT.
SHARRAE, YOU'RE MOST COMFORTABLE USING THIS TECHNOLOGY...
YES, DESPITE KNOWING THIS SMALL BOX RADIATES INVISIBLE WAVES WHICH WILL SOMEDAY FILL ME WITH TUMORS...I'LL CALL WHEN WE'RE FINISHED.
GOOD. AND WARLOCK...
I'VE WATCHED MANY FILMS INVOLVING "DRIVING". I'M GOING TO TAME THIS GREAT METAL STEED AND RIDE IT INTO BATTLE AGAINST EVIL.
THATTA BOY. I'M PROUD OF YOU.
THANK YOU--
--YOU GREAT CRIMSON TWAT. WON'T YOU BE BLOODY PROUD WHEN I MAKE A LOIN CLOTH OF YOUR SNOUT?

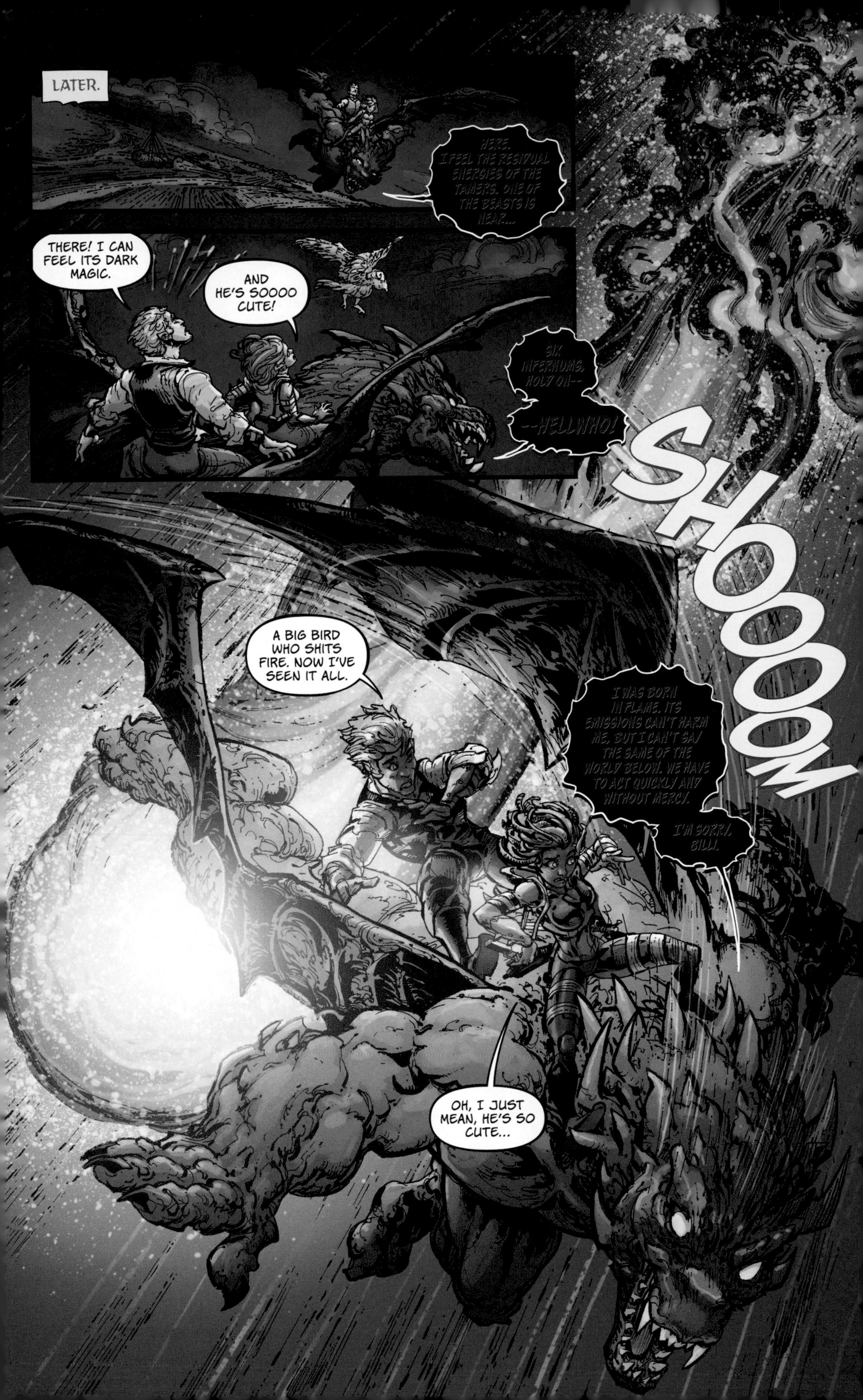
LATER.
HERE. I FEEL THE RESIDUAL ENERGIES OF THE TAMERS. ONE OF THE BEASTS IS NEAR...
THERE! I CAN FEEL ITS DARK MAGIC.
AND HE'S SOOOO CUTE!
SIX INFERNUMS, HOLD ON--
--HELLWHO!
SHOOOOOM
A BIG BIRD WHO SHITS FIRE. NOW I'VE SEEN IT ALL.
I WAS BORN IN FLAME. ITS EMISSIONS CAN'T HARM ME, BUT I CAN'T SAY THE SAME OF THE WORLD BELOW. WE HAVE TO ACT QUICKLY AND WITHOUT MERCY.
I'M SORRY, BILL.
OH, I JUST MEAN, HE'S SO CUTE...

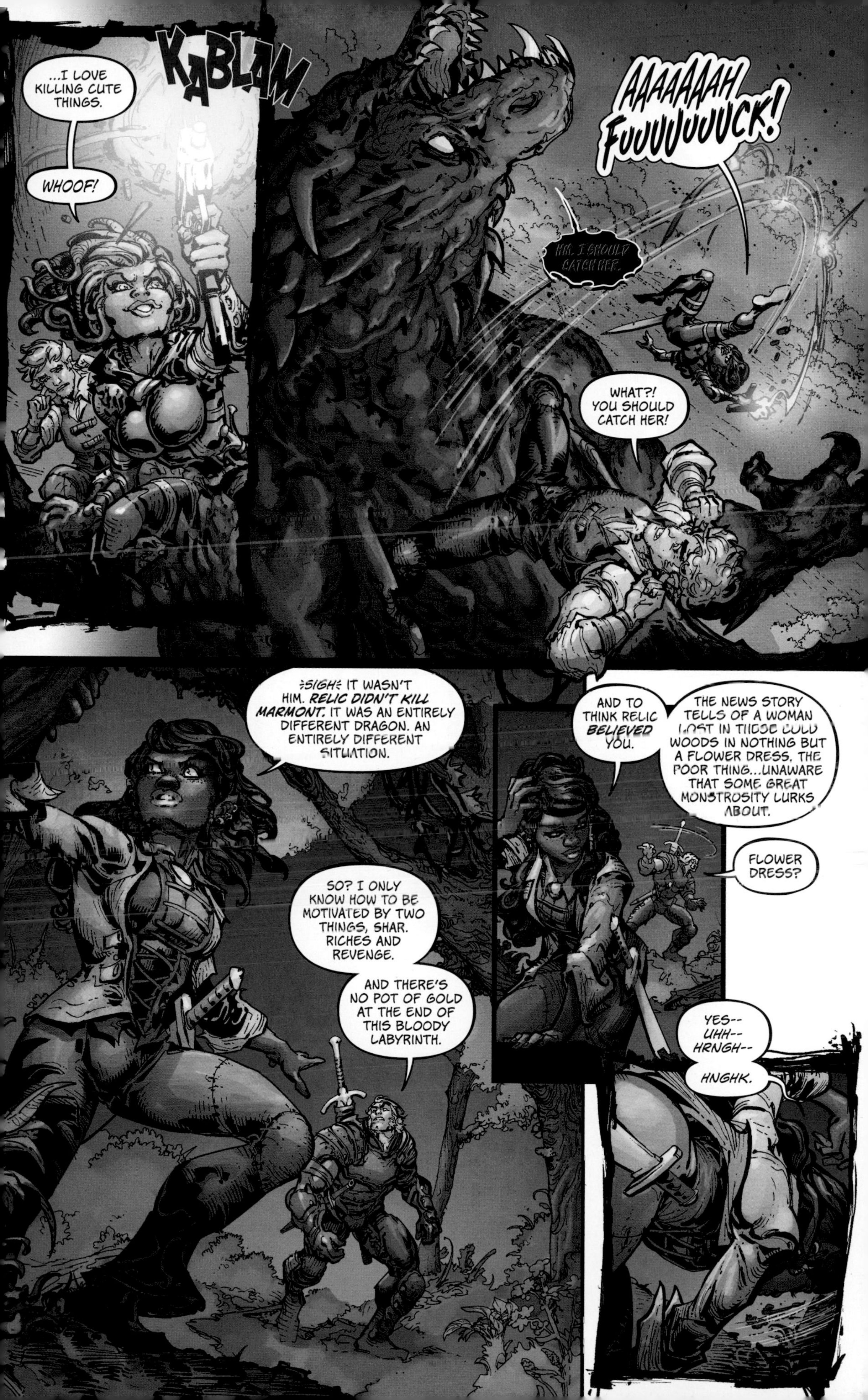

KABLAM
...I LOVE KILLING CUTE THINGS.
WHOOF!
AAAAAAAH FUUUUUUUCK!
HM. I SHOULD CATCH HER.
WHAT?! YOU SHOULD CATCH HER!
SIGH IT WASN'T HIM. RELIC DIDN'T KILL MARMONT. IT WAS AN ENTIRELY DIFFERENT DRAGON. AN ENTIRELY DIFFERENT SITUATION.
SO? I ONLY KNOW HOW TO BE MOTIVATED BY TWO THINGS, SHAR. RICHES AND REVENGE.
AND THERE'S NO POT OF GOLD AT THE END OF THIS BLOODY LABYRINTH.
AND TO THINK RELIC BELIEVED YOU.
THE NEWS STORY TELLS OF A WOMAN LOST IN THOSE COLD WOODS IN NOTHING BUT A FLOWER DRESS. THE POOR THING...UNAWARE THAT SOME GREAT MONSTROSITY LURKS ABOUT.
FLOWER DRESS?
YES-- UHH-- HRNGH--
HNGHK.

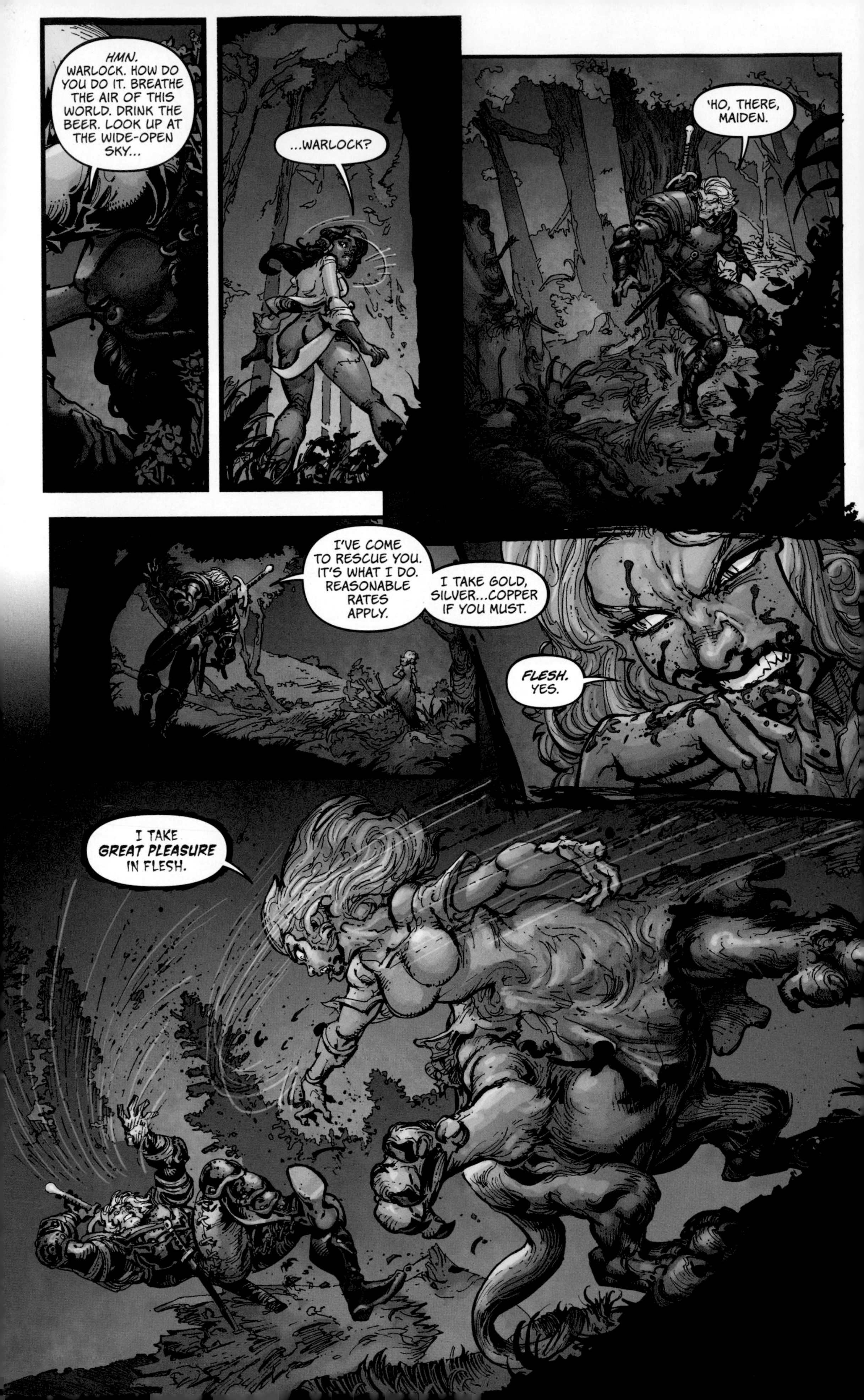
HMN. WARLOCK. HOW DO YOU DO IT. BREATHE THE AIR OF THIS WORLD. DRINK THE BEER. LOOK UP AT THE WIDE-OPEN SKY...
...WARLOCK?
'HO, THERE, MAIDEN.
I'VE COME TO RESCUE YOU. IT'S WHAT I DO. REASONABLE RATES APPLY.
I TAKE GOLD, SILVER...COPPER IF YOU MUST.
FLESH. YES.
I TAKE GREAT PLEASURE IN FLESH.

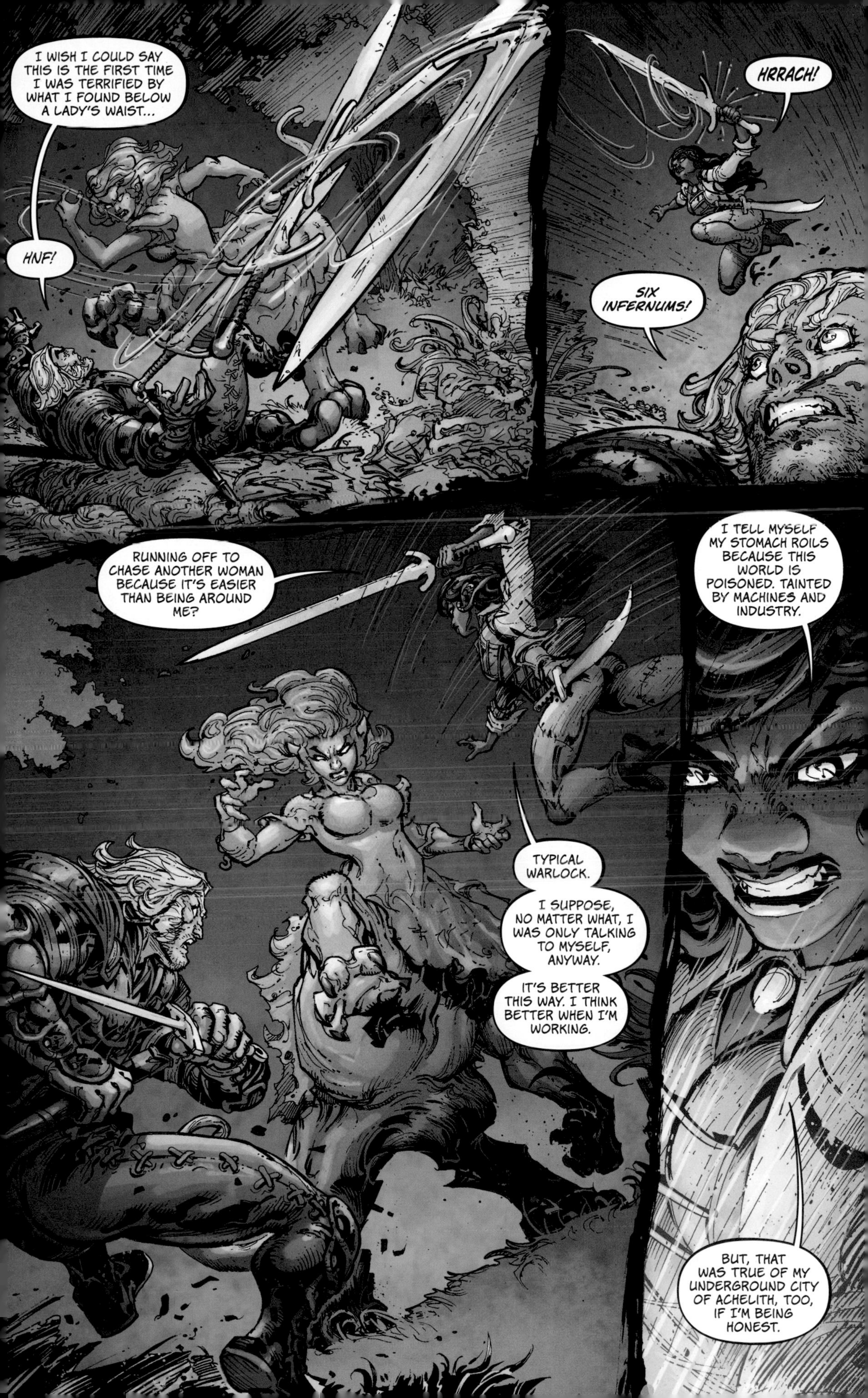
I WISH I COULD SAY THIS IS THE FIRST TIME I WAS TERRIFIED BY WHAT I FOUND BELOW A LADY'S WAIST...
HNF!
HRRACH!
SIX INFERNUMS!
RUNNING OFF TO CHASE ANOTHER WOMAN BECAUSE IT'S EASIER THAN BEING AROUND ME?
I TELL MYSELF MY STOMACH ROILS BECAUSE THIS WORLD IS POISONED. TAINTED BY MACHINES AND INDUSTRY.
TYPICAL WARLOCK.
I SUPPOSE, NO MATTER WHAT, I WAS ONLY TALKING TO MYSELF, ANYWAY.
IT'S BETTER THIS WAY. I THINK BETTER WHEN I'M WORKING.
BUT, THAT WAS TRUE OF MY UNDERGROUND CITY OF ACHELITH, TOO, IF I'M BEING HONEST.

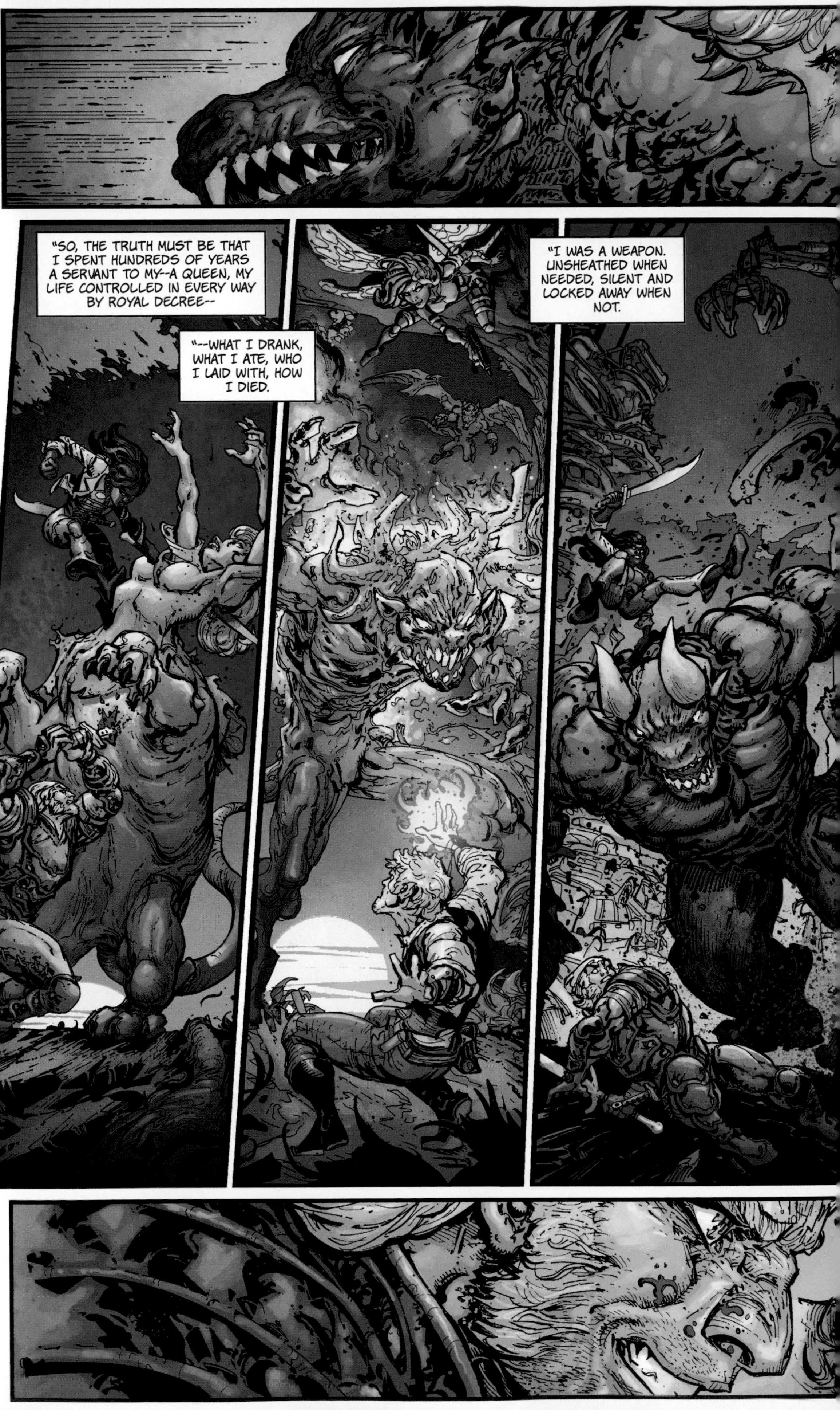
"SO, THE TRUTH MUST BE THAT I SPENT HUNDREDS OF YEARS A SERVANT TO MY--A QUEEN, MY LIFE CONTROLLED IN EVERY WAY BY ROYAL DECREE--
"--WHAT I DRANK, WHAT I ATE, WHO I LAID WITH, HOW I DIED.
"I WAS A WEAPON. UNSHEATHED WHEN NEEDED, SILENT AND LOCKED AWAY WHEN NOT.

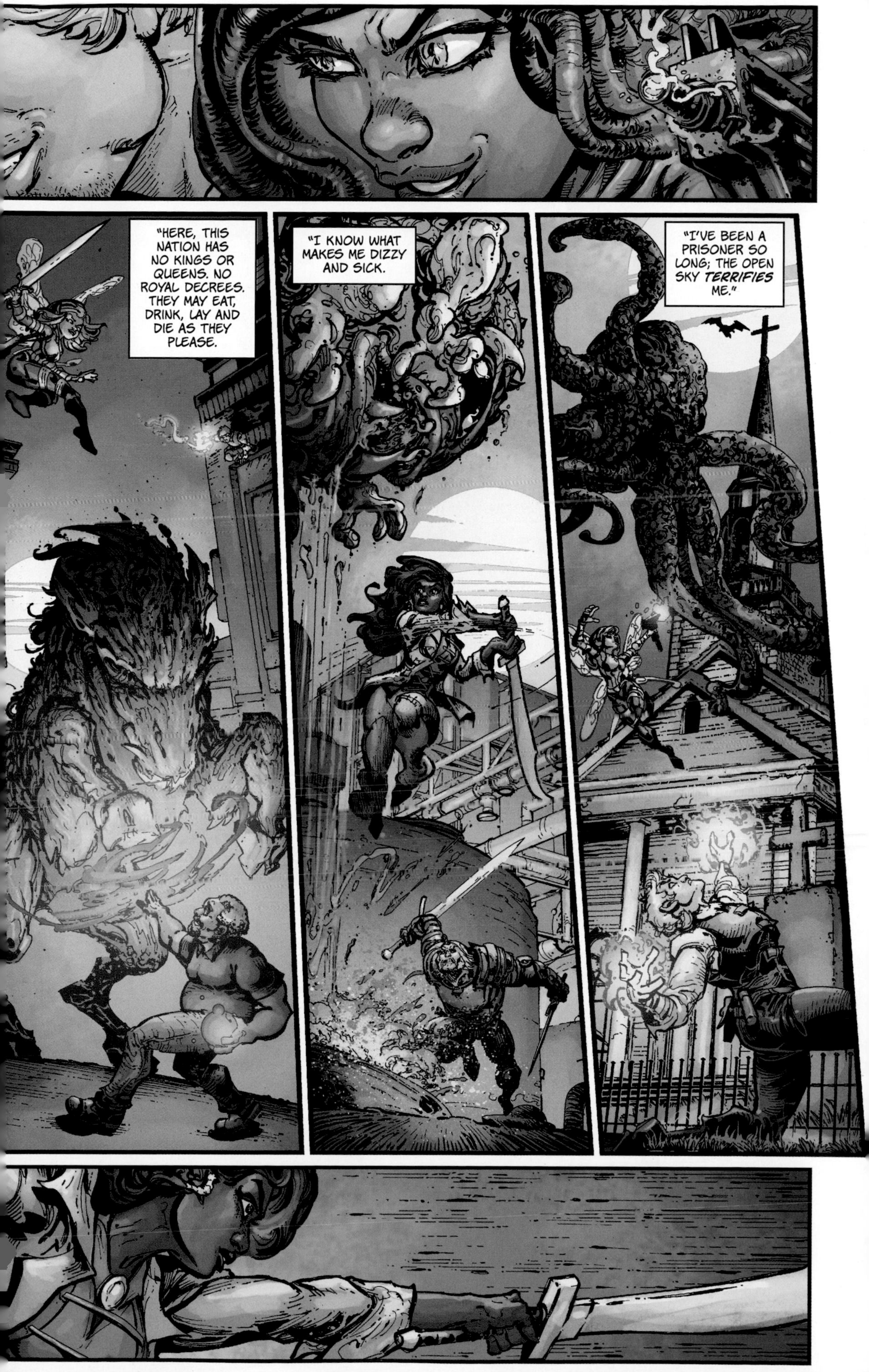
"HERE, THIS NATION HAS NO KINGS OR QUEENS. NO ROYAL DECREES. THEY MAY EAT, DRINK, LAY AND DIE AS THEY PLEASE.
"I KNOW WHAT MAKES ME DIZZY AND SICK.
"I'VE BEEN A PRISONER SO LONG; THE OPEN SKY TERRIFIES ME."

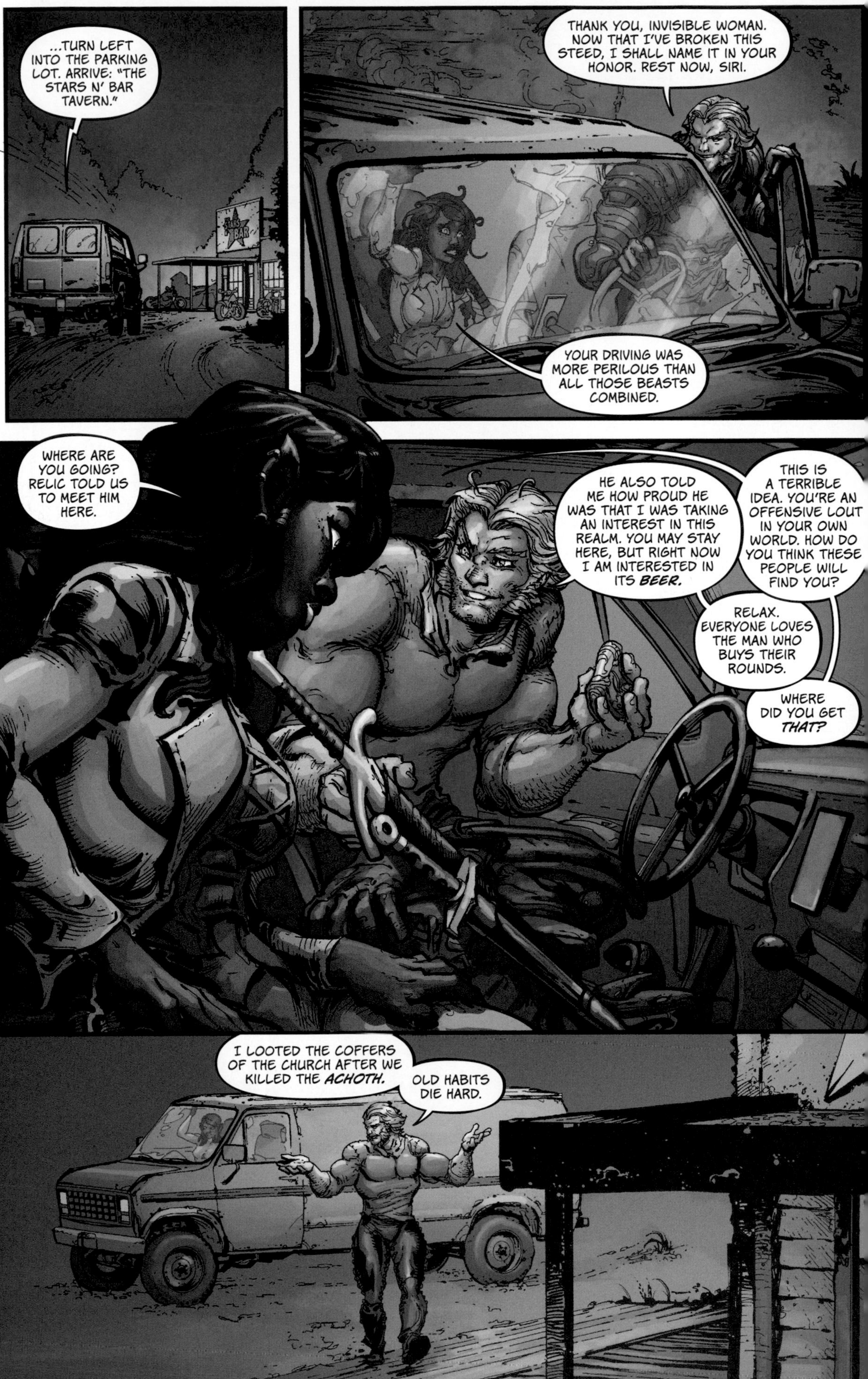

...TURN LEFT INTO THE PARKING LOT. ARRIVE: "THE STARS N' BAR TAVERN."
STARS N' BAR
THANK YOU, INVISIBLE WOMAN. NOW THAT I'VE BROKEN THIS STEED, I SHALL NAME IT IN YOUR HONOR. REST NOW, SIRI.
YOUR DRIVING WAS MORE PERILOUS THAN ALL THOSE BEASTS COMBINED.
WHERE ARE YOU GOING? RELIC TOLD US TO MEET HIM HERE.
HE ALSO TOLD ME HOW PROUD HE WAS THAT I WAS TAKING AN INTEREST IN THIS REALM. YOU MAY STAY HERE, BUT RIGHT NOW I AM INTERESTED IN ITS *BEER.*
THIS IS A TERRIBLE IDEA. YOU'RE AN OFFENSIVE LOUT IN YOUR OWN WORLD. HOW DO YOU THINK THESE PEOPLE WILL FIND YOU?
RELAX. EVERYONE LOVES THE MAN WHO BUYS THEIR ROUNDS.
WHERE DID YOU GET *THAT?*
I LOOTED THE COFFERS OF THE CHURCH AFTER WE KILLED THE *ACHOTH.*
OLD HABITS DIE HARD.

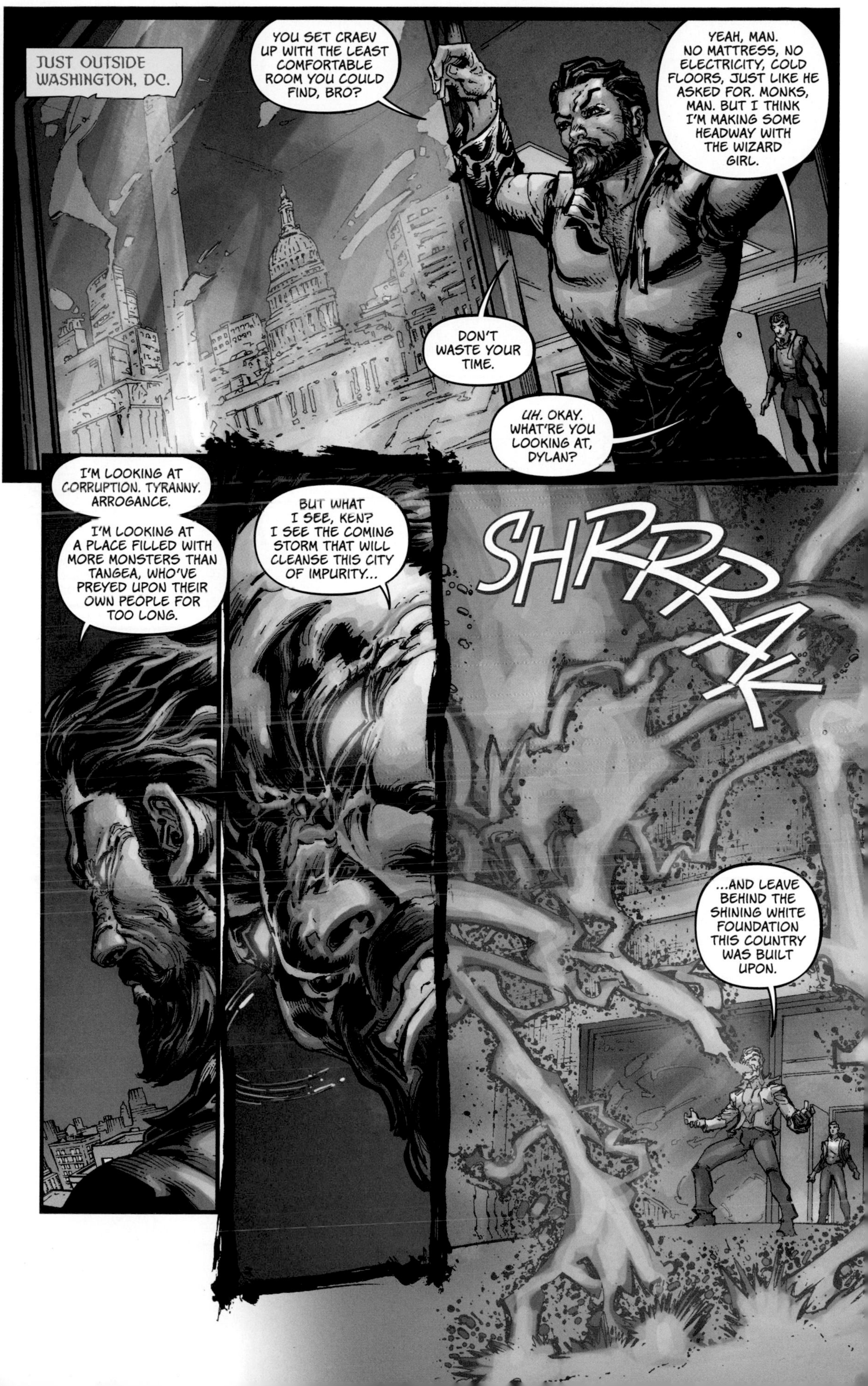
JUST OUTSIDE WASHINGTON, DC.
YOU SET CRAEV UP WITH THE LEAST COMFORTABLE ROOM YOU COULD FIND, BRO?
YEAH, MAN. NO MATTRESS, NO ELECTRICITY, COLD FLOORS, JUST LIKE HE ASKED FOR. MONKS, MAN. BUT I THINK I'M MAKING SOME HEADWAY WITH THE WIZARD GIRL.
DON'T WASTE YOUR TIME.
UH. OKAY. WHAT'RE YOU LOOKING AT, DYLAN?
I'M LOOKING AT CORRUPTION. TYRANNY. ARROGANCE.
I'M LOOKING AT A PLACE FILLED WITH MORE MONSTERS THAN TANGEA, WHO'VE PREYED UPON THEIR OWN PEOPLE FOR TOO LONG.
BUT WHAT I SEE, KEN? I SEE THE COMING STORM THAT WILL CLEANSE THIS CITY OF IMPURITY...
SHRRRAK
...AND LEAVE BEHIND THE SHINING WHITE FOUNDATION THIS COUNTRY WAS BUILT UPON.

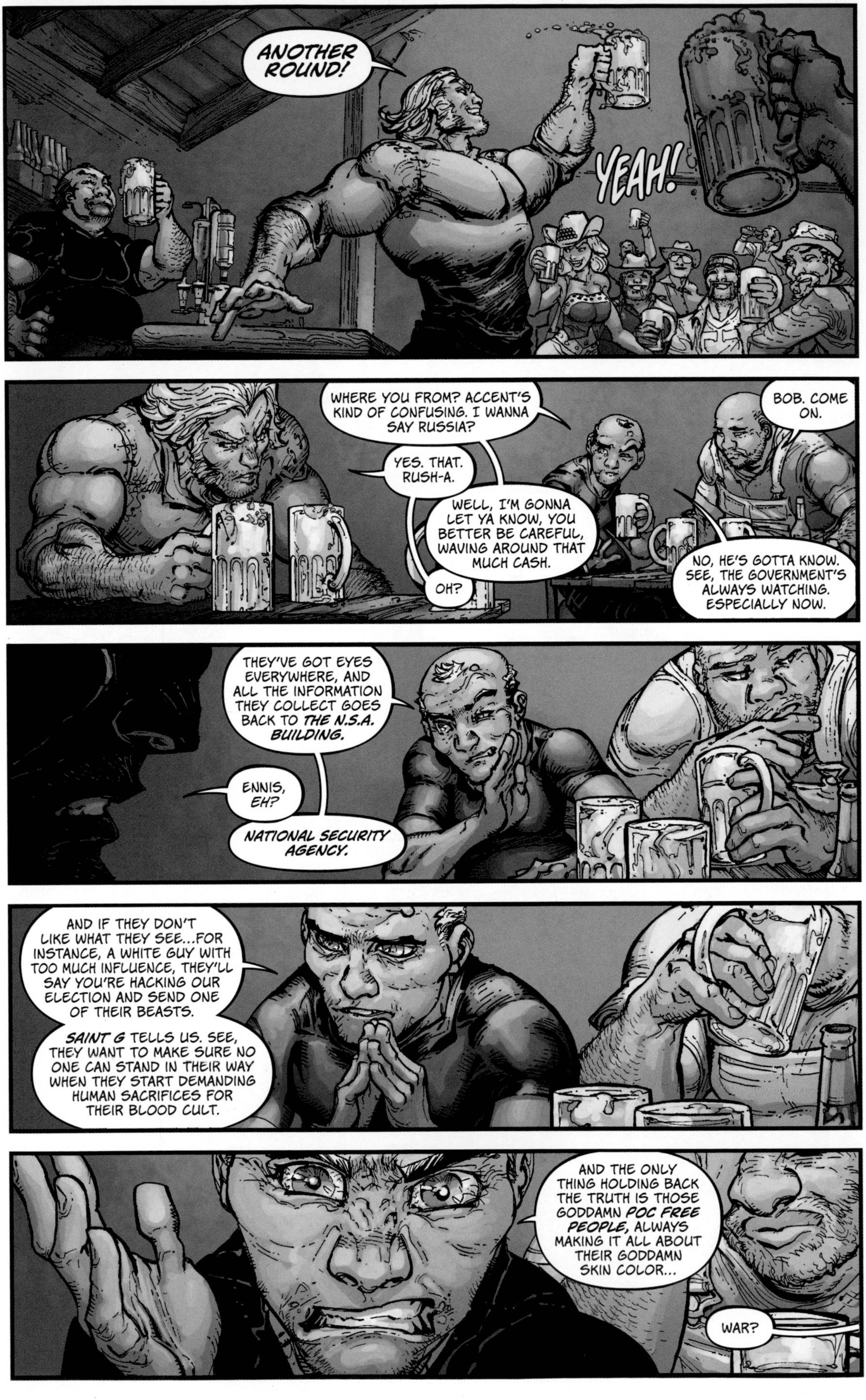
ANOTHER ROUND!
YEAH!
WHERE YOU FROM? ACCENT'S KIND OF CONFUSING. I WANNA SAY RUSSIA?
YES. THAT. RUSH-A.
BOB. COME ON.
WELL, I'M GONNA LET YA KNOW, YOU BETTER BE CAREFUL, WAVING AROUND THAT MUCH CASH.
OH?
NO, HE'S GOTTA KNOW. SEE, THE GOVERNMENT'S ALWAYS WATCHING. ESPECIALLY NOW.
THEY'VE GOT EYES EVERYWHERE, AND ALL THE INFORMATION THEY COLLECT GOES BACK TO THE N.S.A. BUILDING.
ENNIS, EH?
NATIONAL SECURITY AGENCY.
AND IF THEY DON'T LIKE WHAT THEY SEE...FOR INSTANCE, A WHITE GUY WITH TOO MUCH INFLUENCE, THEY'LL SAY YOU'RE HACKING OUR ELECTION AND SEND ONE OF THEIR BEASTS.
SAINT G TELLS US. SEE, THEY WANT TO MAKE SURE NO ONE CAN STAND IN THEIR WAY WHEN THEY START DEMANDING HUMAN SACRIFICES FOR THEIR BLOOD CULT.
AND THE ONLY THING HOLDING BACK THE TRUTH IS THOSE GODDAMN POC FREE PEOPLE, ALWAYS MAKING IT ALL ABOUT THEIR GODDAMN SKIN COLOR...
WAR?

EVERYONE'S HERE. BILLI SAID SHE WANTS TO SHOW YOU SOMETHING.
SAID IT REMINDS HER OF YOU WHEN YOU'VE HAD MANY BEERS AND PICKLED EGGS. I DIDN'T WANT MORE EXPLANATION.
HRNPH.
IS THERE A PROBLEM, FRIEND?
YEAH. YOU COME OVER FROM A PLACE THAT'S GOT THOSE PEOPLE UNDER CONTROL, SO YOU CAN CALL ONE A FRIEND?
YOU'RE A TRAITOR TO YOUR RACE.
THAT, OR YOU'VE LOST YOUR *DAMN MIND.*
WOK
WARLOCK. THIS IS NOT THE TIME--
YOU HEARD WHAT HE SAID?
ABOUT ME? YES.
OH--YES! ABOUT *YOU!*

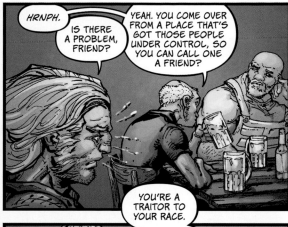

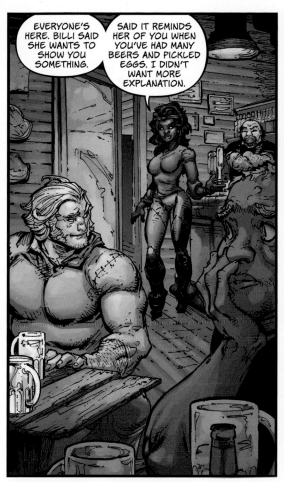

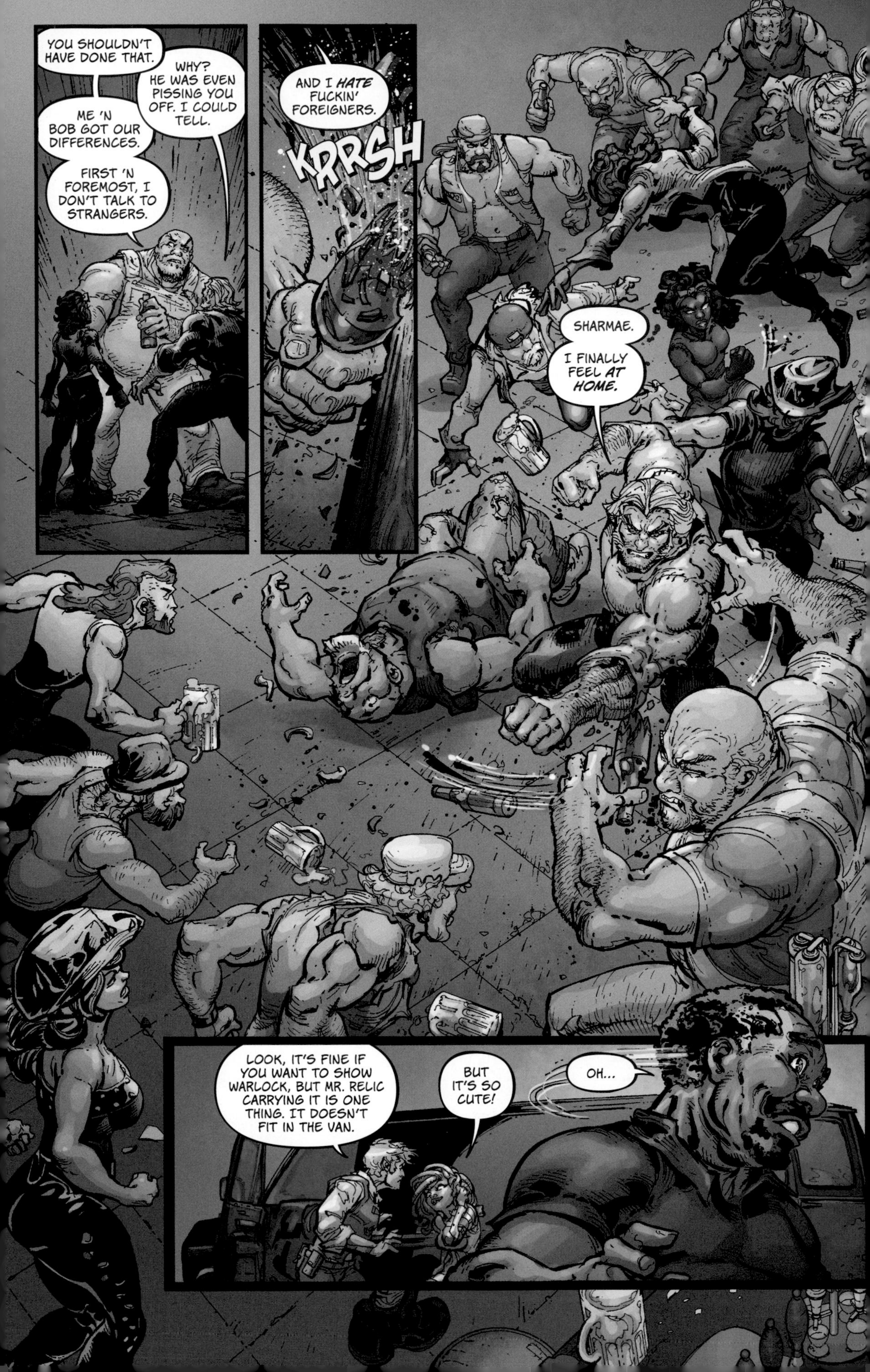
YOU SHOULDN'T HAVE DONE THAT.
WHY? HE WAS EVEN PISSING YOU OFF. I COULD TELL.
ME 'N BOB GOT OUR DIFFERENCES.
FIRST 'N FOREMOST, I DON'T TALK TO STRANGERS.
AND I *HATE* FUCKIN' FOREIGNERS.
KRRSH
SHARMAE.
I FINALLY FEEL *AT HOME.*
LOOK, IT'S FINE IF YOU WANT TO SHOW WARLOCK, BUT MR. RELIC CARRYING IT IS ONE THING. IT DOESN'T FIT IN THE VAN.
BUT IT'S SO CUTE!
OH...

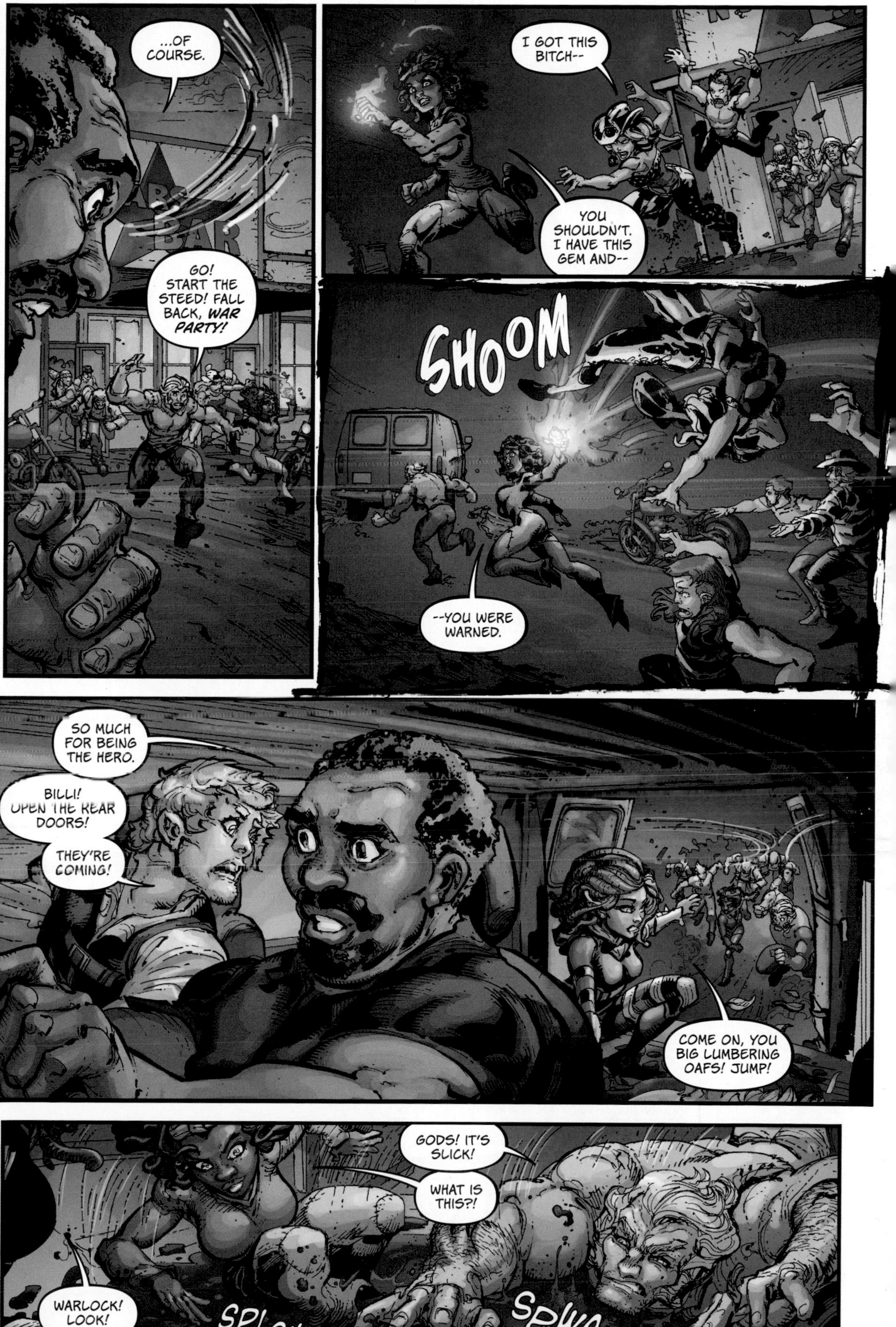
...OF COURSE.
GO! START THE STEED! FALL BACK, WAR PARTY!
I GOT THIS BITCH--
YOU SHOULDN'T. I HAVE THIS GEM AND--
SHOOM
--YOU WERE WARNED.
SO MUCH FOR BEING THE HERO.
BILLI! OPEN THE REAR DOORS!
THEY'RE COMING!
COME ON, YOU BIG LUMBERING OAFS! JUMP!
WARLOCK! LOOK!
GODS! IT'S SLICK!
WHAT IS THIS?!
SPLSH
SPWAT

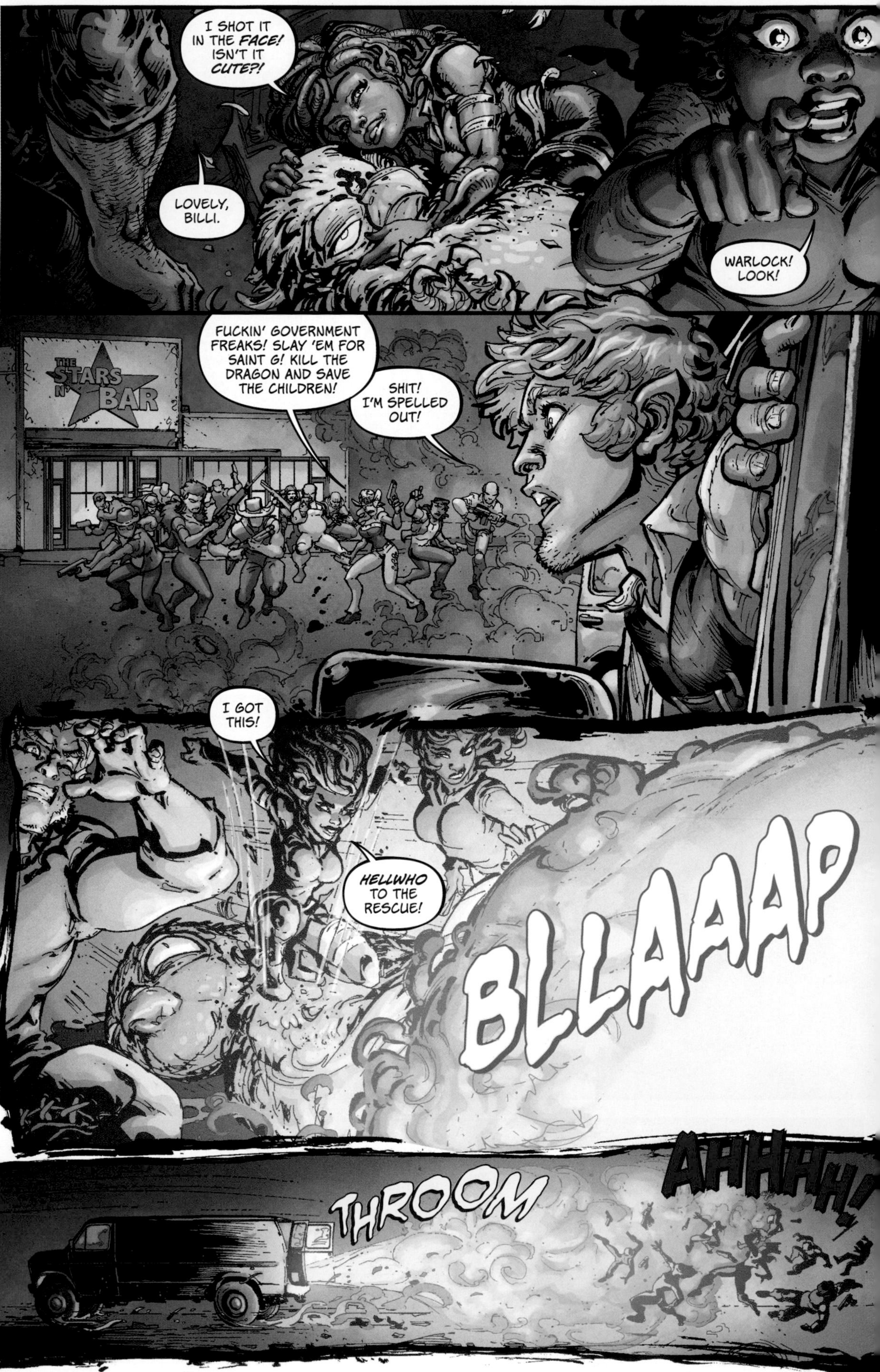
I SHOT IT IN THE *FACE!* ISN'T IT *CUTE?!*
LOVELY, BILLI.
WARLOCK! LOOK!
THE STARS N' BAR
FUCKIN' GOVERNMENT FREAKS! SLAY 'EM FOR SAINT G! KILL THE DRAGON AND SAVE THE CHILDREN!
SHIT! I'M SPELLED OUT!
I GOT THIS!
HELLWHO TO THE RESCUE!
BLLAAAP
THROOM
AHHHH

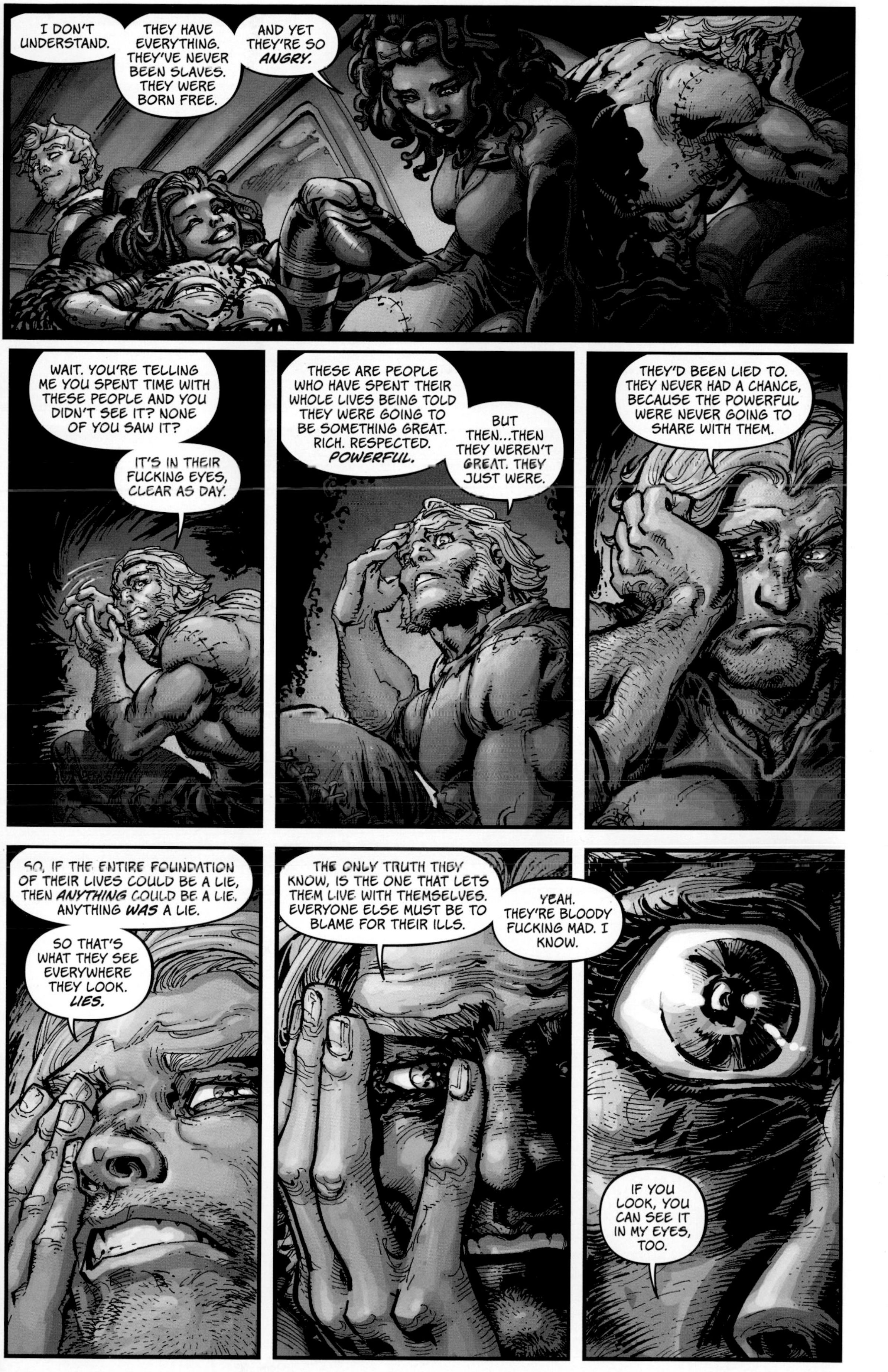
I DON'T UNDERSTAND.
THEY HAVE EVERYTHING. THEY'VE NEVER BEEN SLAVES. THEY WERE BORN FREE.
AND YET THEY'RE SO *ANGRY.*
WAIT. YOU'RE TELLING ME YOU SPENT TIME WITH THESE PEOPLE AND YOU DIDN'T SEE IT? NONE OF YOU SAW IT?
IT'S IN THEIR FUCKING EYES, CLEAR AS DAY.
THESE ARE PEOPLE WHO HAVE SPENT THEIR WHOLE LIVES BEING TOLD THEY WERE GOING TO BE SOMETHING GREAT. RICH. RESPECTED. *POWERFUL.*
BUT THEN...THEN THEY WEREN'T GREAT. THEY JUST WERE.
THEY'D BEEN LIED TO. THEY NEVER HAD A CHANCE, BECAUSE THE POWERFUL WERE NEVER GOING TO SHARE WITH THEM.
SO, IF THE ENTIRE FOUNDATION OF THEIR LIVES COULD BE A LIE, THEN *ANYTHING* COULD BE A LIE. ANYTHING *WAS* A LIE.
SO THAT'S WHAT THEY SEE EVERYWHERE THEY LOOK. *LIES.*
THE ONLY TRUTH THEY KNOW, IS THE ONE THAT LETS THEM LIVE WITH THEMSELVES. EVERYONE ELSE MUST BE TO BLAME FOR THEIR ILLS.
YEAH. THEY'RE BLOODY FUCKING MAD. I KNOW.
IF YOU LOOK, YOU CAN SEE IT IN MY EYES, TOO.

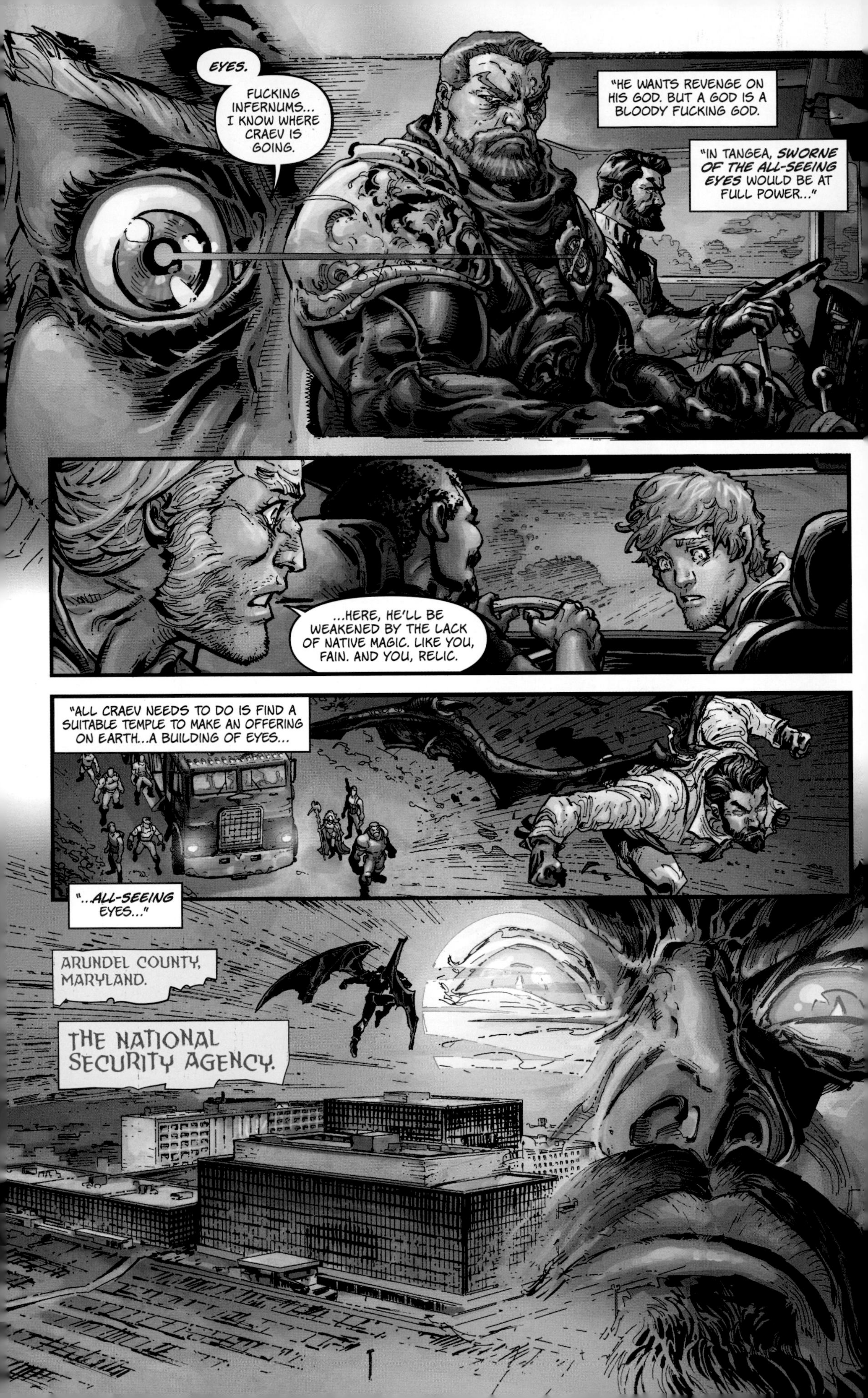
EYES.
FUCKING INFERNUMS... I KNOW WHERE CRAEV IS GOING.
"HE WANTS REVENGE ON HIS GOD. BUT A GOD IS A BLOODY FUCKING GOD.
"IN TANGEA, SWORNE OF THE ALL-SEEING EYES WOULD BE AT FULL POWER..."
...HERE, HE'LL BE WEAKENED BY THE LACK OF NATIVE MAGIC. LIKE YOU, FAIN. AND YOU, RELIC.
"ALL CRAEV NEEDS TO DO IS FIND A SUITABLE TEMPLE TO MAKE AN OFFERING ON EARTH...A BUILDING OF EYES...
"...ALL-SEEING EYES..."
ARUNDEL COUNTY, MARYLAND.
THE NATIONAL SECURITY AGENCY.

4

FOR THE GREATER CHAOTIC GOOD

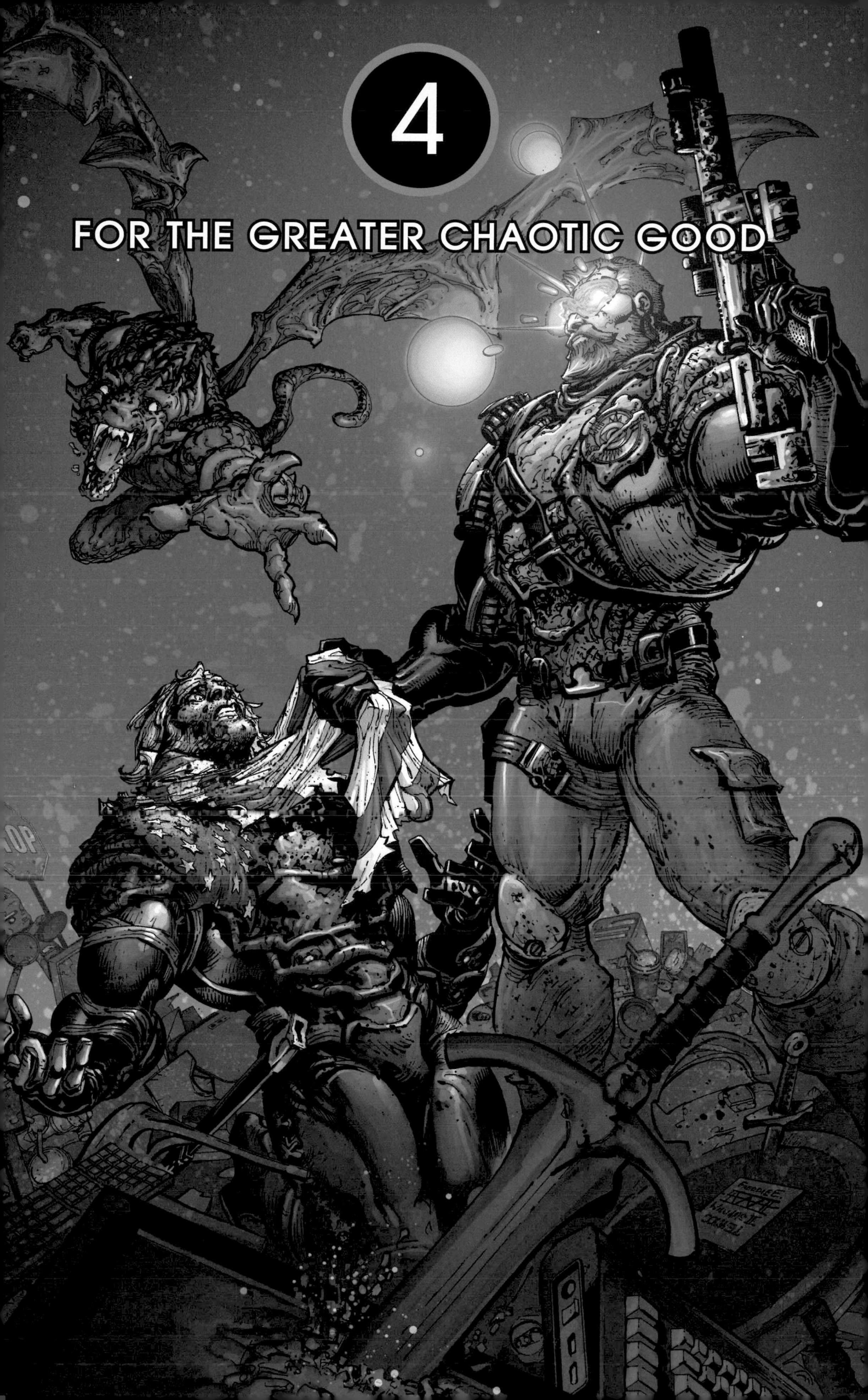

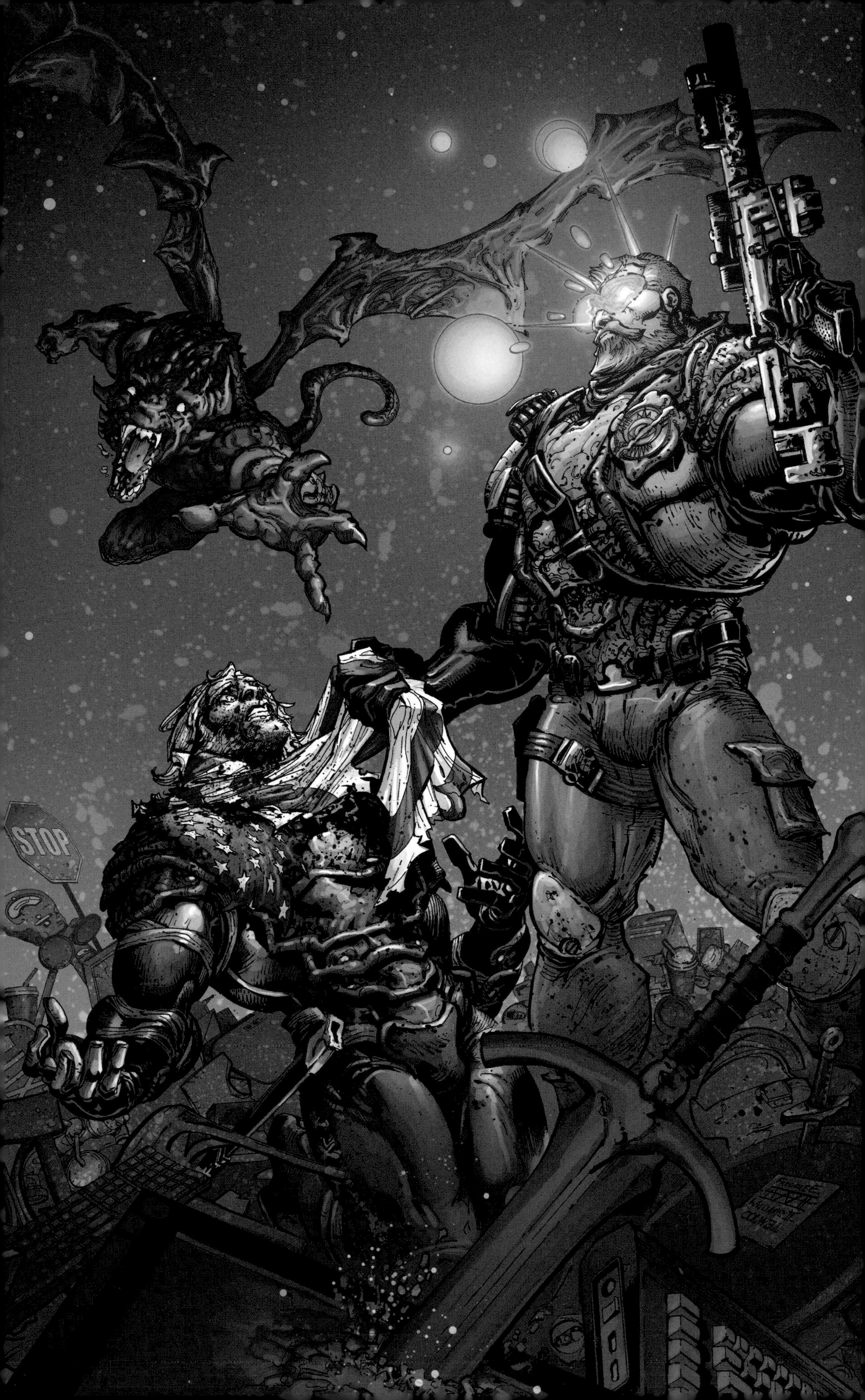
STOP

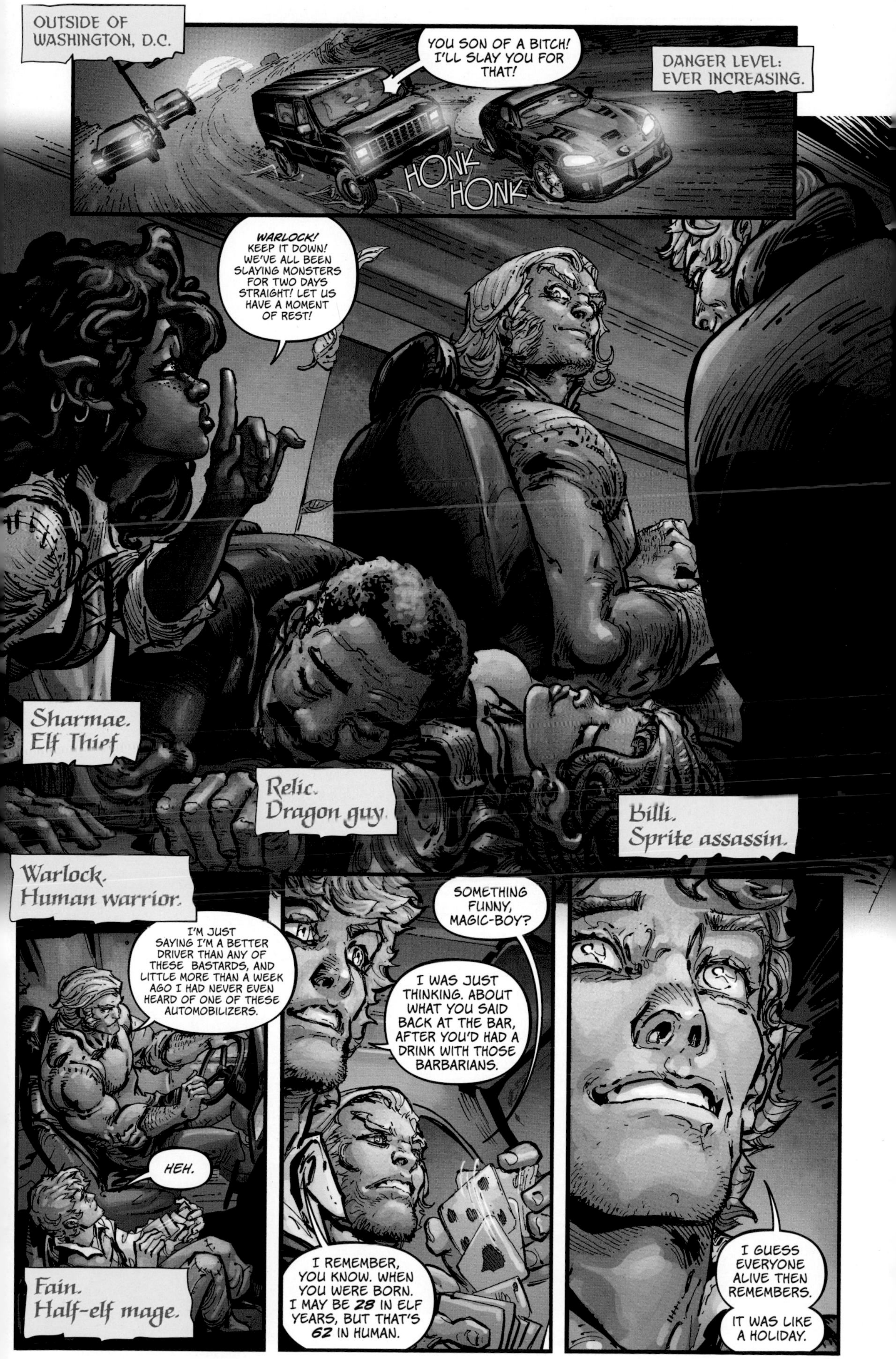

OUTSIDE OF WASHINGTON, D.C.
YOU SON OF A BITCH! I'LL SLAY YOU FOR THAT!
DANGER LEVEL: EVER INCREASING.
HONK HONK
WARLOCK! KEEP IT DOWN! WE'VE ALL BEEN SLAYING MONSTERS FOR TWO DAYS STRAIGHT! LET US HAVE A MOMENT OF REST!
Sharmae. Elf Thief
Relic. Dragon guy.
Billi. Sprite assassin.
Warlock. Human warrior.
I'M JUST SAYING I'M A BETTER DRIVER THAN ANY OF THESE BASTARDS, AND LITTLE MORE THAN A WEEK AGO I HAD NEVER EVEN HEARD OF ONE OF THESE AUTOMOBILIZERS.
HEH.
Fain. Half-elf mage.
SOMETHING FUNNY, MAGIC-BOY?
I WAS JUST THINKING. ABOUT WHAT YOU SAID BACK AT THE BAR, AFTER YOU'D HAD A DRINK WITH THOSE BARBARIANS.
I REMEMBER, YOU KNOW. WHEN YOU WERE BORN. I MAY BE 28 IN ELF YEARS, BUT THAT'S 62 IN HUMAN.
I GUESS EVERYONE ALIVE THEN REMEMBERS.
IT WAS LIKE A HOLIDAY.

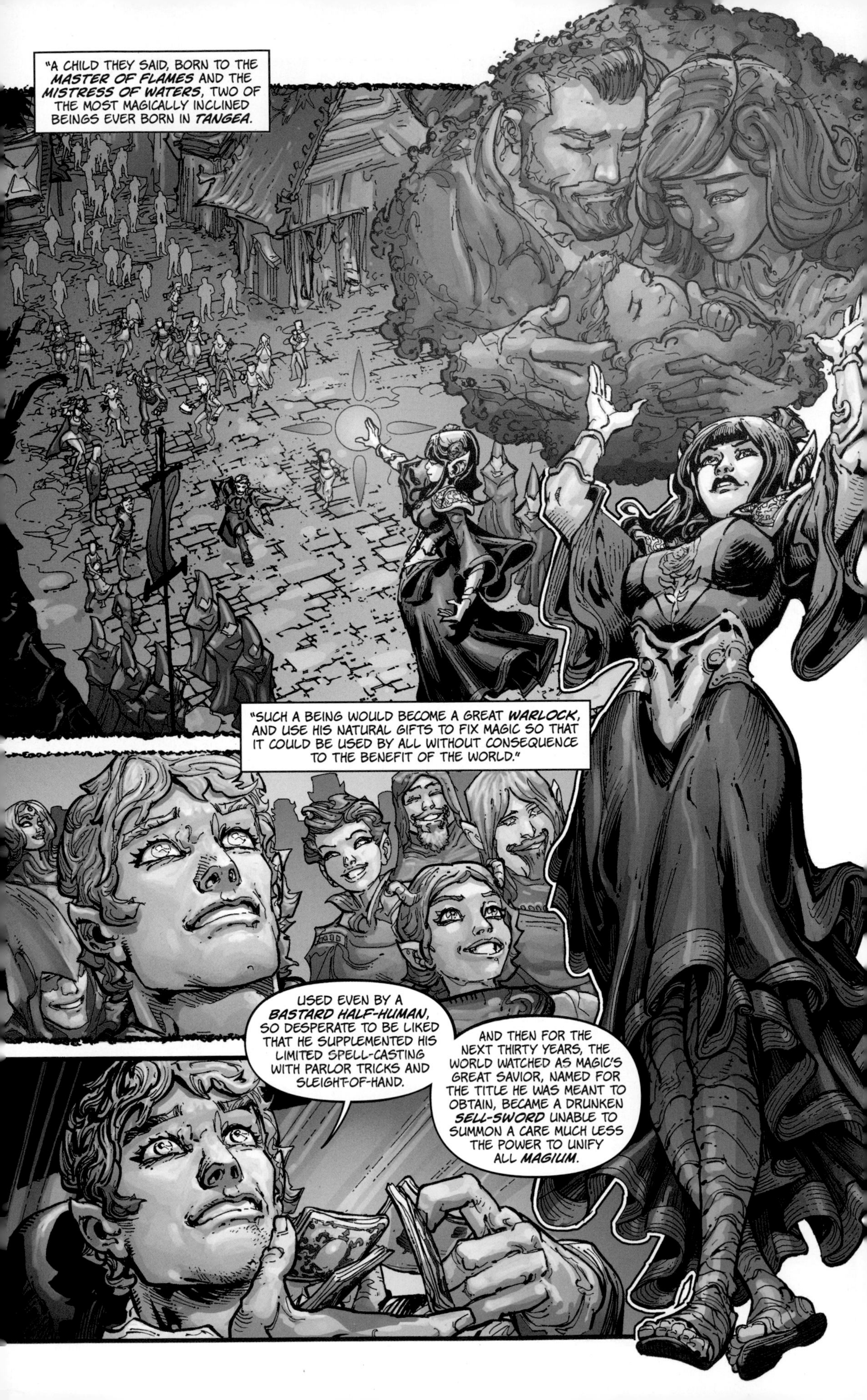
"A CHILD THEY SAID, BORN TO THE MASTER OF FLAMES AND THE MISTRESS OF WATERS, TWO OF THE MOST MAGICALLY INCLINED BEINGS EVER BORN IN TANGEA.
"SUCH A BEING WOULD BECOME A GREAT WARLOCK, AND USE HIS NATURAL GIFTS TO FIX MAGIC SO THAT IT COULD BE USED BY ALL WITHOUT CONSEQUENCE TO THE BENEFIT OF THE WORLD."
USED EVEN BY A BASTARD HALF-HUMAN, SO DESPERATE TO BE LIKED THAT HE SUPPLEMENTED HIS LIMITED SPELL-CASTING WITH PARLOR TRICKS AND SLEIGHT-OF-HAND.
AND THEN FOR THE NEXT THIRTY YEARS, THE WORLD WATCHED AS MAGIC'S GREAT SAVIOR, NAMED FOR THE TITLE HE WAS MEANT TO OBTAIN, BECAME A DRUNKEN SELL-SWORD UNABLE TO SUMMON A CARE MUCH LESS THE POWER TO UNIFY ALL MAGIUM.

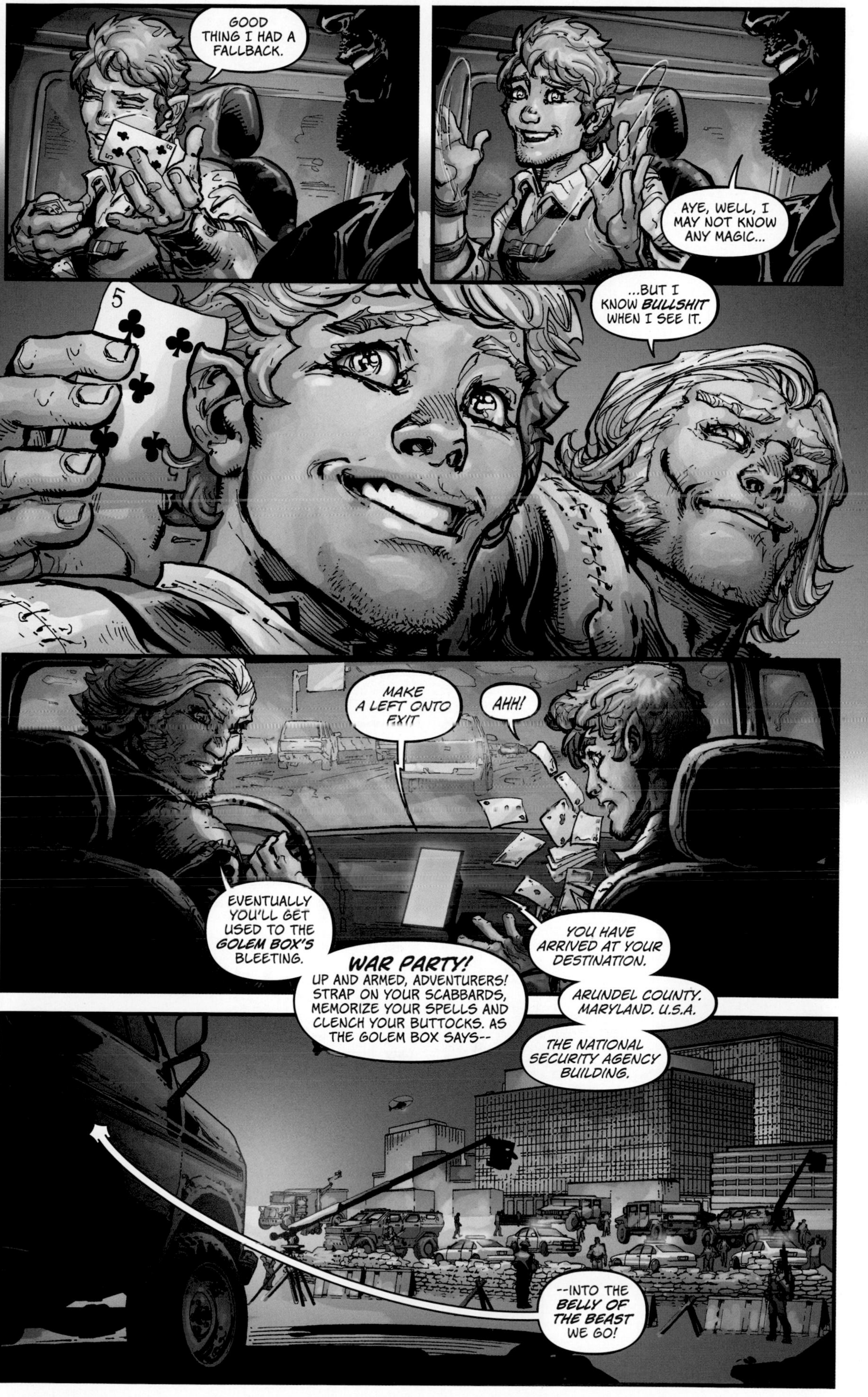
GOOD THING I HAD A FALLBACK.
AYE, WELL, I MAY NOT KNOW ANY MAGIC...
...BUT I KNOW BULLSHIT WHEN I SEE IT.
5
MAKE A LEFT ONTO EXIT
AHH!
EVENTUALLY YOU'LL GET USED TO THE GOLEM BOX'S BLEETING.
YOU HAVE ARRIVED AT YOUR DESTINATION.
WAR PARTY!
UP AND ARMED, ADVENTURERS! STRAP ON YOUR SCABBARDS, MEMORIZE YOUR SPELLS AND CLENCH YOUR BUTTOCKS. AS THE GOLEM BOX SAYS--
ARUNDEL COUNTY. MARYLAND. U.S.A.
THE NATIONAL SECURITY AGENCY BUILDING.
--INTO THE BELLY OF THE BEAST WE GO!

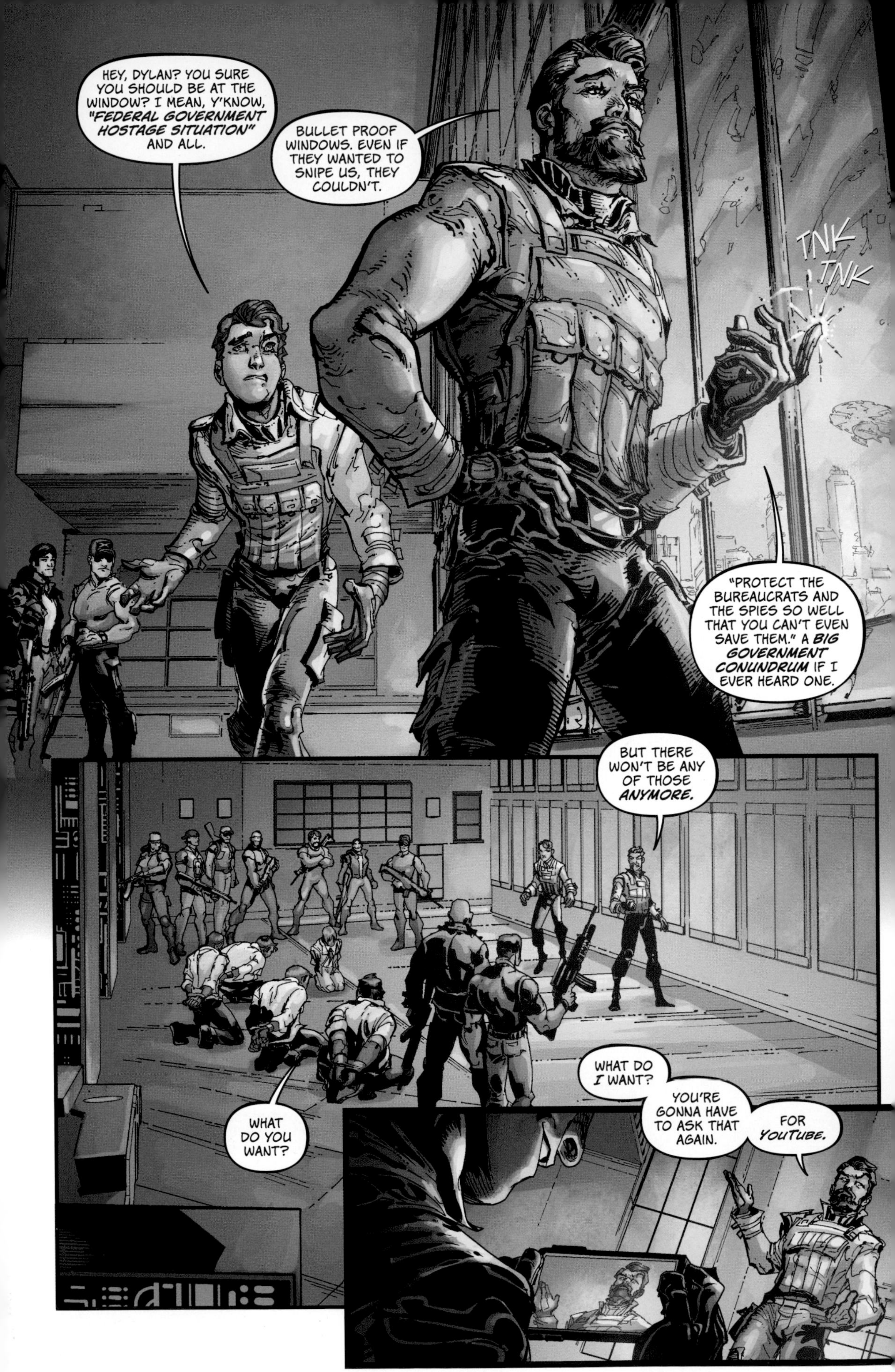
HEY, DYLAN? YOU SURE YOU SHOULD BE AT THE WINDOW? I MEAN, Y'KNOW, "FEDERAL GOVERNMENT HOSTAGE SITUATION" AND ALL.
BULLET PROOF WINDOWS. EVEN IF THEY WANTED TO SNIPE US, THEY COULDN'T.
TNK TNK
"PROTECT THE BUREAUCRATS AND THE SPIES SO WELL THAT YOU CAN'T EVEN SAVE THEM." A BIG GOVERNMENT CONUNDRUM IF I EVER HEARD ONE.
BUT THERE WON'T BE ANY OF THOSE ANYMORE.
WHAT DO YOU WANT?
WHAT DO I WANT?
YOU'RE GONNA HAVE TO ASK THAT AGAIN.
FOR YOUTUBE.

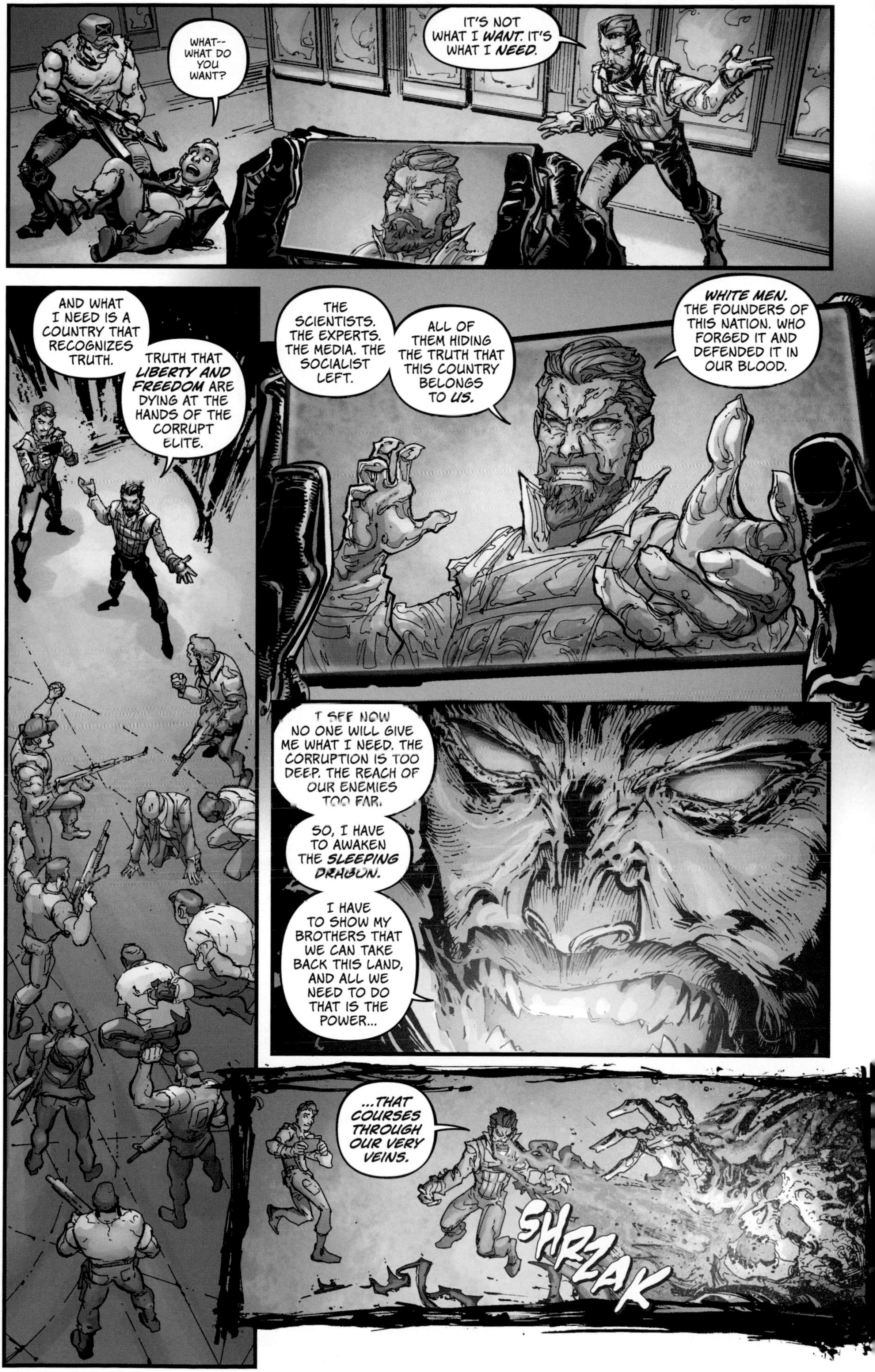
WHAT-- WHAT DO YOU WANT?
IT'S NOT WHAT I *WANT*. IT'S WHAT I *NEED*.
AND WHAT I NEED IS A COUNTRY THAT RECOGNIZES TRUTH.
TRUTH THAT *LIBERTY AND FREEDOM* ARE DYING AT THE HANDS OF THE CORRUPT ELITE.
THE SCIENTISTS. THE EXPERTS. THE MEDIA. THE SOCIALIST LEFT.
ALL OF THEM HIDING THE TRUTH THAT THIS COUNTRY BELONGS TO *US*.
WHITE MEN. THE FOUNDERS OF THIS NATION. WHO FORGED IT AND DEFENDED IT IN OUR BLOOD.
I SEE NOW NO ONE WILL GIVE ME WHAT I NEED. THE CORRUPTION IS TOO DEEP. THE REACH OF OUR ENEMIES TOO FAR.
SO, I HAVE TO AWAKEN THE *SLEEPING DRAGON*.
I HAVE TO SHOW MY BROTHERS THAT WE CAN TAKE BACK THIS LAND, AND ALL WE NEED TO DO THAT IS THE POWER...
...THAT COURSES THROUGH OUR VERY VEINS.
SHRZAK

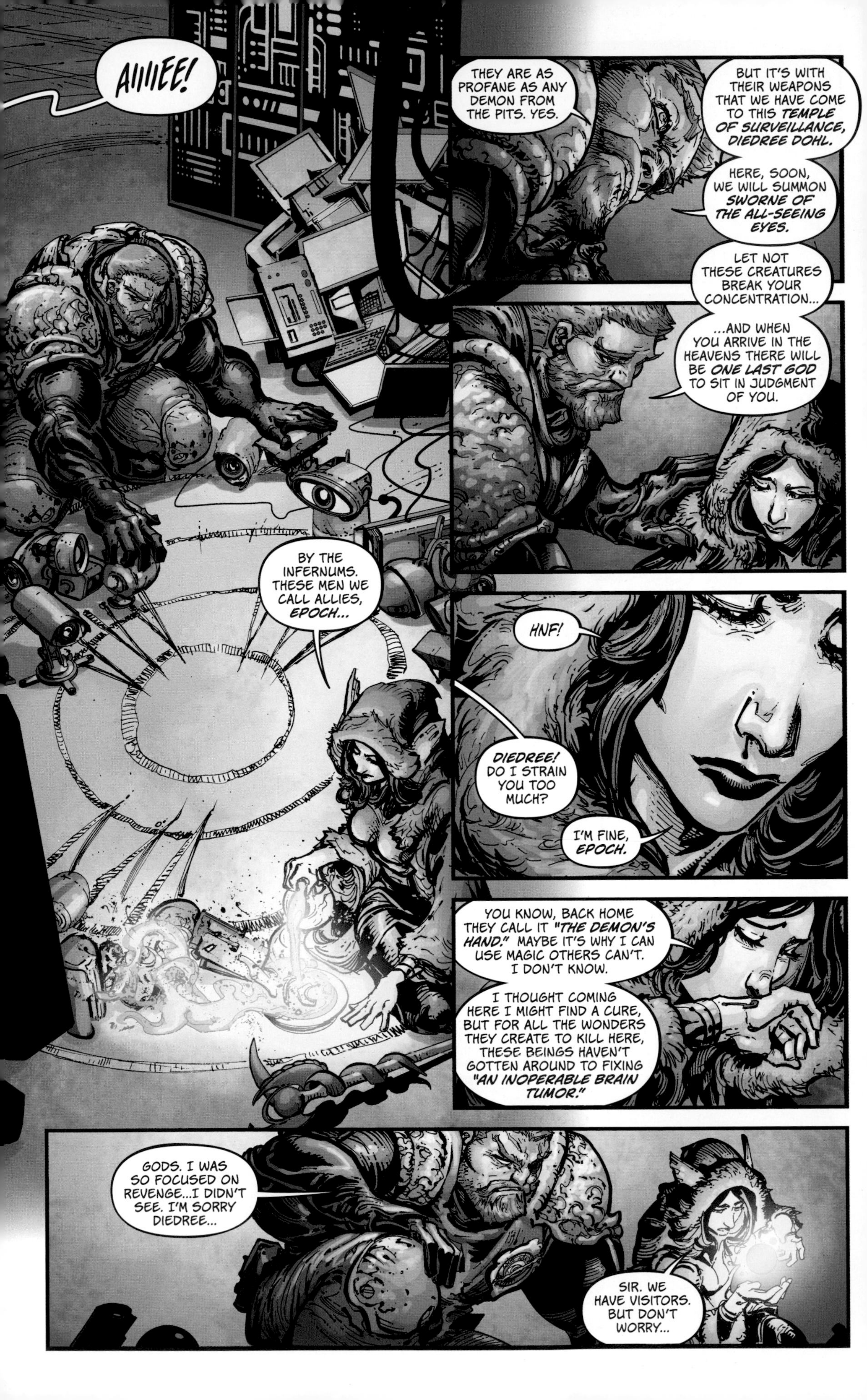
AIIIIEE!
THEY ARE AS PROFANE AS ANY DEMON FROM THE PITS. YES.
BUT IT'S WITH THEIR WEAPONS THAT WE HAVE COME TO THIS TEMPLE OF SURVEILLANCE, DIEDREE DOHL.
HERE, SOON, WE WILL SUMMON SWORNE OF THE ALL-SEEING EYES.
LET NOT THESE CREATURES BREAK YOUR CONCENTRATION...
...AND WHEN YOU ARRIVE IN THE HEAVENS THERE WILL BE ONE LAST GOD TO SIT IN JUDGMENT OF YOU.
BY THE INFERNUMS. THESE MEN WE CALL ALLIES, EPOCH...
HNF!
DIEDREE! DO I STRAIN YOU TOO MUCH?
I'M FINE, EPOCH.
YOU KNOW, BACK HOME THEY CALL IT "THE DEMON'S HAND." MAYBE IT'S WHY I CAN USE MAGIC OTHERS CAN'T. I DON'T KNOW.
I THOUGHT COMING HERE I MIGHT FIND A CURE, BUT FOR ALL THE WONDERS THEY CREATE TO KILL HERE, THESE BEINGS HAVEN'T GOTTEN AROUND TO FIXING "AN INOPERABLE BRAIN TUMOR."
GODS. I WAS SO FOCUSED ON REVENGE...I DIDN'T SEE. I'M SORRY DIEDREE...
SIR. WE HAVE VISITORS. BUT DON'T WORRY...

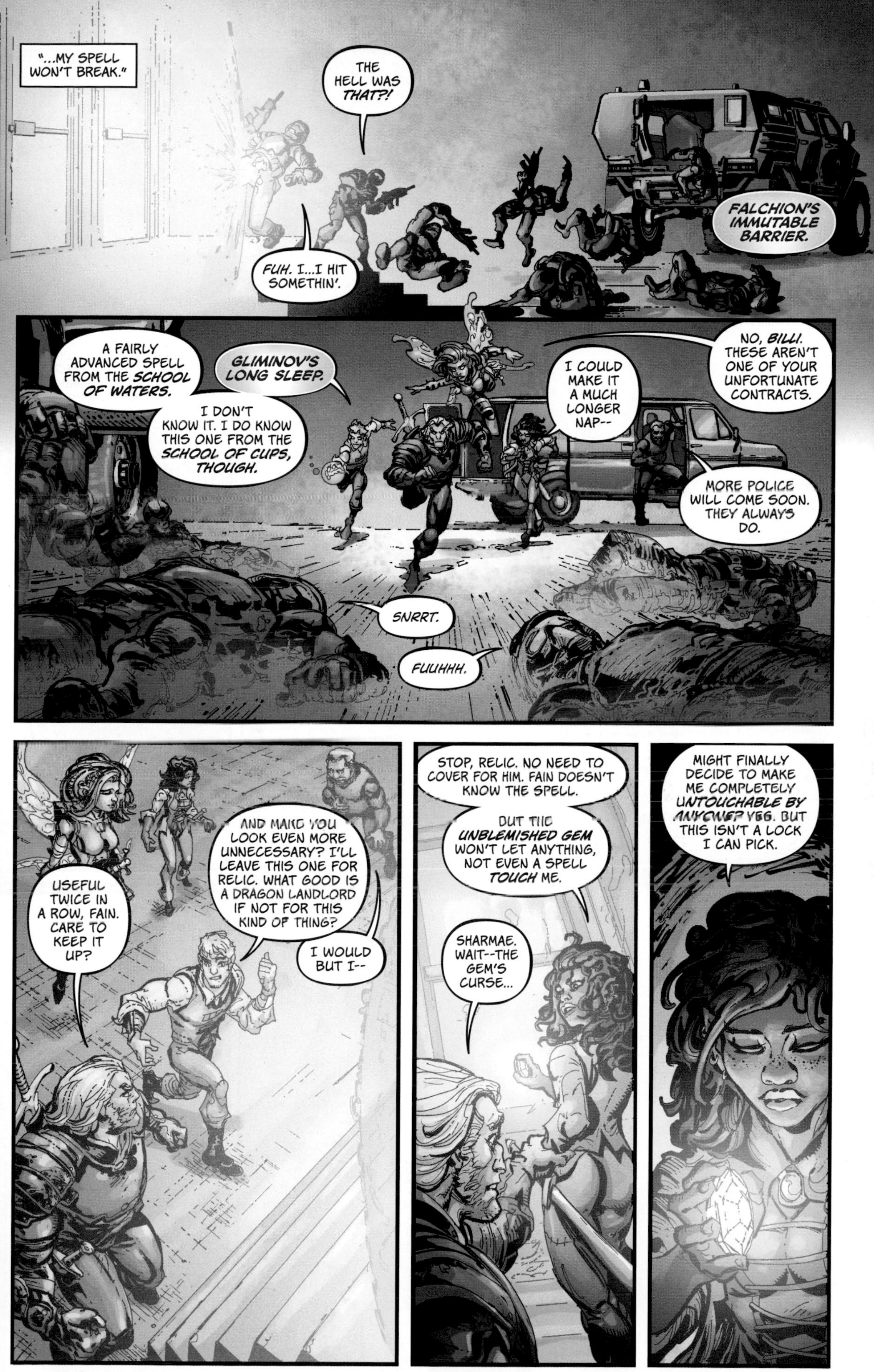
"...MY SPELL WON'T BREAK."
THE HELL WAS *THAT?!*
FUH. I...I HIT SOMETHIN'.
FALCHION'S IMMUTABLE BARRIER.
A FAIRLY ADVANCED SPELL FROM THE *SCHOOL OF WATERS.*
GLIMINOV'S LONG SLEEP.
I DON'T KNOW IT. I DO KNOW THIS ONE FROM THE *SCHOOL OF CUPS, THOUGH.*
I COULD MAKE IT A MUCH LONGER NAP--
NO, *BILLI.* THESE AREN'T ONE OF YOUR UNFORTUNATE CONTRACTS.
MORE POLICE WILL COME SOON. THEY ALWAYS DO.
SNRRT.
FUUHHH.
USEFUL TWICE IN A ROW, FAIN. CARE TO KEEP IT UP?
AND MAKE YOU LOOK EVEN MORE UNNECESSARY? I'LL LEAVE THIS ONE FOR RELIC. WHAT GOOD IS A DRAGON LANDLORD IF NOT FOR THIS KIND OF THING?
I WOULD BUT I--
STOP, RELIC. NO NEED TO COVER FOR HIM. FAIN DOESN'T KNOW THE SPELL.
BUT THE *UNBLEMISHED GEM* WON'T LET ANYTHING, NOT EVEN A SPELL *TOUCH* ME.
SHARMAE. WAIT--THE GEM'S CURSE...
MIGHT FINALLY DECIDE TO MAKE ME COMPLETELY *UNTOUCHABLE BY ANYONE?* YES. BUT THIS ISN'T A LOCK I CAN PICK.

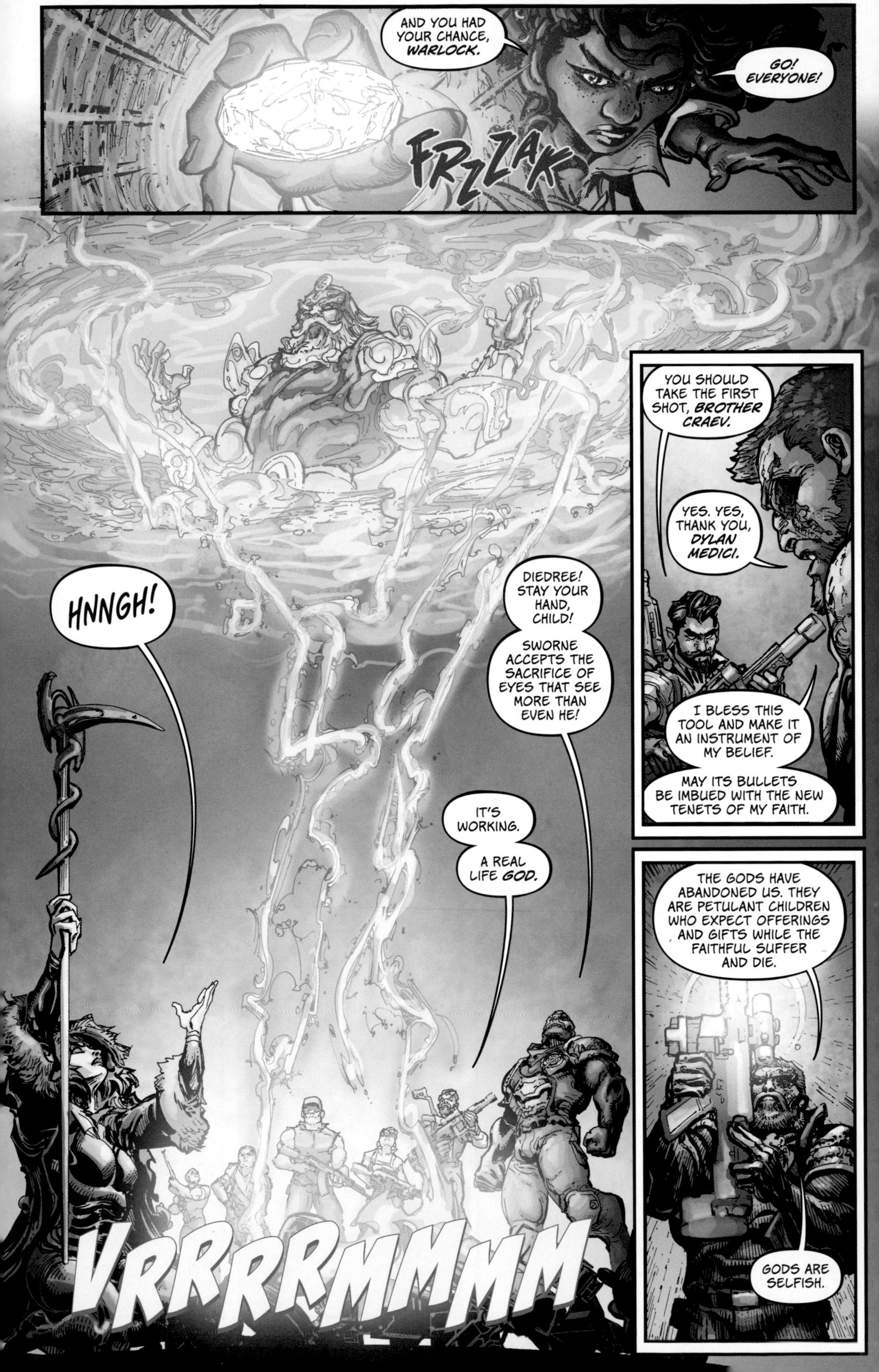
AND YOU HAD YOUR CHANCE, WARLOCK.
GO! EVERYONE!
FRZZZAK
YOU SHOULD TAKE THE FIRST SHOT, BROTHER CRAEV.
YES. YES, THANK YOU, DYLAN MEDICI.
I BLESS THIS TOOL AND MAKE IT AN INSTRUMENT OF MY BELIEF.
MAY ITS BULLETS BE IMBUED WITH THE NEW TENETS OF MY FAITH.
HNNGH!
DIEDREE! STAY YOUR HAND, CHILD!
SWORNE ACCEPTS THE SACRIFICE OF EYES THAT SEE MORE THAN EVEN HE!
IT'S WORKING.
A REAL LIFE GOD.
VRRRRMMMMM
THE GODS HAVE ABANDONED US. THEY ARE PETULANT CHILDREN WHO EXPECT OFFERINGS AND GIFTS WHILE THE FAITHFUL SUFFER AND DIE.
GODS ARE SELFISH.

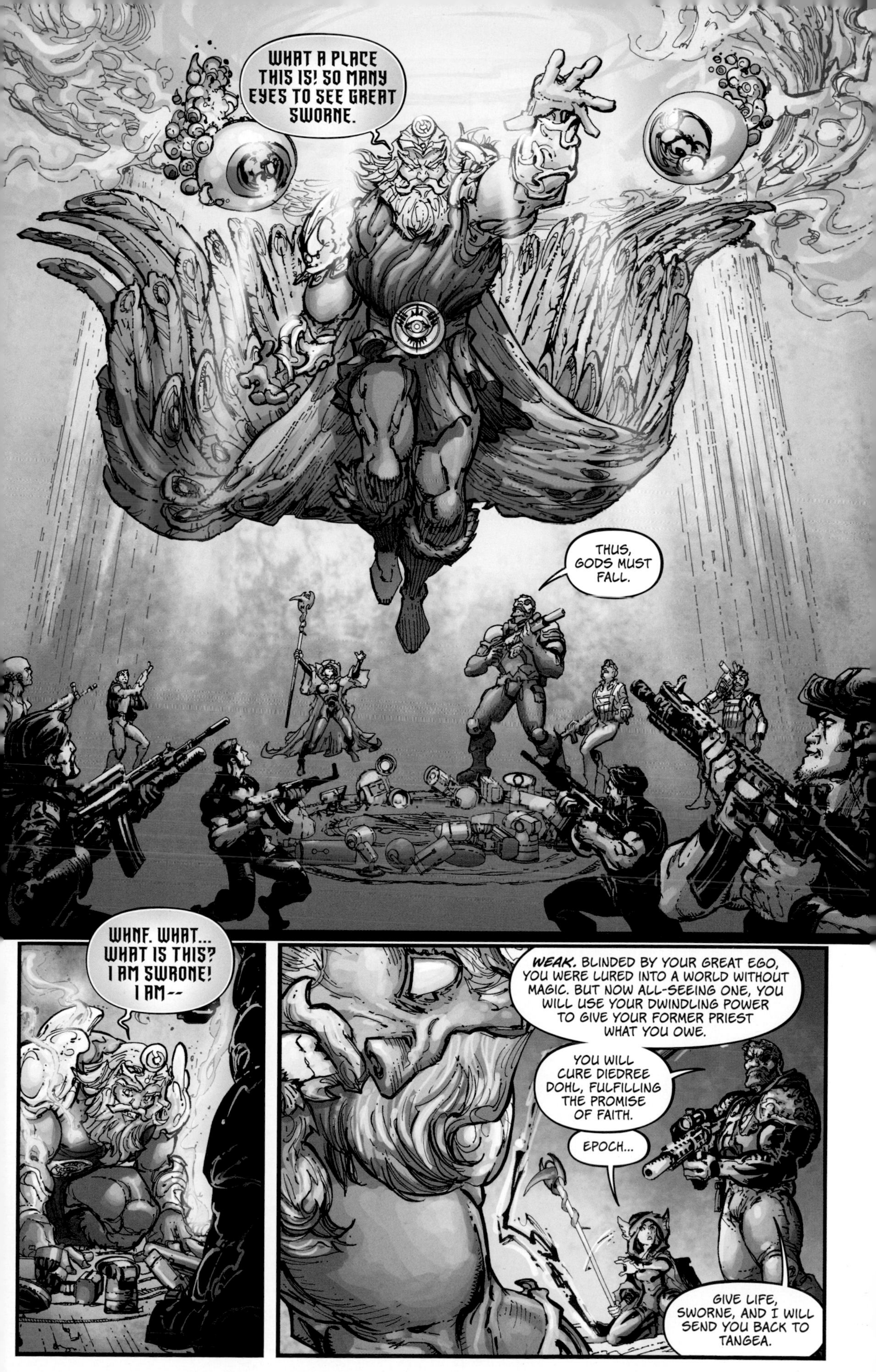
WHAT A PLACE THIS IS! SO MANY EYES TO SEE GREAT SWORNE.
THUS, GODS MUST FALL.
WHNF. WHAT... WHAT IS THIS? I AM SWRONE! I AM--
WEAK. BLINDED BY YOUR GREAT EGO, YOU WERE LURED INTO A WORLD WITHOUT MAGIC. BUT NOW ALL-SEEING ONE, YOU WILL USE YOUR DWINDLING POWER TO GIVE YOUR FORMER PRIEST WHAT YOU OWE.
YOU WILL CURE DIEDREE DOHL, FULFILLING THE PROMISE OF FAITH.
EPOCH...
GIVE LIFE, SWORNE, AND I WILL SEND YOU BACK TO TANGEA.

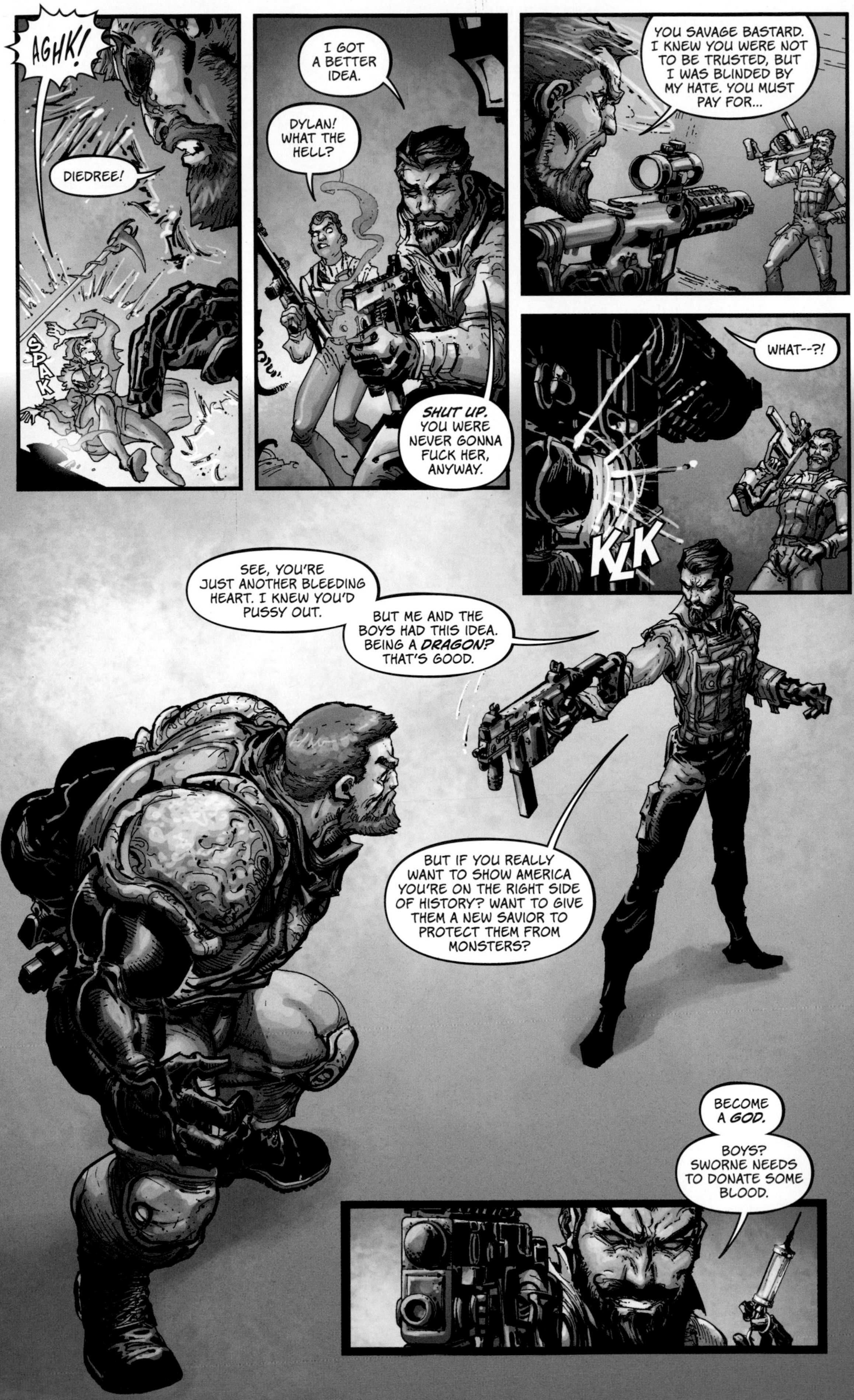
AGHK!
DIEDREE!
SPAK
I GOT A BETTER IDEA.
DYLAN! WHAT THE HELL?
SHUT UP. YOU WERE NEVER GONNA FUCK HER, ANYWAY.
YOU SAVAGE BASTARD. I KNEW YOU WERE NOT TO BE TRUSTED, BUT I WAS BLINDED BY MY HATE. YOU MUST PAY FOR...
WHAT--?!
KLK
SEE, YOU'RE JUST ANOTHER BLEEDING HEART. I KNEW YOU'D PUSSY OUT.
BUT ME AND THE BOYS HAD THIS IDEA. BEING A DRAGON? THAT'S GOOD.
BUT IF YOU REALLY WANT TO SHOW AMERICA YOU'RE ON THE RIGHT SIDE OF HISTORY? WANT TO GIVE THEM A NEW SAVIOR TO PROTECT THEM FROM MONSTERS?
BECOME A GOD.
BOYS? SWORNE NEEDS TO DONATE SOME BLOOD.

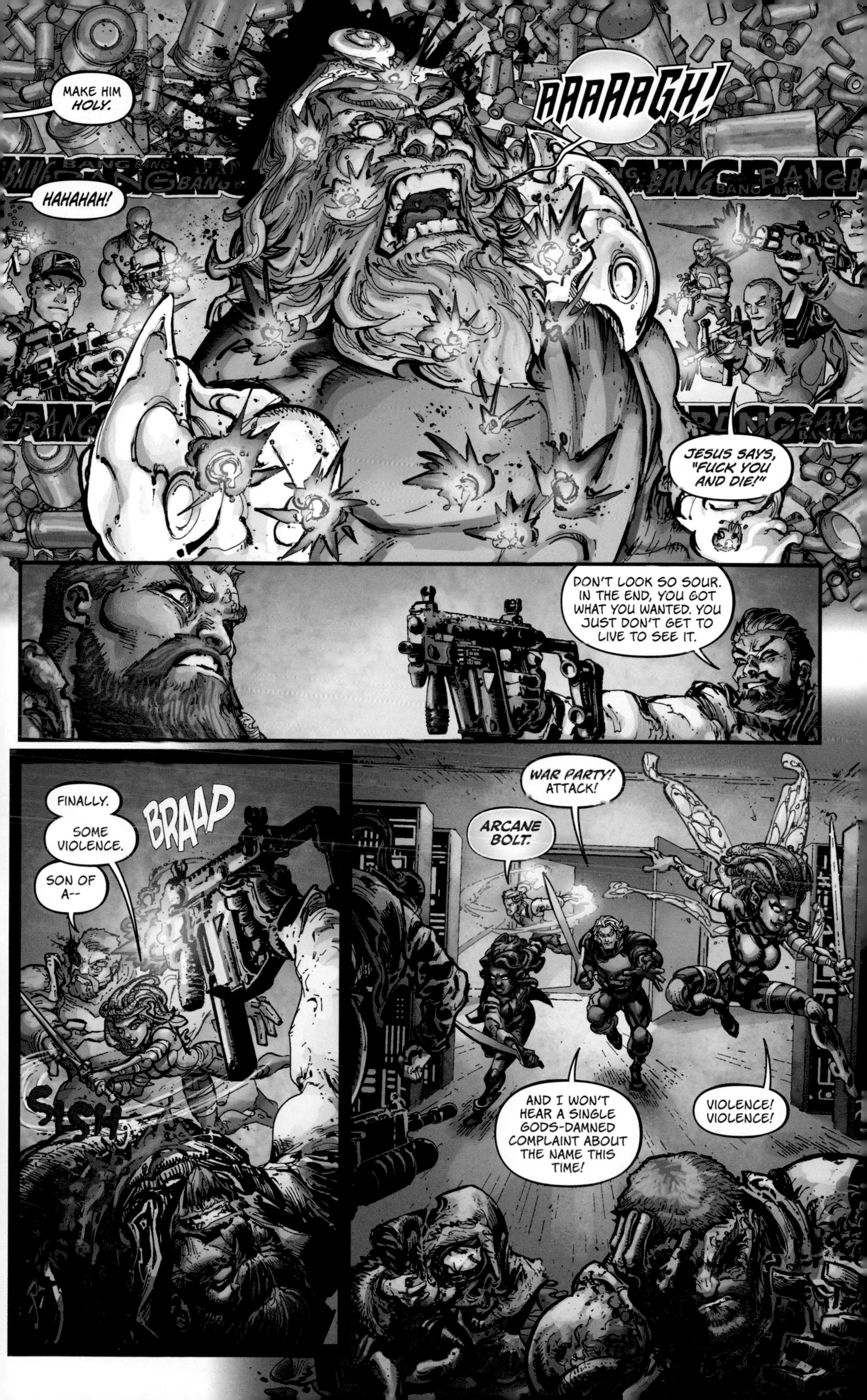
MAKE HIM HOLY.
AAAAAGH!
BANG BANG BANG BANG
HAHAHAH!
BANG BANG BANG
JESUS SAYS, "FUCK YOU AND DIE!"
DON'T LOOK SO SOUR. IN THE END, YOU GOT WHAT YOU WANTED. YOU JUST DON'T GET TO LIVE TO SEE IT.
FINALLY.
SOME VIOLENCE.
SON OF A--
BRAAP
SLISH
WAR PARTY! ATTACK!
ARCANE BOLT.
AND I WON'T HEAR A SINGLE GODS-DAMNED COMPLAINT ABOUT THE NAME THIS TIME!
VIOLENCE! VIOLENCE!

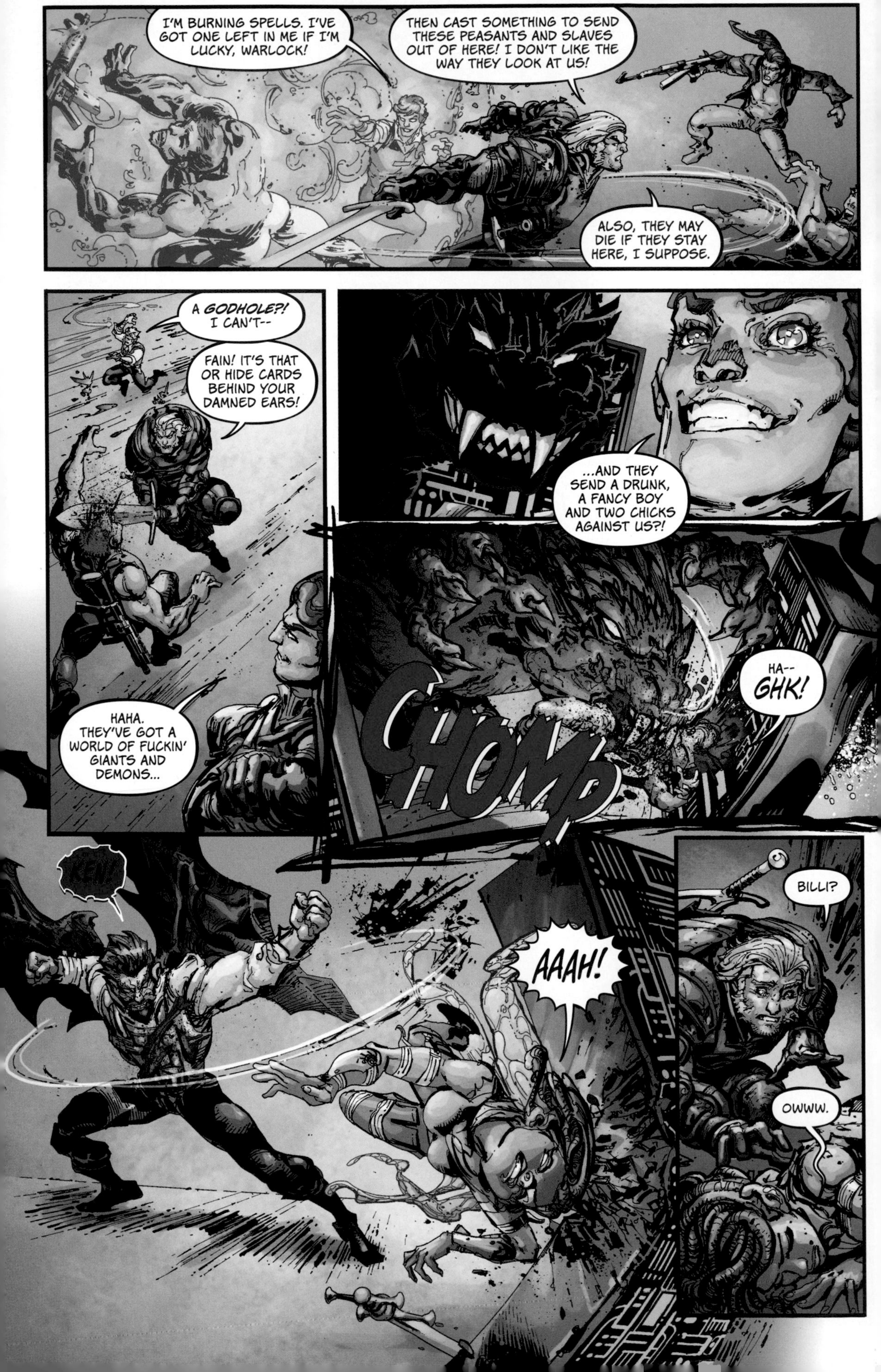
I'M BURNING SPELLS. I'VE GOT ONE LEFT IN ME IF I'M LUCKY, WARLOCK!
THEN CAST SOMETHING TO SEND THESE PEASANTS AND SLAVES OUT OF HERE! I DON'T LIKE THE WAY THEY LOOK AT US!
ALSO, THEY MAY DIE IF THEY STAY HERE, I SUPPOSE.
A GODHOLE?! I CAN'T--
FAIN! IT'S THAT OR HIDE CARDS BEHIND YOUR DAMNED EARS!
HAHA. THEY'VE GOT A WORLD OF FUCKIN' GIANTS AND DEMONS...
...AND THEY SEND A DRUNK, A FANCY BOY AND TWO CHICKS AGAINST US?!
CHOMP
HA-- GHK!
AAAH!
BILLI?
OWWW.

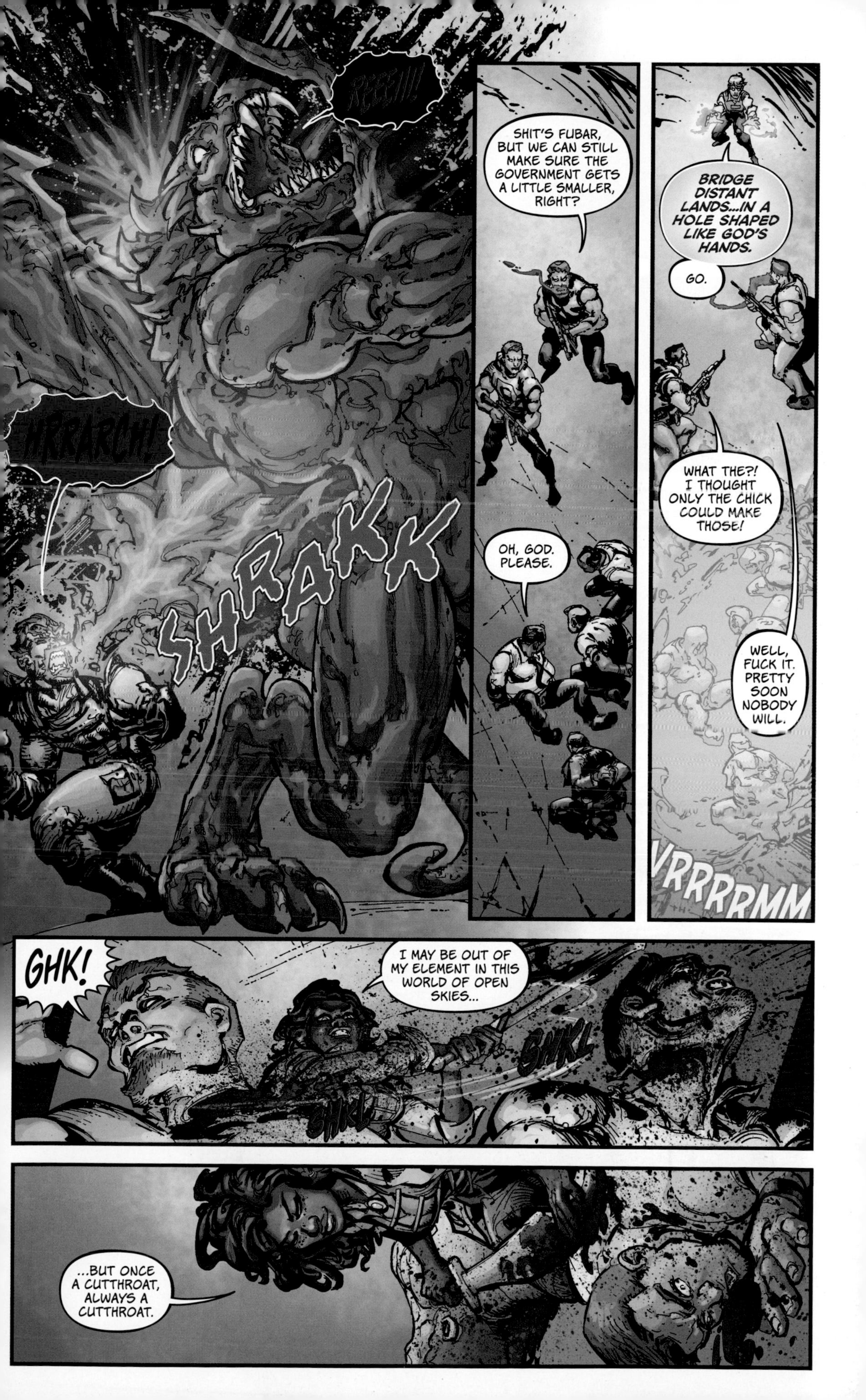
REEEE!!!
HRRARGH!
SHRAKK
SHIT'S FUBAR, BUT WE CAN STILL MAKE SURE THE GOVERNMENT GETS A LITTLE SMALLER, RIGHT?
OH, GOD. PLEASE.
BRIDGE DISTANT LANDS...IN A HOLE SHAPED LIKE GOD'S HANDS.
GO.
WHAT THE?! I THOUGHT ONLY THE CHICK COULD MAKE THOSE!
WELL, FUCK IT. PRETTY SOON NOBODY WILL.
VRRRRMM
GHK!
I MAY BE OUT OF MY ELEMENT IN THIS WORLD OF OPEN SKIES...
SHKL
SHKL
...BUT ONCE A CUTTHROAT, ALWAYS A CUTTHROAT.

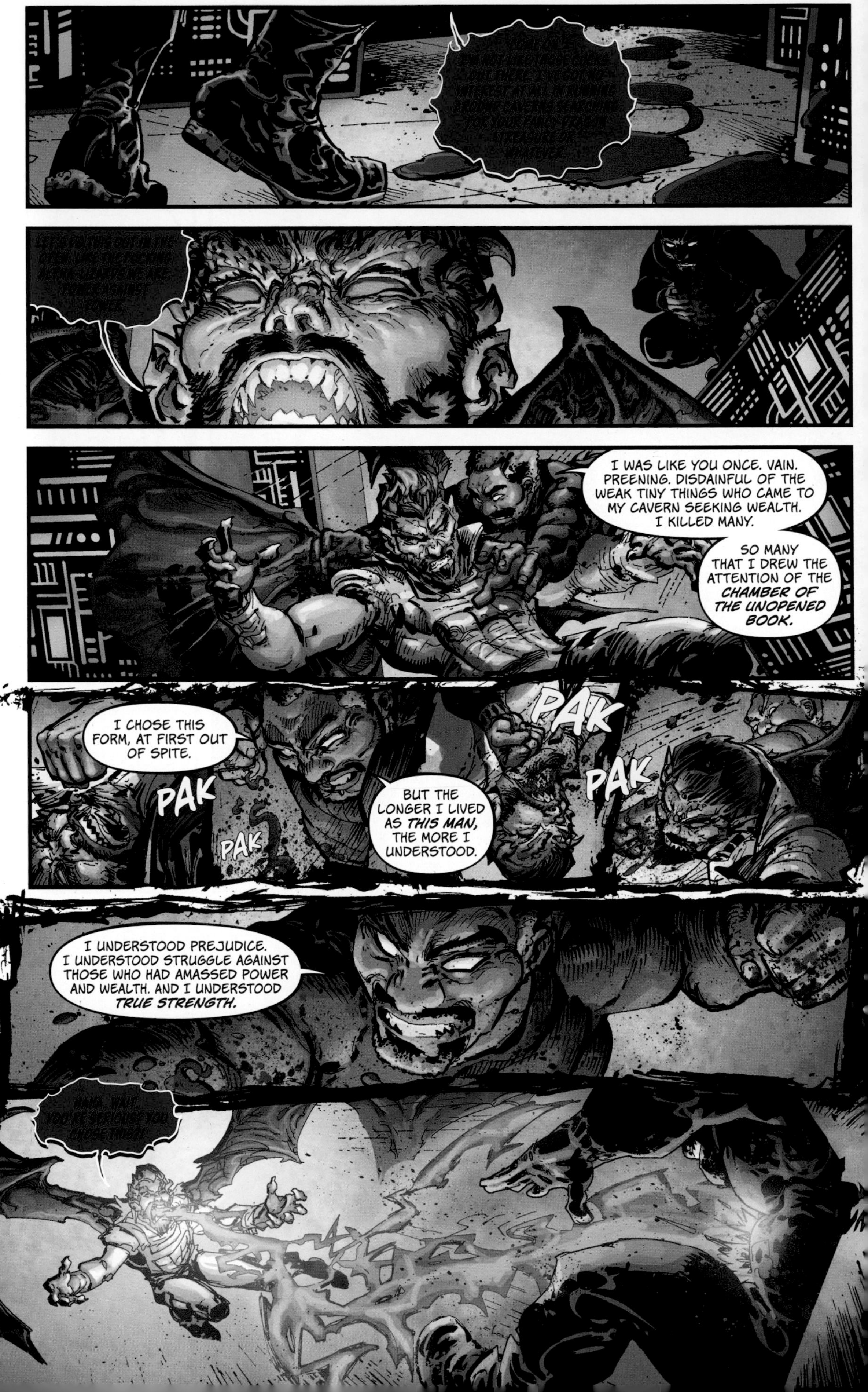

I WAS LIKE YOU ONCE. VAIN. PREENING. DISDAINFUL OF THE WEAK TINY THINGS WHO CAME TO MY CAVERN SEEKING WEALTH. I KILLED MANY.
SO MANY THAT I DREW THE ATTENTION OF THE CHAMBER OF THE UNOPENED BOOK.
I CHOSE THIS FORM, AT FIRST OUT OF SPITE.
PAK
PAK
BUT THE LONGER I LIVED AS THIS MAN, THE MORE I UNDERSTOOD.
PAK
PAK
I UNDERSTOOD PREJUDICE. I UNDERSTOOD STRUGGLE AGAINST THOSE WHO HAD AMASSED POWER AND WEALTH. AND I UNDERSTOOD TRUE STRENGTH.

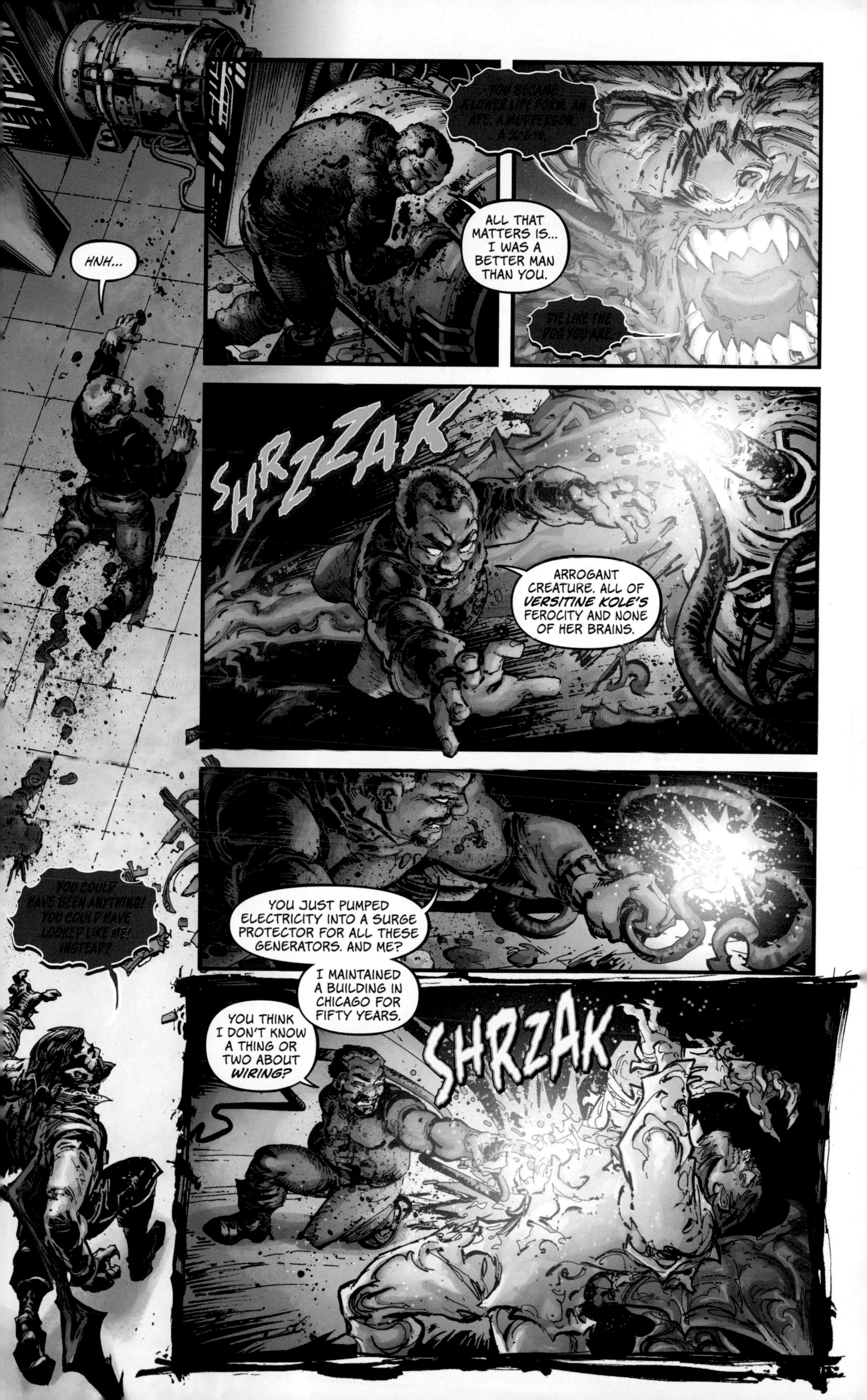
ALL THAT MATTERS IS... I WAS A BETTER MAN THAN YOU.
HNH...
SHRZZAK
ARROGANT CREATURE. ALL OF VERSITINE KOLE'S FEROCITY AND NONE OF HER BRAINS.
YOU JUST PUMPED ELECTRICITY INTO A SURGE PROTECTOR FOR ALL THESE GENERATORS. AND ME?
I MAINTAINED A BUILDING IN CHICAGO FOR FIFTY YEARS.
YOU THINK I DON'T KNOW A THING OR TWO ABOUT WIRING?
SHRZAK

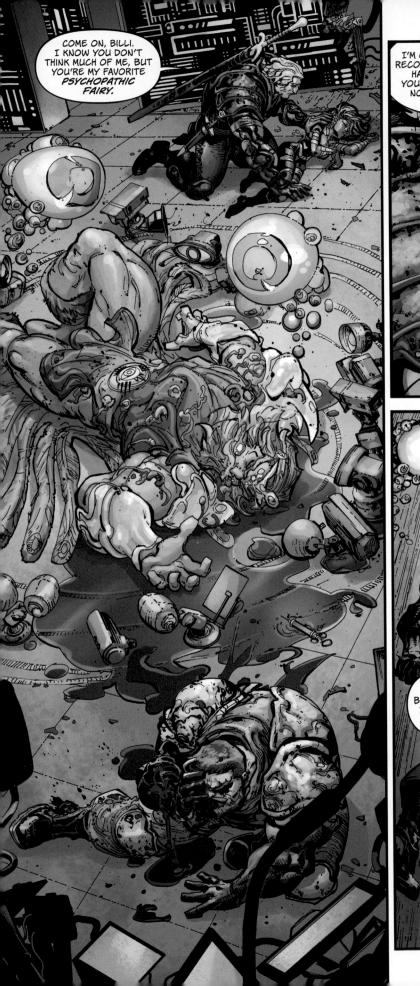

COME ON, BILLI. I KNOW YOU DON'T THINK MUCH OF ME, BUT YOU'RE MY FAVORITE *PSYCHOPATHIC FAIRY.*

I'M GOING TO NEED YOU TO RECOVER, BECAUSE WE DON'T HAVE A CLERIC TO HEAL YOU ANYMORE. HE DIED. BUT NOT BECAUSE OF SOME ROTTING DRAGON.

HNGH.

GARTHODD.

BECAUSE OF ME. BECAUSE I'M NOT A SAVIOR. I'M NOT A LEADER. I CAN'T EVEN ROB FUCKING TOMBS WELL.

I...

...I SEE NOW.

WITH JUST A DROP OF THE BLOOD OF SWORNE, I SEE THAT WHICH I'VE BEEN BLIND TO.

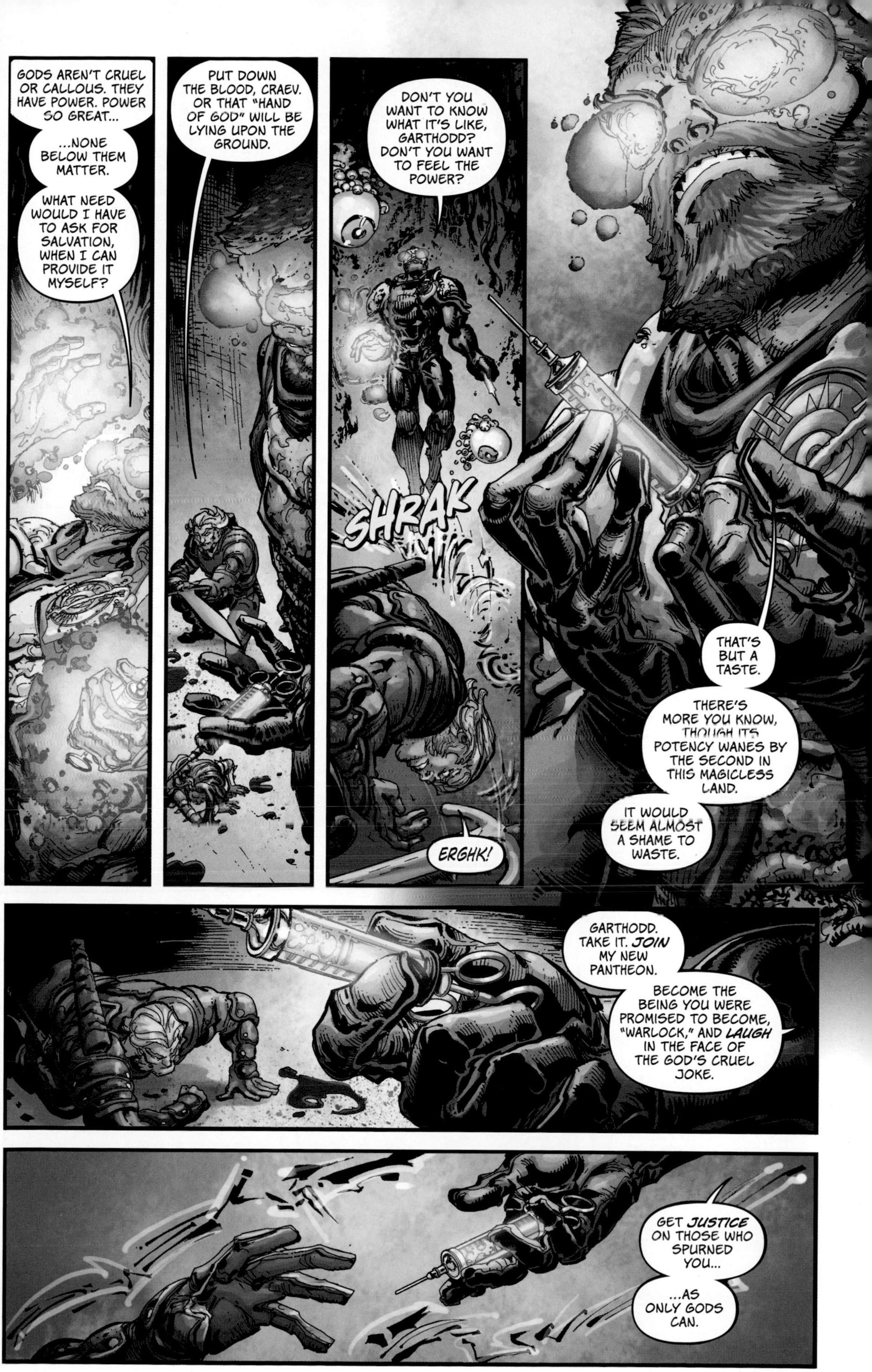
GODS AREN'T CRUEL OR CALLOUS. THEY HAVE POWER. POWER SO GREAT...
...NONE BELOW THEM MATTER.
WHAT NEED WOULD I HAVE TO ASK FOR SALVATION, WHEN I CAN PROVIDE IT MYSELF?
PUT DOWN THE BLOOD, CRAEV. OR THAT "HAND OF GOD" WILL BE LYING UPON THE GROUND.
DON'T YOU WANT TO KNOW WHAT IT'S LIKE, GARTHODD? DON'T YOU WANT TO FEEL THE POWER?
SHRAK
ERGHK!
THAT'S BUT A TASTE.
THERE'S MORE YOU KNOW, THOUGH ITS POTENCY WANES BY THE SECOND IN THIS MAGICLESS LAND.
IT WOULD SEEM ALMOST A SHAME TO WASTE.
GARTHODD. TAKE IT. JOIN MY NEW PANTHEON.
BECOME THE BEING YOU WERE PROMISED TO BECOME, "WARLOCK," AND LAUGH IN THE FACE OF THE GOD'S CRUEL JOKE.
GET JUSTICE ON THOSE WHO SPURNED YOU...
...AS ONLY GODS CAN.

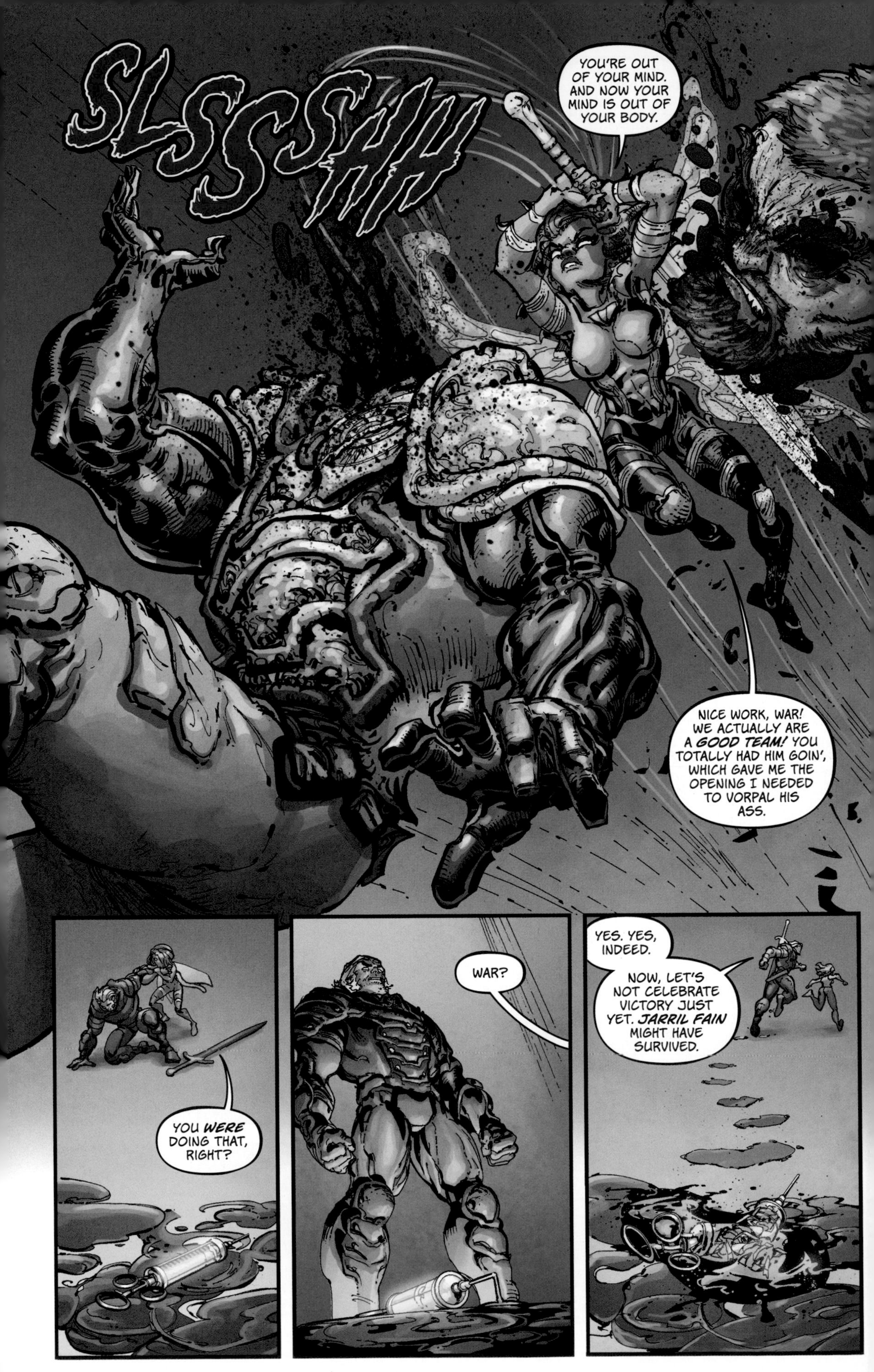
SLSSHH
YOU'RE OUT OF YOUR MIND. AND NOW YOUR MIND IS OUT OF YOUR BODY.
NICE WORK, WAR! WE ACTUALLY ARE A GOOD TEAM! YOU TOTALLY HAD HIM GOIN', WHICH GAVE ME THE OPENING I NEEDED TO VORPAL HIS ASS.
YOU WERE DOING THAT, RIGHT?
WAR?
YES. YES, INDEED.
NOW, LET'S NOT CELEBRATE VICTORY JUST YET. JARRIL FAIN MIGHT HAVE SURVIVED.

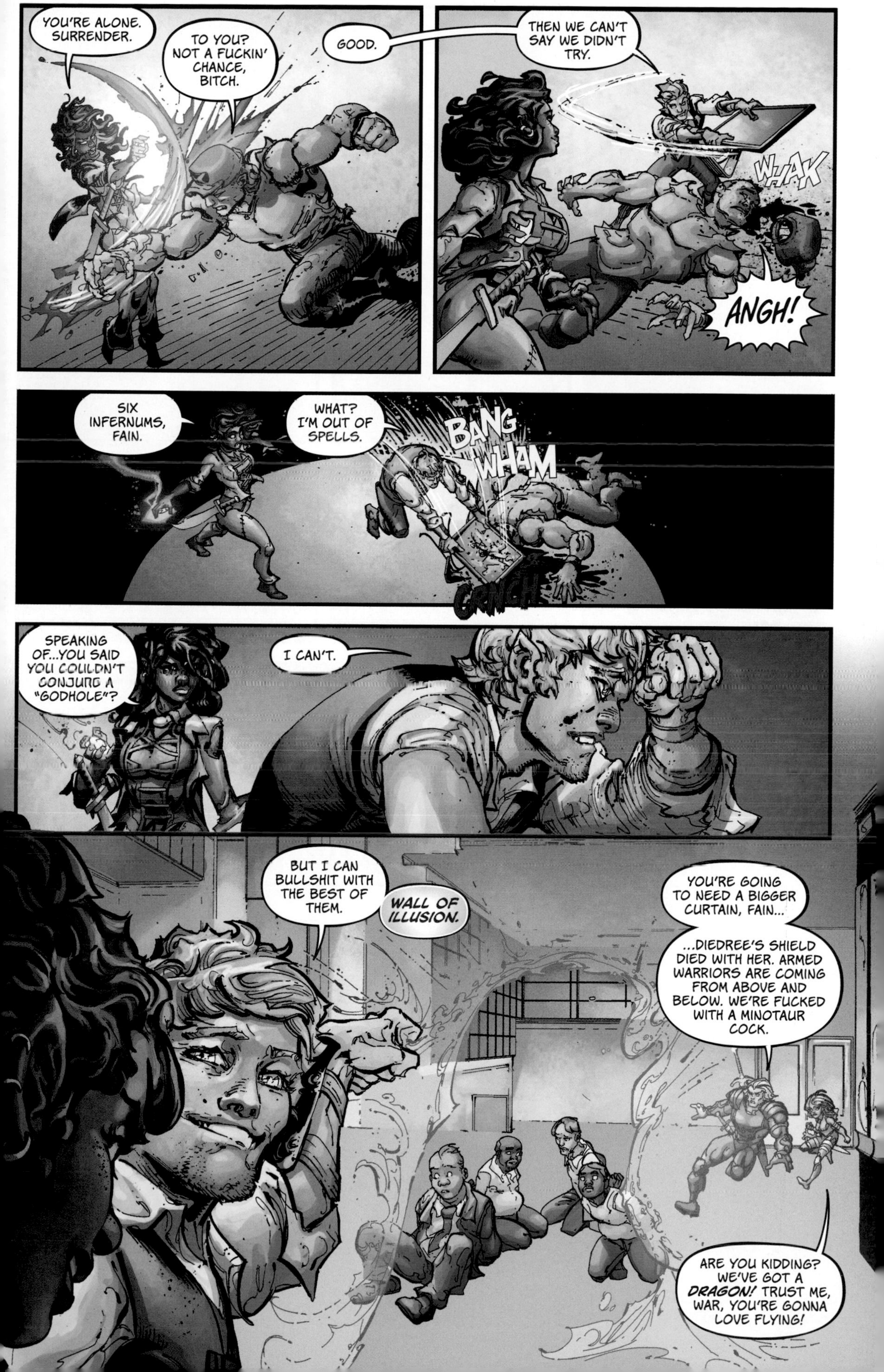
YOU'RE ALONE. SURRENDER.
TO YOU? NOT A FUCKIN' CHANCE, BITCH.
GOOD.
THEN WE CAN'T SAY WE DIDN'T TRY.
WHAK
ANGH!
SIX INFERNUMS, FAIN.
WHAT? I'M OUT OF SPELLS.
BANG
WHAM
CRNCH
SPEAKING OF...YOU SAID YOU COULDN'T CONJURE A "GODHOLE"?
I CAN'T.
BUT I CAN BULLSHIT WITH THE BEST OF THEM.
WALL OF ILLUSION.
YOU'RE GOING TO NEED A BIGGER CURTAIN, FAIN...
...DIEDREE'S SHIELD DIED WITH HER. ARMED WARRIORS ARE COMING FROM ABOVE AND BELOW. WE'RE FUCKED WITH A MINOTAUR COCK.
ARE YOU KIDDING? WE'VE GOT A DRAGON! TRUST ME, WAR, YOU'RE GONNA LOVE FLYING!

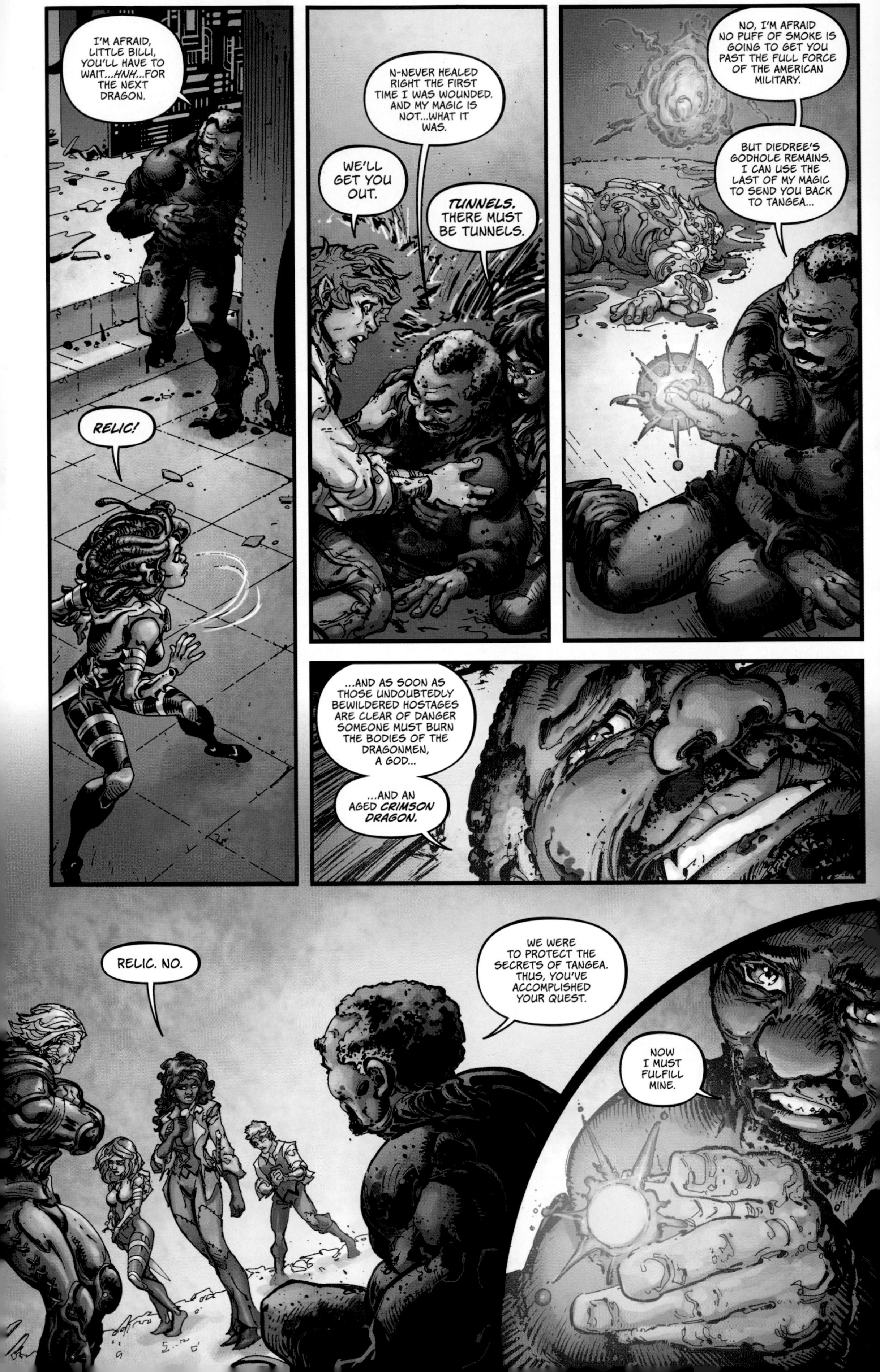
I'M AFRAID, LITTLE BILLI, YOU'LL HAVE TO WAIT...*HNH*...FOR THE NEXT DRAGON.
RELIC!
N-NEVER HEALED RIGHT THE FIRST TIME I WAS WOUNDED. AND MY MAGIC IS NOT...WHAT IT WAS.
WE'LL GET YOU OUT.
TUNNELS. THERE MUST BE TUNNELS.
NO, I'M AFRAID NO PUFF OF SMOKE IS GOING TO GET YOU PAST THE FULL FORCE OF THE AMERICAN MILITARY.
BUT DIEDREE'S GODHOLE REMAINS. I CAN USE THE LAST OF MY MAGIC TO SEND YOU BACK TO TANGEA...
...AND AS SOON AS THOSE UNDOUBTEDLY BEWILDERED HOSTAGES ARE CLEAR OF DANGER SOMEONE MUST BURN THE BODIES OF THE DRAGONMEN, A GOD...
...AND AN AGED *CRIMSON DRAGON.*
RELIC. NO.
WE WERE TO PROTECT THE SECRETS OF TANGEA. THUS, YOU'VE ACCOMPLISHED YOUR QUEST.
NOW I MUST FULFILL MINE.

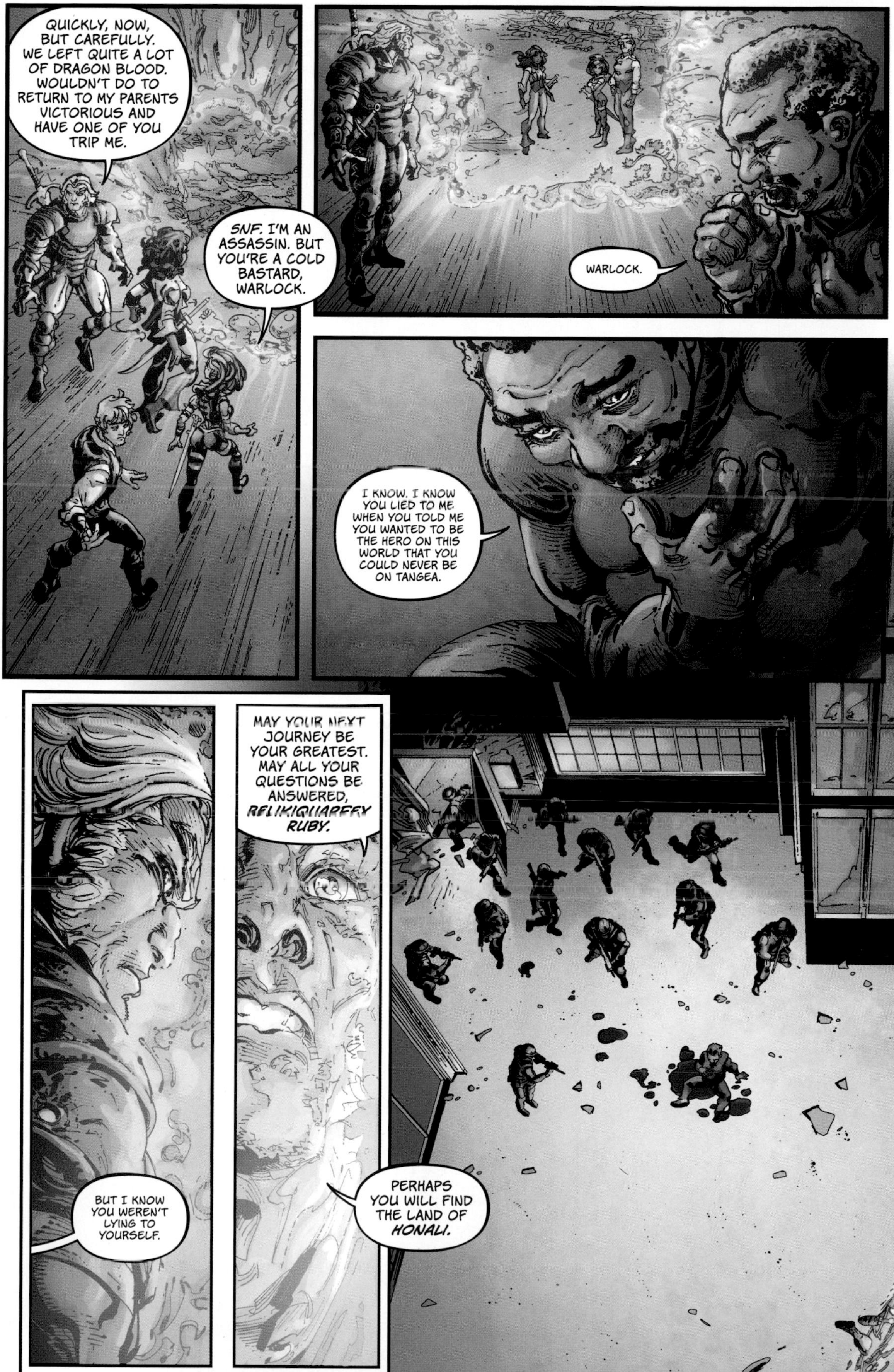
QUICKLY, NOW, BUT CAREFULLY. WE LEFT QUITE A LOT OF DRAGON BLOOD. WOULDN'T DO TO RETURN TO MY PARENTS VICTORIOUS AND HAVE ONE OF YOU TRIP ME.
SNF. I'M AN ASSASSIN. BUT YOU'RE A COLD BASTARD, WARLOCK.
WARLOCK.
I KNOW. I KNOW YOU LIED TO ME WHEN YOU TOLD ME YOU WANTED TO BE THE HERO ON THIS WORLD THAT YOU COULD NEVER BE ON TANGEA.
BUT I KNOW YOU WEREN'T LYING TO YOURSELF.
MAY YOUR NEXT JOURNEY BE YOUR GREATEST. MAY ALL YOUR QUESTIONS BE ANSWERED, *RELIKIQUAREFY RUBY.*
PERHAPS YOU WILL FIND THE LAND OF *HONALI.*

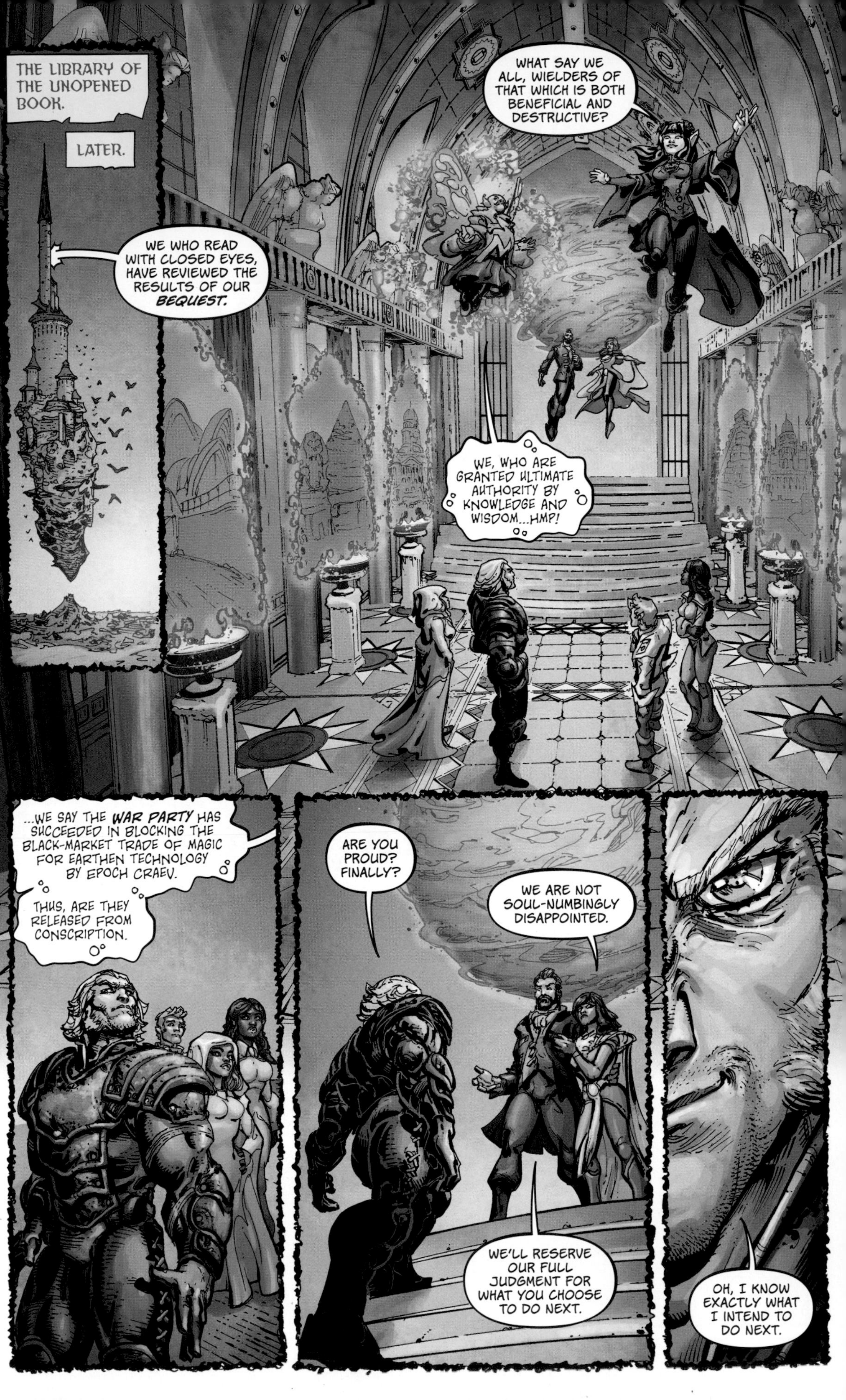
THE LIBRARY OF THE UNOPENED BOOK.
LATER.
WHAT SAY WE ALL, WIELDERS OF THAT WHICH IS BOTH BENEFICIAL AND DESTRUCTIVE?
WE WHO READ WITH CLOSED EYES, HAVE REVIEWED THE RESULTS OF OUR BEQUEST.
WE, WHO ARE GRANTED ULTIMATE AUTHORITY BY KNOWLEDGE AND WISDOM...HMP!
...WE SAY THE WAR PARTY HAS SUCCEEDED IN BLOCKING THE BLACK-MARKET TRADE OF MAGIC FOR EARTHEN TECHNOLOGY BY EPOCH CRAEV.
THUS, ARE THEY RELEASED FROM CONSCRIPTION.
ARE YOU PROUD? FINALLY?
WE ARE NOT SOUL-NUMBINGLY DISAPPOINTED.
WE'LL RESERVE OUR FULL JUDGMENT FOR WHAT YOU CHOOSE TO DO NEXT.
OH, I KNOW EXACTLY WHAT I INTEND TO DO NEXT.

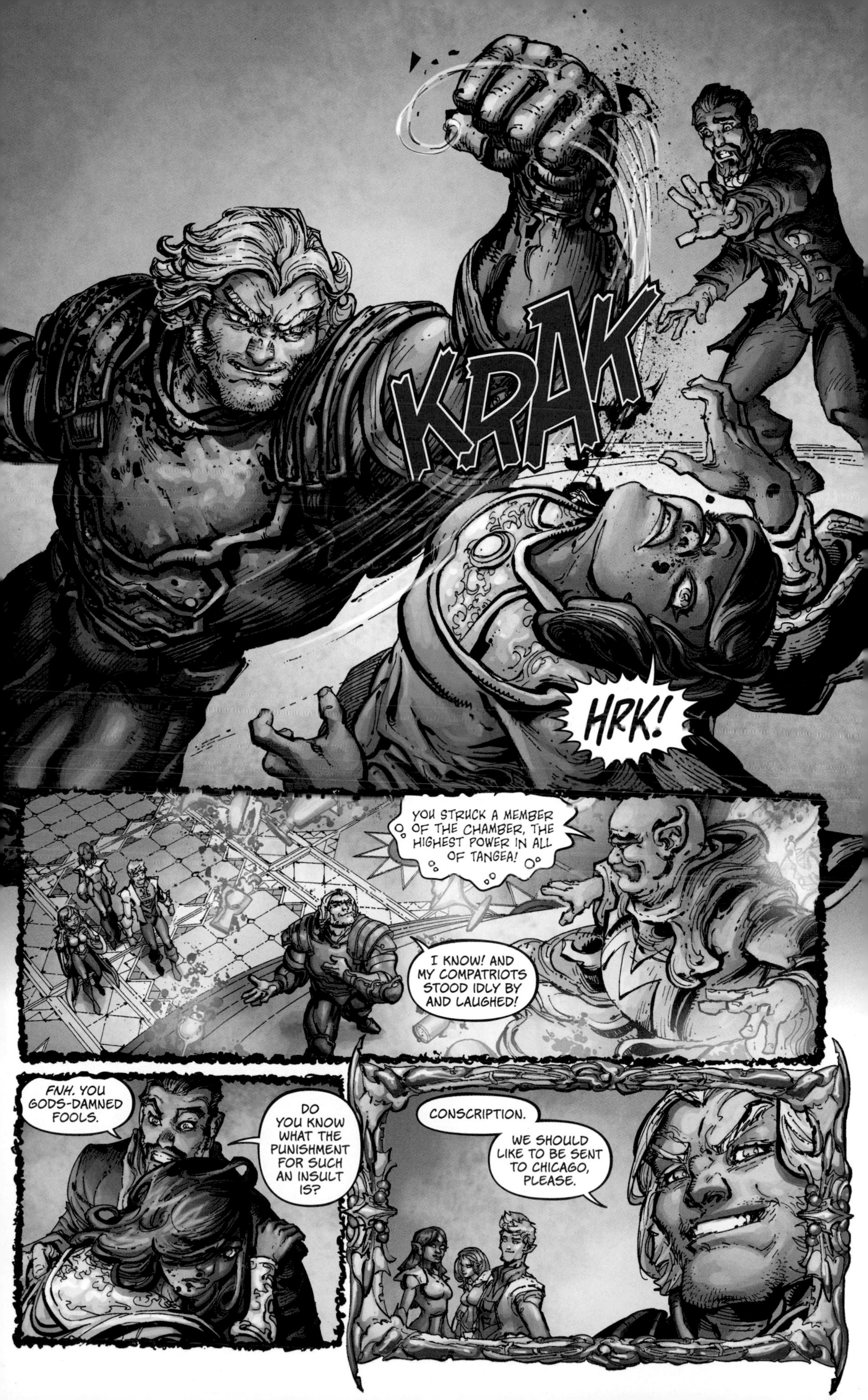
KRAK
HRK!
YOU STRUCK A MEMBER OF THE CHAMBER, THE HIGHEST POWER IN ALL OF TANGEA!
I KNOW! AND MY COMPATRIOTS STOOD IDLY BY AND LAUGHED!
FNH. YOU GODS-DAMNED FOOLS.
DO YOU KNOW WHAT THE PUNISHMENT FOR SUCH AN INSULT IS?
CONSCRIPTION.
WE SHOULD LIKE TO BE SENT TO CHICAGO, PLEASE.

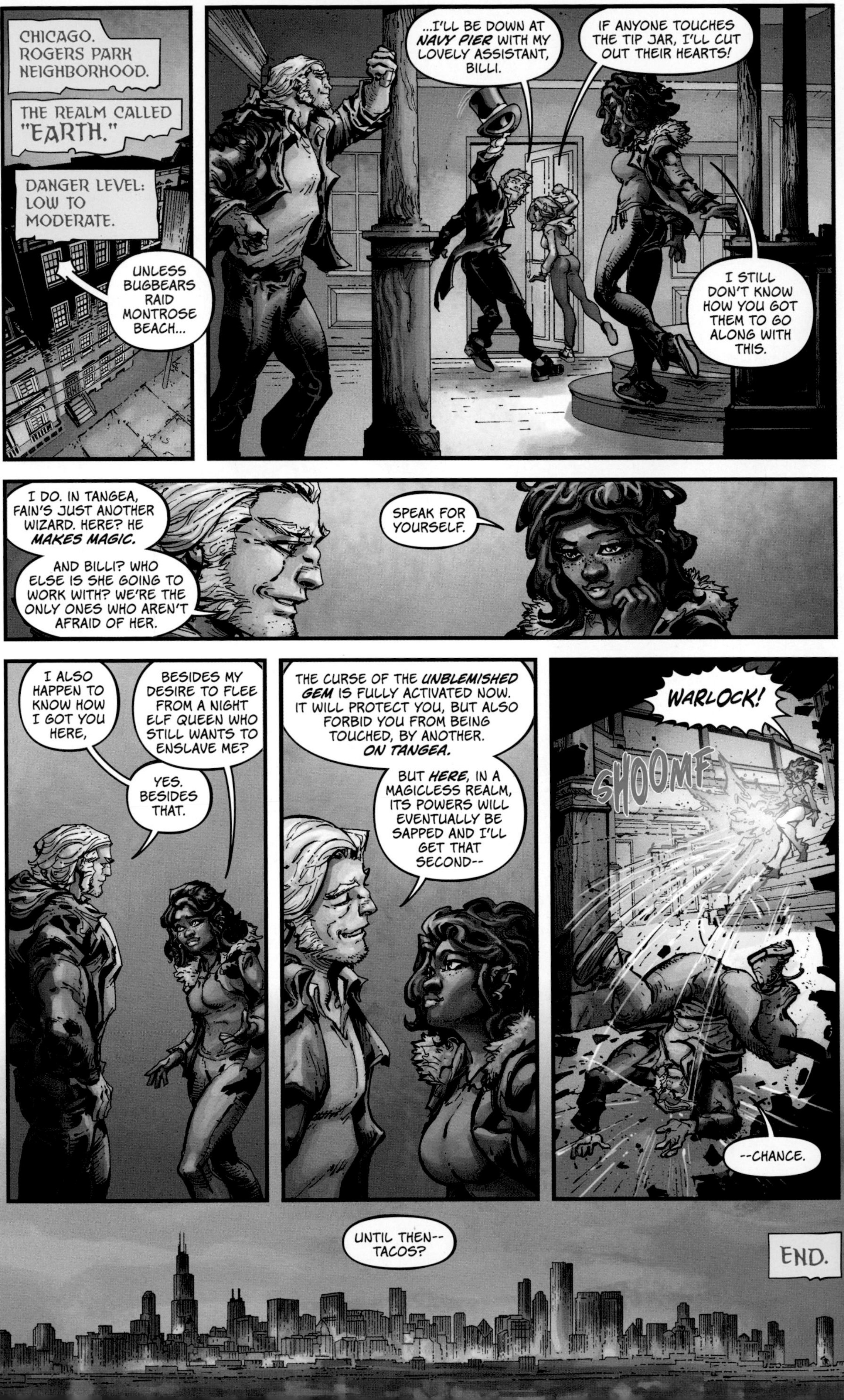
CHICAGO. ROGERS PARK NEIGHBORHOOD.
THE REALM CALLED "EARTH."
DANGER LEVEL: LOW TO MODERATE.
UNLESS BUGBEARS RAID MONTROSE BEACH...
...I'LL BE DOWN AT NAVY PIER WITH MY LOVELY ASSISTANT, BILLI.
IF ANYONE TOUCHES THE TIP JAR, I'LL CUT OUT THEIR HEARTS!
I STILL DON'T KNOW HOW YOU GOT THEM TO GO ALONG WITH THIS.
I DO. IN TANGEA, FAIN'S JUST ANOTHER WIZARD. HERE? HE MAKES MAGIC.
AND BILLI? WHO ELSE IS SHE GOING TO WORK WITH? WE'RE THE ONLY ONES WHO AREN'T AFRAID OF HER.
SPEAK FOR YOURSELF.
I ALSO HAPPEN TO KNOW HOW I GOT YOU HERE,
BESIDES MY DESIRE TO FLEE FROM A NIGHT ELF QUEEN WHO STILL WANTS TO ENSLAVE ME?
YES. BESIDES THAT.
THE CURSE OF THE UNBLEMISHED GEM IS FULLY ACTIVATED NOW. IT WILL PROTECT YOU, BUT ALSO FORBID YOU FROM BEING TOUCHED, BY ANOTHER. ON TANGEA.
BUT HERE, IN A MAGICLESS REALM, ITS POWERS WILL EVENTUALLY BE SAPPED AND I'LL GET THAT SECOND--
WARLOCK!
SHOOMF
--CHANCE.
UNTIL THEN-- TACOS?
END.

The Bequest™

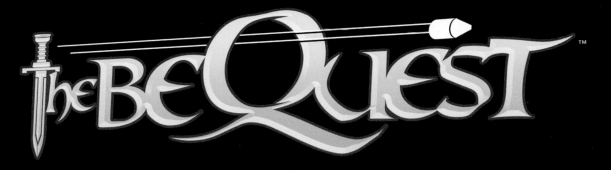

COVER GALLERY

Issue 1
TYLER WALPOLE
Incentive Cover

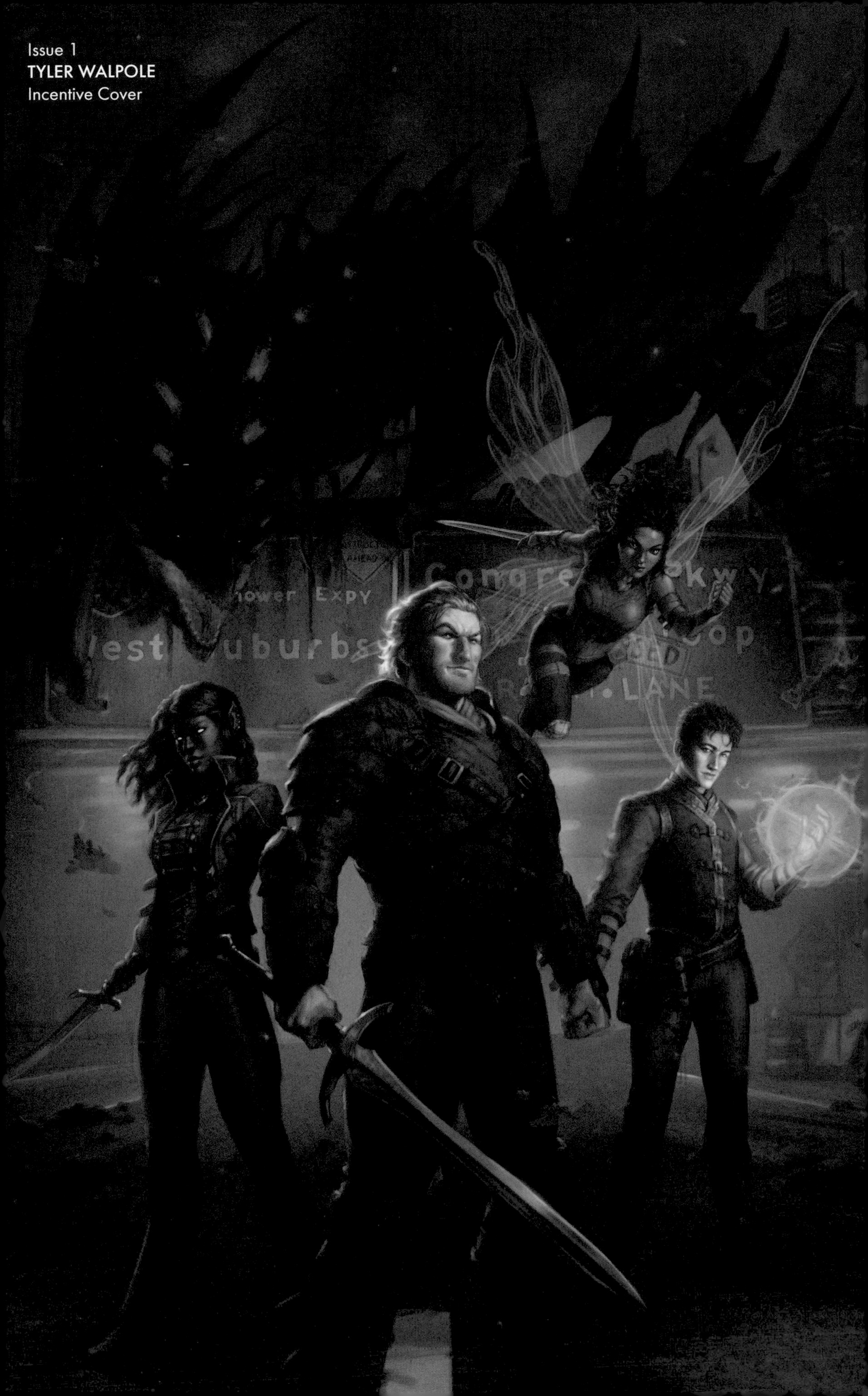

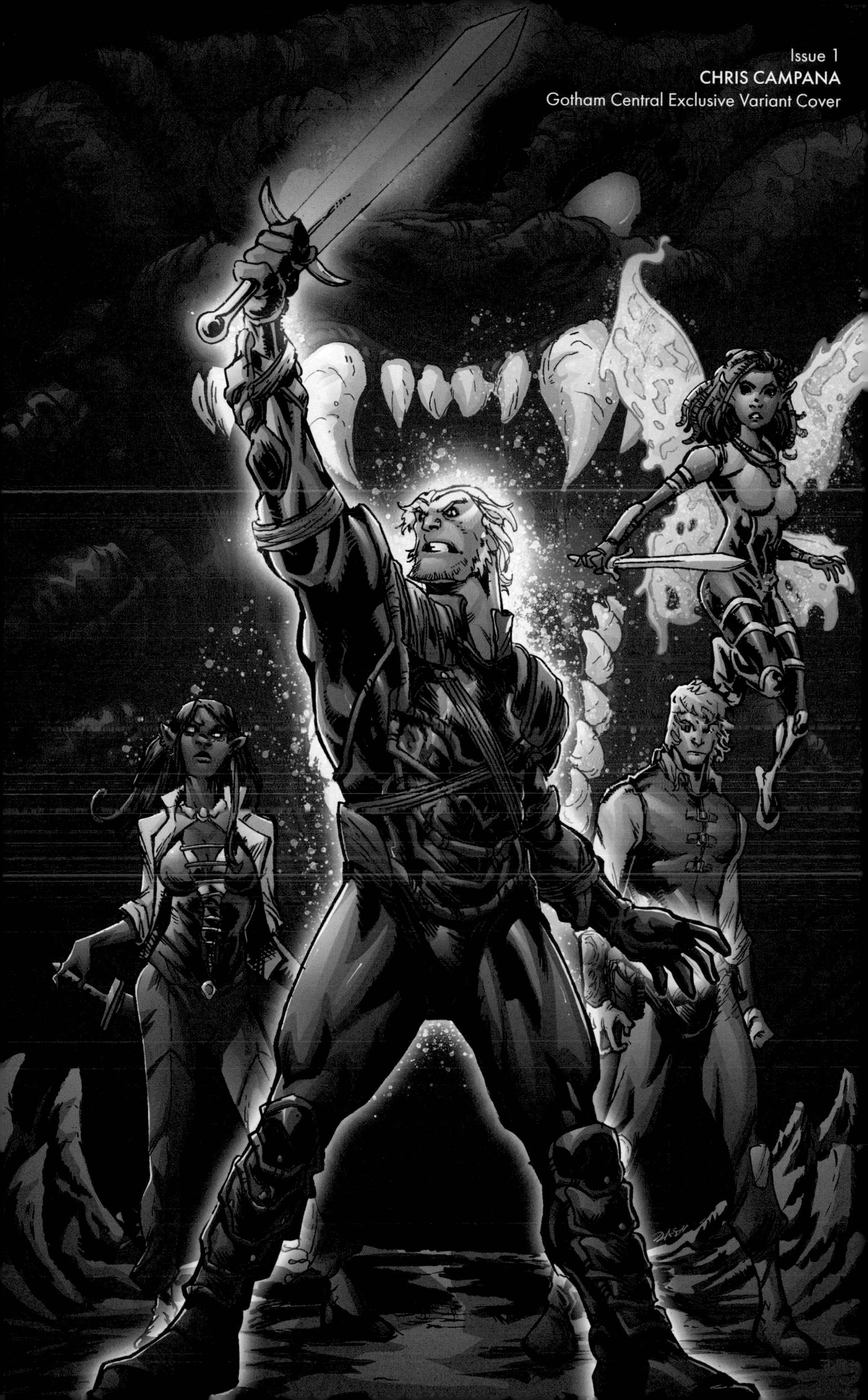

Issue 1
CHRIS CAMPANA
Gotham Central Exclusive Variant Cover

BEHIND THE SCENES & EXTRAS

CHARACTER SHEET

WARLOCK GARTHODD
Character Name

TIM SEELEY
Player's Name

NEUTRAL
Alignment

WARRIOR **5**
Class   Level

MIKEY MARTS
Dungeon Master

4
Armor Class

42
Hit Points

ABILITIES

16	Strength Adjustment:	+4
9	Intelligence Adjustment:	-3
8	Wisdom Adjustment:	-1
15	Dexterity Adjustment:	+3
16	Constitution Adjustment:	+4
9	Charisma Adjustment:	—

SPECIAL ABILITIES

EXPERT SWORDSMAN
THIEF TRAINING
PICCISING
KNOWLEDGE OF MAGIC
 • MODIFIED BY DISTASTE/
  HATRED OF MAGIC AND
  WIZARDS!

SWORD + 2 AGAINST MACES

SAVING

11 Poison or Death Ray	13 Magic Wand	12 Paralysis	13 Dragon Breath	14 Spells or Magic

AC TO HIT

11	12	13	14	15	16	17	18	19	20
9	8	7	6	5	4	3	2	1	0

CREATURES & CAVERNS

JARRIL FAIN
Character Name

TIM SEELEY
Player's Name

NEUTRAL GOOD
Alignment

MAGE   8
Class   Level

CHRISTINA HARRINGTON
Dungeon Master

6
Armor Class

29
Hit Points

ABILITIES

11	Strength	−1
	Adjustment:	
17	Intelligence	15
	Adjustment:	
12	Wisdom	—
	Adjustment:	
15	Dexterity	+3
	Adjustment:	
11	Constitution	−1
	Adjustment:	
17	Charisma	+5
	Adjustment:	

SPECIAL ABILITIES

HALF ELF

- SCHOOL OF SCLEIGHT OF HAND +8 — UNAFFILLATE
- SCHOOL OF ILLUSION +3 — WATERS
- SCHOOL OF DIVINATION −4 — CUPS
  (DOESN'T WANT TO KNOW FUTURE)
- SCHOOL OF DEFENSE +2 — ROSES
- SCHOOL OF ATTACK +1 — FLAMES
- SPEAKS - ELVISH (ALL), DRAGON
- IN ♡ WITH MISTRESS OF THE ROSE

SAVING

13	Poison or Death Ray	
9	Magic Wand	
11	Paralysis	
13	Dragon Breath	
10	Spells or Magic	

AC TO HIT

12	13	14	15	16	17	18	19	20	−
9	8	7	6	5	4	3	2	1	0

CREATURES & CAVERNS

CHARACTER SHEET

BILLI UFT-IMP
Character Name

TIM SEELEY
Player's Name

NEUTRAL EVIL
Alignment

ASSASSIN   3
Class   Level

CHRISTINA HARRINGTON
Dungeon Master

5
Armor
Class

28
Hit
Points

ABILITIES   SPECIAL ABILITIES

| 11 | Strength | -1 |
Adjustment: -1

| 17 | Intelligence +5 |
Adjustment:

| 7 | Wisdom -5 |
Adjustment:

| 19 | Dexterity +7 |
Adjustment:

| 12 | Constitution - |
Adjustment:

| 13 | Charisma +1 |
Adjustment:

- SPRITE, ASSASSIN GUILD MEMBER

- LIMITED FLIGHT W/ FAIRY WINGS

- DAGGER +4 AGAINST HUMANS & ELVES

- RAGE FIT. +4 ON STRENGTH & DEX, -5 ON INT & WIS.

SAVING

(13) Poison or Death Ray   (14) Magic Wand   (12) Paralysis   (16) Dragon Breath   (15) Spells or Magic

AC TO HIT

11	12	13	14	15	16	17	18	19	20
9	8	7	6	5	4	3	2	1	0

CHARACTER SHEET

CREEDUX SHARNAE
Character Name

TIM SEELEY
Player's Name

CHAOTIC GOOD
Alignment

THIEF   **7**
Class   Level

MIKEY MARTS
Dungeon Master

6
Armor Class

① WITH UNBLEMISHED GEM!

35
Hit Points

ABILITIES

9	**Strength** Adjustment:	−3
16	**Intelligence** Adjustment:	+4
13	**Wisdom** Adjustment:	+1
18	**Dexterity** Adjustment:	+5
10	**Constitution** Adjustment:	−2
16	**Charisma** Adjustment:	+4

SPECIAL ABILITIES

- NIGHT ELF FORMER ASSASSIN
- KNOWLEDGE OF POLITICS, SPYING, SEDUCTION, THE UNDERGROUND.
- POSSESSES 'THE UNBLEMISHED GEM' — POSSESSIVE ARTIFACT
- SPEAKS ORC, NIGHT ELF, WOOD ELF, DEEP TONGUE.
- DAGGER, +1 AGAINST DEEP WALKERS

SAVING

| 12 | Poison or Death Ray | 12 | Magic Wand | 11 | Paralysis | 15 | Dragon Breath | 13 | Spells or Magic |

AC TO HIT

11	12	13	14	15	16	17	18	19	20
9	8	7	6	5	4	3	2	1	0

CHARACTER SHEET

MARMONT THE STONE EYED
Character Name

TIM SEELEY
Player's Name

LAWFUL GOOD
Alignment

CLERIC   **8**
Class   Level

MIKEY MARTS
Dungeon Master

2
Armor Class

51
Hit Points

ABILITIES

14	Strength	+2
	Adjustment:	
11	Intelligence	-1
	Adjustment:	
18	Wisdom	+5
	Adjustment:	
8	Dexterity	-1
	Adjustment:	
18	Constitution	+6
	Adjustment:	
15	Charisma	+3
	Adjustment:	

SPECIAL ABILITIES

KNOWLEDGE OF UNDERGROUND, DWARVEN HISTORY, ALL RELIGIONS.

SPEAKS DWARVEN, COMMON, NIGHT ELF

· PROSELTYZING

· +4 MAGIC AXE
  +5 AGAINST NIGHT ELVES

SAVING

 1 Poison or Death Ray   11 Magic Wand   10 Paralysis   13 Dragon Breath   12 Spells or Magic

AC TO HIT

10	11	12	13	14	15	16	17	18	19
9	8	7	6	5	4	3	2	1	0

Writer Interview:
TIM SEELEY

AFTERSHOCK COMICS: Where did the inspiration for THE BEQUEST characters come from?

TIM SEELEY: Warlock Garthodd was my actual D&D character when I was thirteen! And, yes, he was totally the arrogant, cowardly jerk then as he was in the comic. The rest were created to be great foils for specific issues I wanted to address.

ASC: What was your favorite character interaction to write?

TS: Any scene between Warlock and Fain likely had me giggling to myself in my office.

ASC: What is your process when fleshing out characters for stories like THE BEQUEST?

TS: I try to do a lot of pre-work, but I'll be honest, most of it comes from actually writing scripts. I kind of need to bounce characters off each other before I know them. This can work against me, but I'm an improv comedian at heart, not a stand-up.

ASC: If you had to be roommates with one of the characters from THE BEQUEST, who would you choose?

TS: Definitely Sharmae. She's pretty and very tidy. And pretty much everyone else would kill you, either accidentally or on purpose.

The BeQuest

Artist Interview:
FREDDIE E. WILLIAMS II

AFTERSHOCK COMICS: What was your favorite part about illustrating THE BEQUEST?

FREDDIE E. WILLIAMS II: Having the freedom to draw whatever I'd like for the script — much more freedom in that — though that sometimes created a bit of paralysis. When there are so many options it can get you 'stuck', but that is an awesome problem to have.

The Bequest
Freddie E. Williams II

ASC: What is your favorite moment, page or panel?

FW: Issue one, pages 18-19, the introduction to Epoch Creav. He's my favorite character (maybe second favorite next to Relic) and this double page spread tells his story in the style of an Illuminated Manuscripts — from security footage to the prophecy of an ancient scroll — suuuuper fun to draw!

The Bequest
Freddie E. Williams II

ASC: What was the most challenging aspect for you when illustrating THE BEQUEST?

FW: For the past five to six years, I've been working in an inkwash style (using diluted India inks to create shades of gray) and for THE BEQUEST, I returned to the more common pen and ink style. Since I had taken such a break from it, I got creative in what techniques I incorporated this time around. More quill? More brush? More scratch? More spatter?

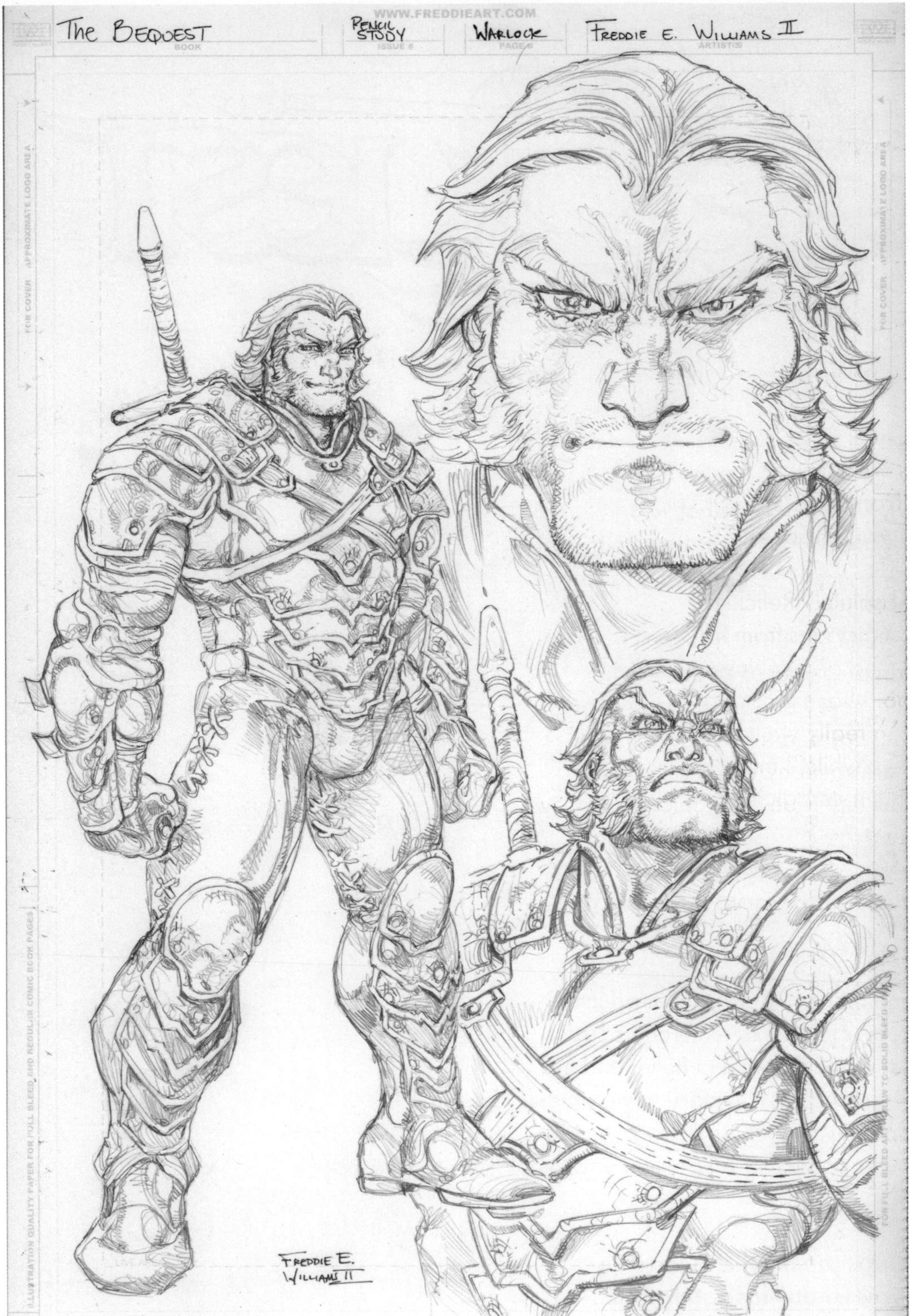
WWW.FREDDIEART.COM
The Bequest
Pencil Study
Warlock
Freddie E. Williams II
Freddie E. Williams II
FOR DOUBLE PAGE SPREAD
CUT AND ABUT
TAPE ON BACK
DO NOT OVERLAP PAGES
WWW.FREDDIEART.COM

▲ **WARLOCK:**

FW: I approached Warlock like a big, good-natured dog that knocks everything off the coffee table with his wagging tail — stinky, loud and clumsy — but lovable!

ASC: How did your experience playing *Dungeons and Dragons* and *Pathfinder* help while bringing the world to life?

FW: I'm an old man now, but in high school, a few friends and I played D&D off and on for two years. Playing those games gave me some useful building blocks and shorthand to the fantasy and fictional worlds we were creating.

ASC: If you had to be roommates with one of the characters from THE BEQUEST, who would you choose?

FW: Relic! Absolutely Relic. I'd listen to his long stories from his ancient past, and be genuinely interested, too! I have a feeling we'd get along really well, and every once in a while, I might get to see him do cool magic stuff, which would be a bonus!

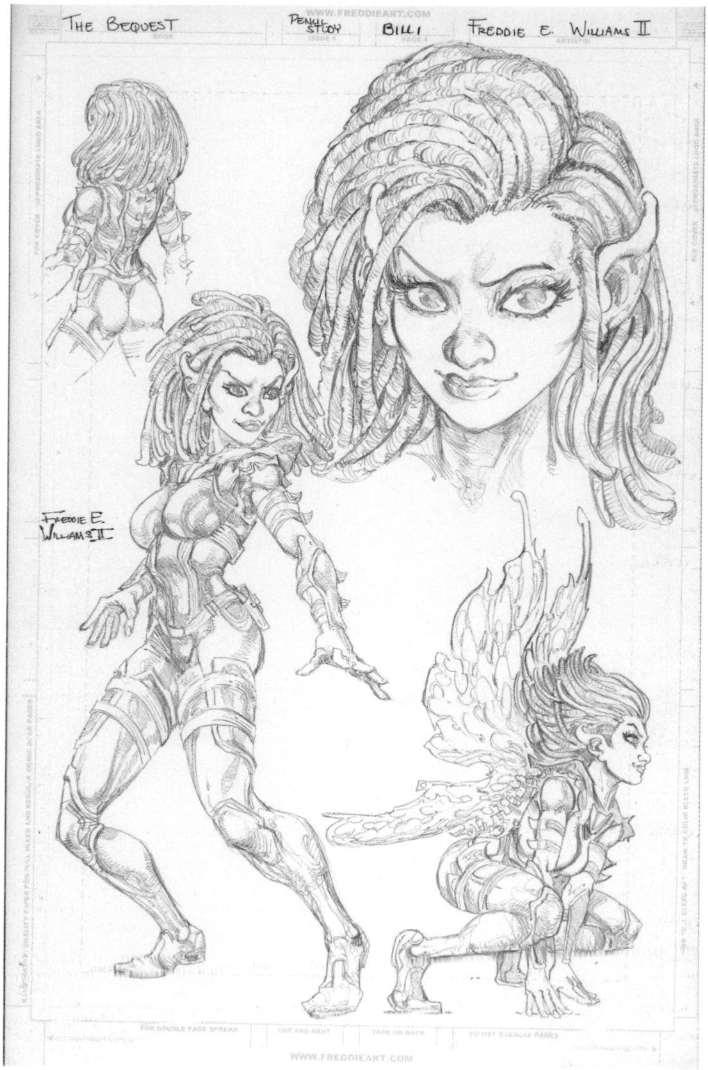

WWW.FREDDIEART.COM
THE BEQUEST
PENCIL STUDY
BILLI
FREDDIE E. WILLIAMS II
FREDDIE E. WILLIAMS II

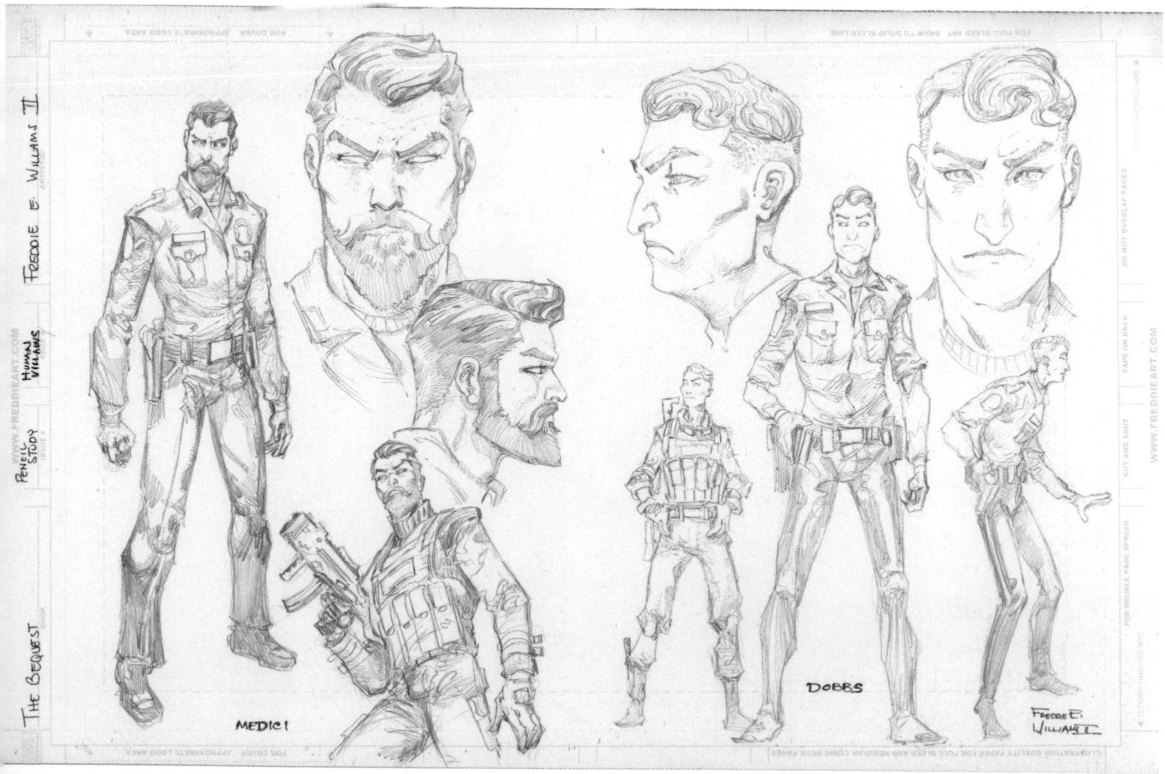

THE BEQUEST
PENCIL STUDY
HUMAN VILLAINS
FREDDIE E. WILLIAMS II
MEDIC
DOBBS
FREDDIE E. WILLIAMS II

▸ FLESH TINKERER:

FW: The Flesh Tinkerer only appears in a few panels, but looking back, I wish I had pushed her design even further. Stuff like beetles for garment clasps and fox heads for shoulder pads — that sort of stuff — but the Flesh Tinkerer was still one of my favorites to draw!

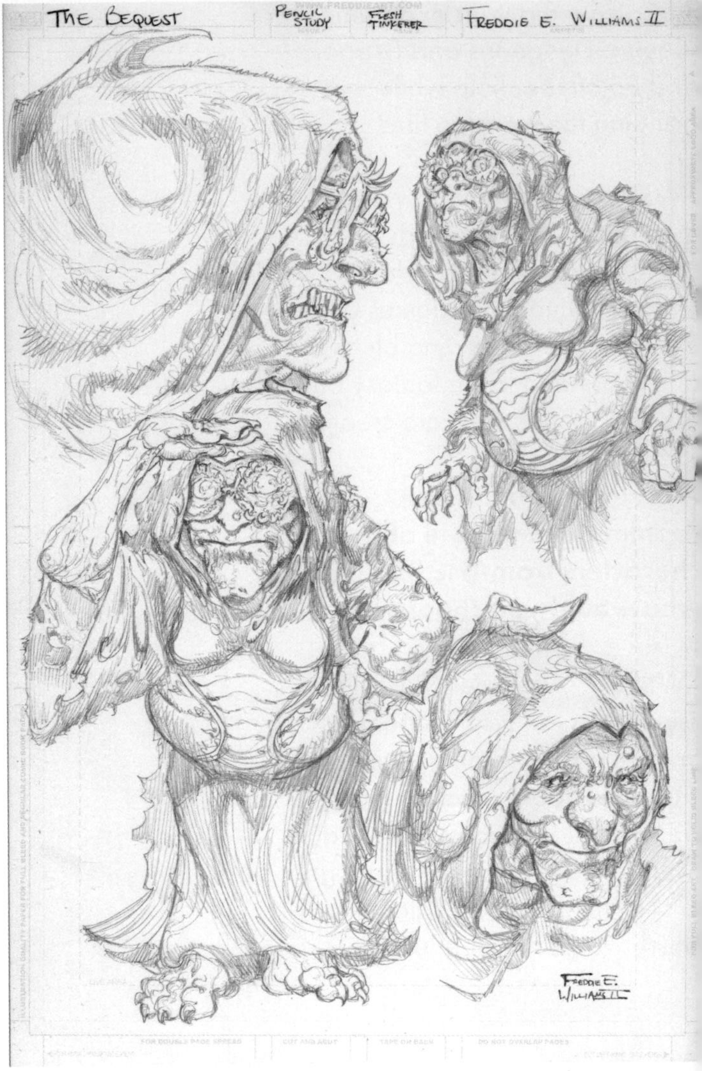
THE BEQUEST
PENCIL STUDY
FLESH TINKERER
FREDDIE E. WILLIAMS II
FREDDIE E. WILLIAMS II

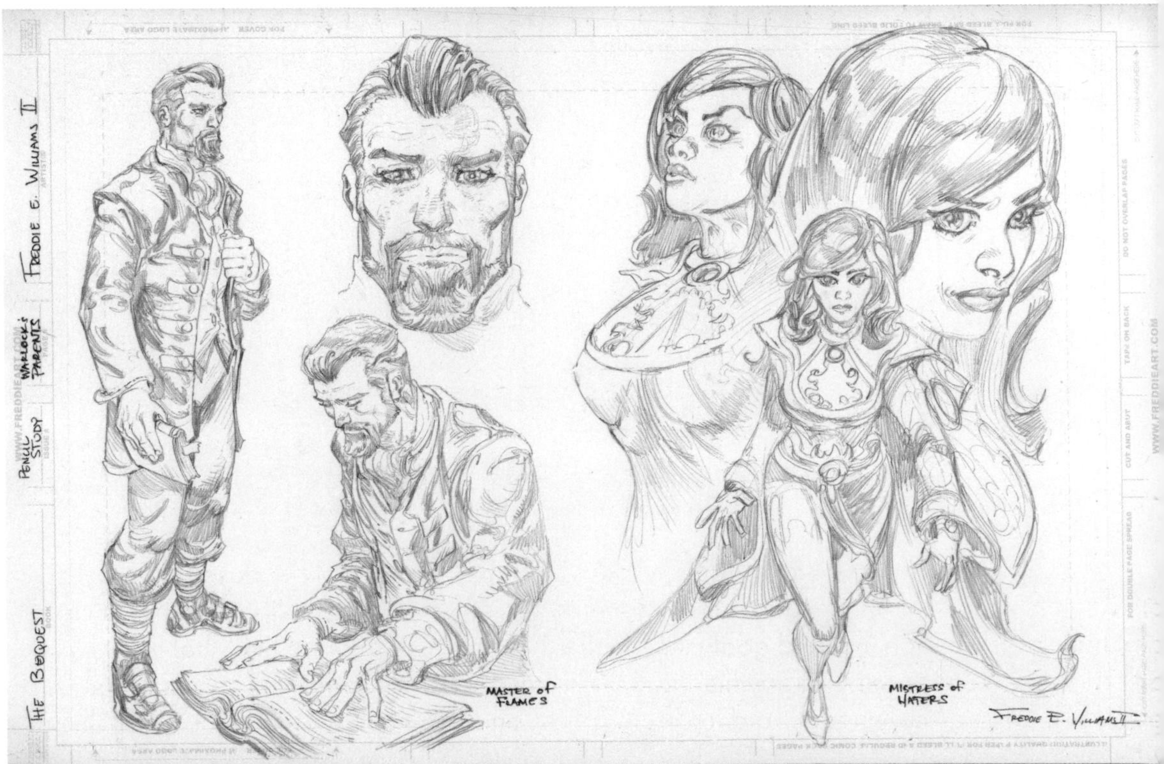
THE BEQUEST
PENCIL STUDY
WARLOCK'S PARENTS
FREDDIE E. WILLIAMS II
MASTER of FLAMES
MISTRESS of WATERS
FREDDIE E. WILLIAMS II

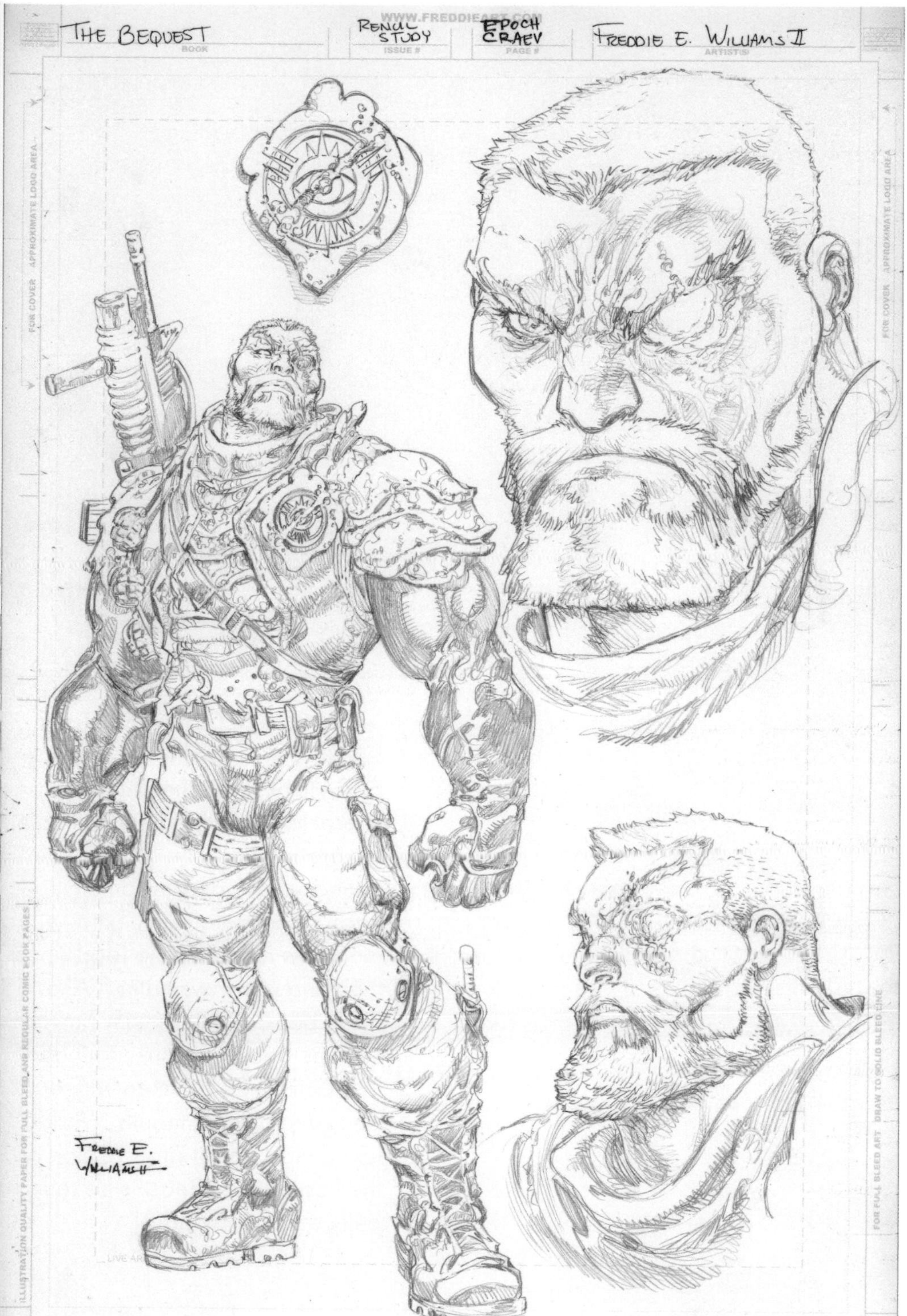
THE BEQUEST
FREDDIE E. WILLIAMS II
WWW.FREDDIEART.COM
BOOK
ISSUE #
PAGE #
ARTIST(S)
FOR DOUBLE PAGE SPREAD
CUT AND ABUT
TAPE ON BACK
DO NOT OVERLAP PAGES
WWW.FREDDIEART.COM

▲ **EPOC:**

FW: Epoc is a bad guy, but I think I connected with him the most. Not because I agree with him or wish to be like him, but because his mission *could* be seen in a noble light. But it's reckless and he's so focused on that end goal (slaying the deity that abandoned him) that he'll make any deal and ally himself with anything to achieve that goal—which is why he's not a *good guy*. I found myself looking forward to drawing him, and wanting to increase his screen time when possible!

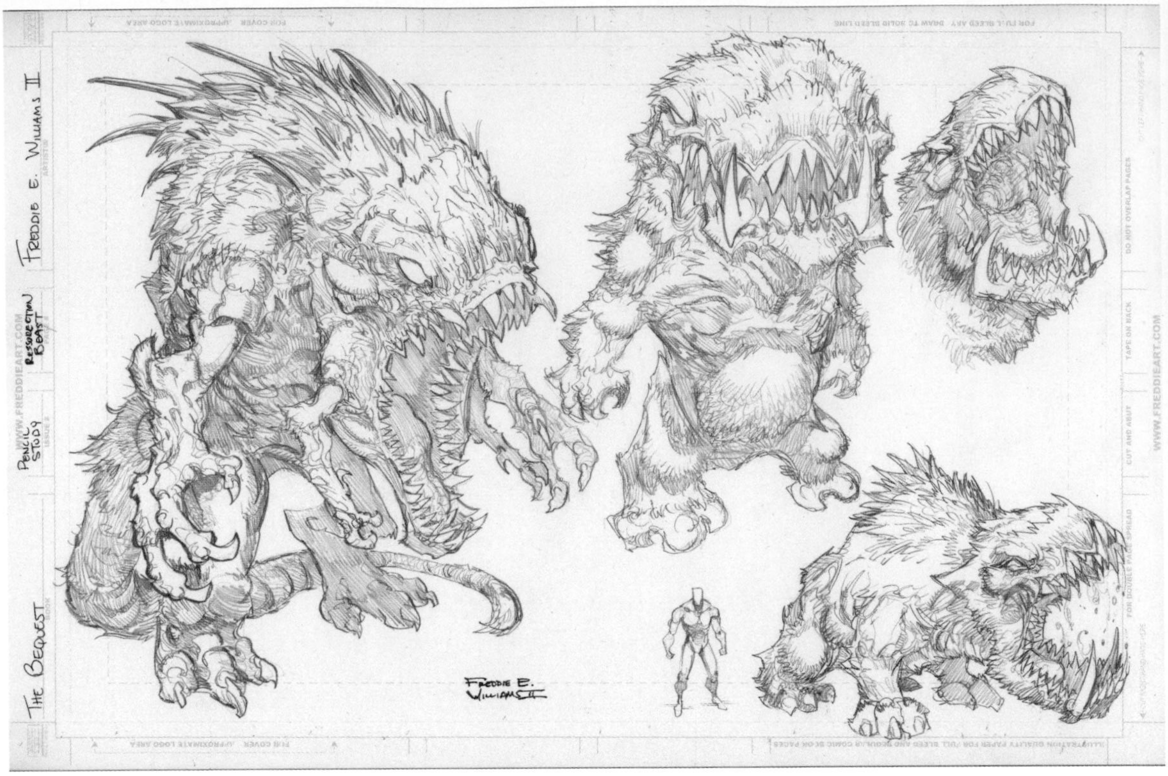
FREDDIE E. WILLIAMS II
RESURRECTION BEAST
PENCIL STUDY
WWW.FREDDIEART.COM
THE BEQUEST
FREDDIE E. WILLIAMS II

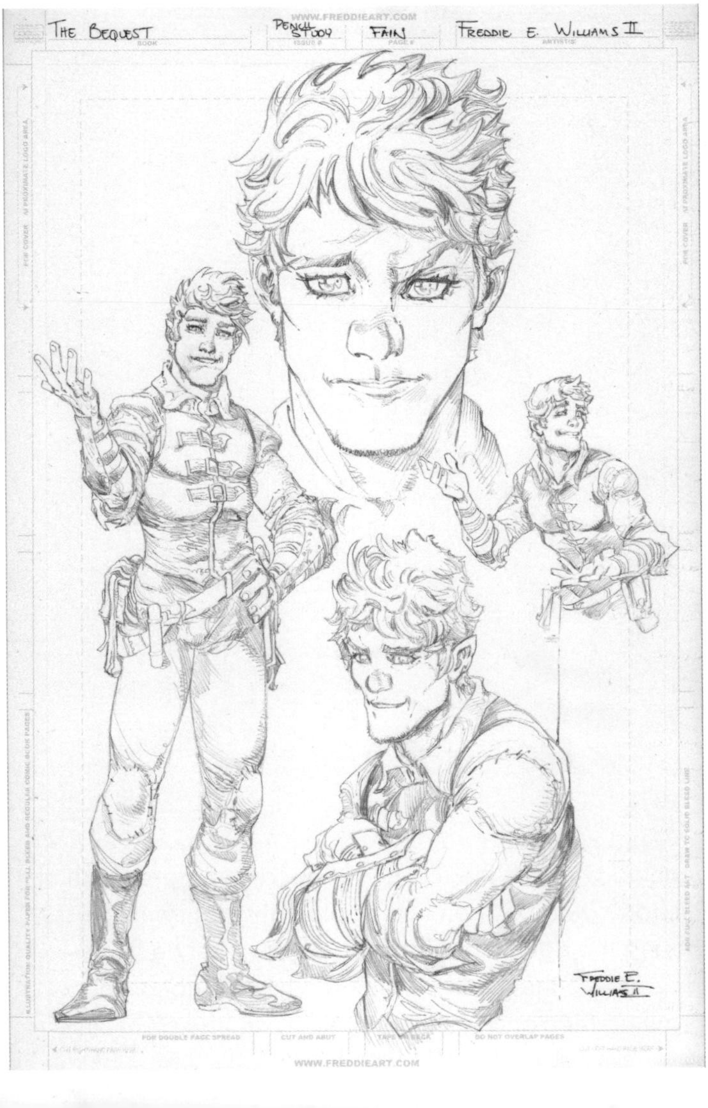
THE BEQUEST
WWW.FREDDIEART.COM
PENCIL STUDY
FAIN!
FREDDIE E. WILLIAMS II
FREDDIE E. WILLIAMS II
WWW.FREDDIEART.COM

▲ RESSURECTION BEAST:

FW: I think this is the only character I designed entirely from the ground up — *twice*! My initial instinct was to design something I hadn't seen before: an extra set of mandible arms to grab food since this thing is always eating! After some back and forth with Tim, he saw the beast as more grounded in a Grizzly bear mixed with a boar and a shark mouth. What I loved most about Tim's version of the Resurrection Beast is his round belly and stubby arms!

◀ **RELIC:**

FW: I love Tim Seeley's take on a Dragon who is powerful and deadly, but has a really good nature and slightly goofy human-looking exterior. It's like making an action star out of a smiling Morgan Freeman. As I drew him in the series, the Dragon version of Relic got more stocky — this could be explained by Relic's ability to shape shift — but it was actually just because I thought he looked cooler that way!

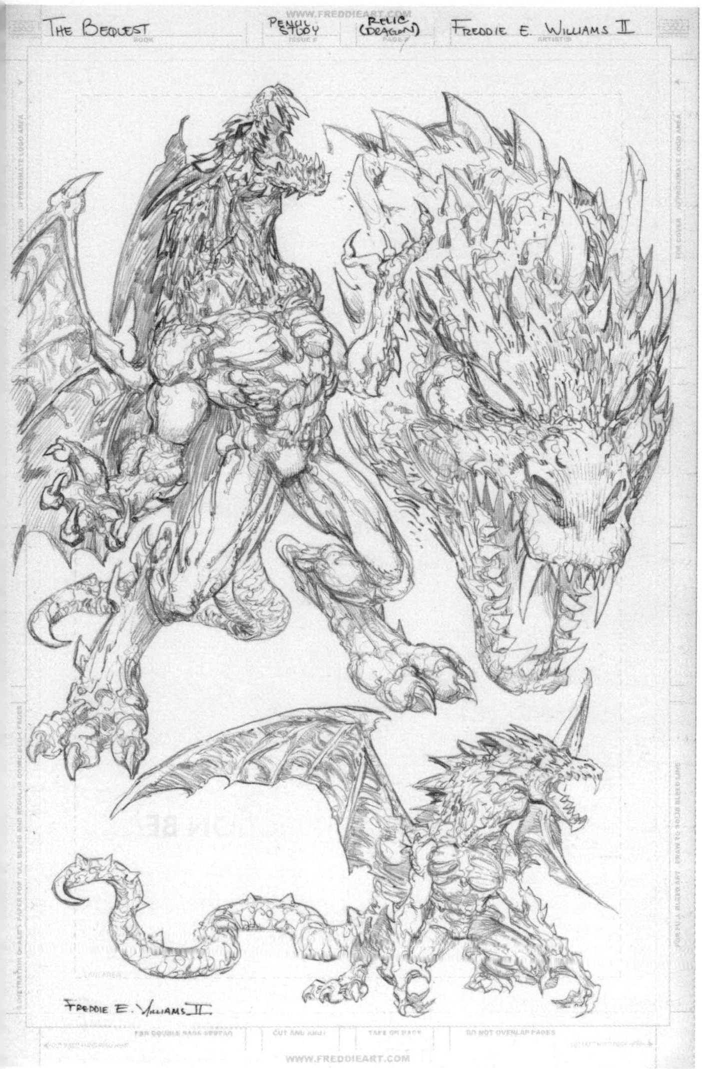
THE BEQUEST
PENCIL STUDY
RELIC (DRAGON)
FREDDIE E. WILLIAMS II
FREDDIE E. WILLIAMS II
WWW.FREDDIEART.COM

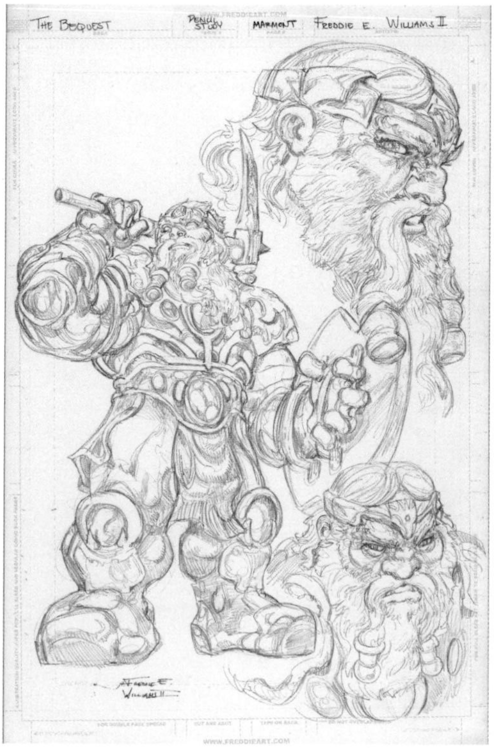
THE BEQUEST
PENCIL STUDY
MARMONT
FREDDIE E. WILLIAMS II

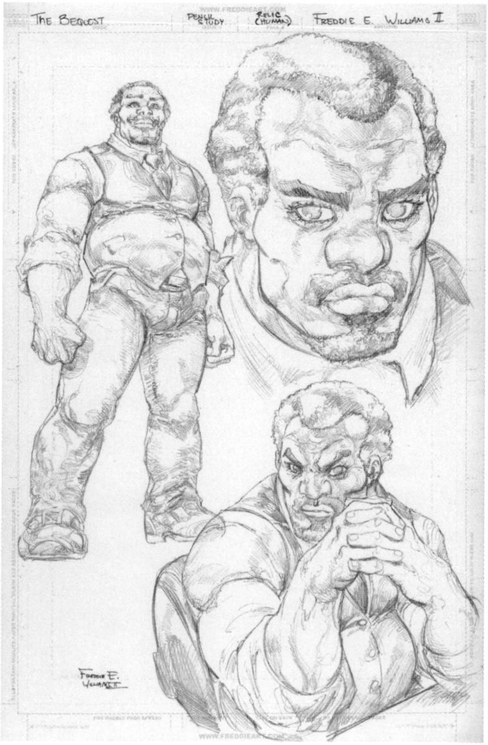
THE BEQUEST
PENCIL STUDY
RELIC (HUMAN)
FREDDIE E. WILLIAMS II
FREDDIE E. WILLIAMS II

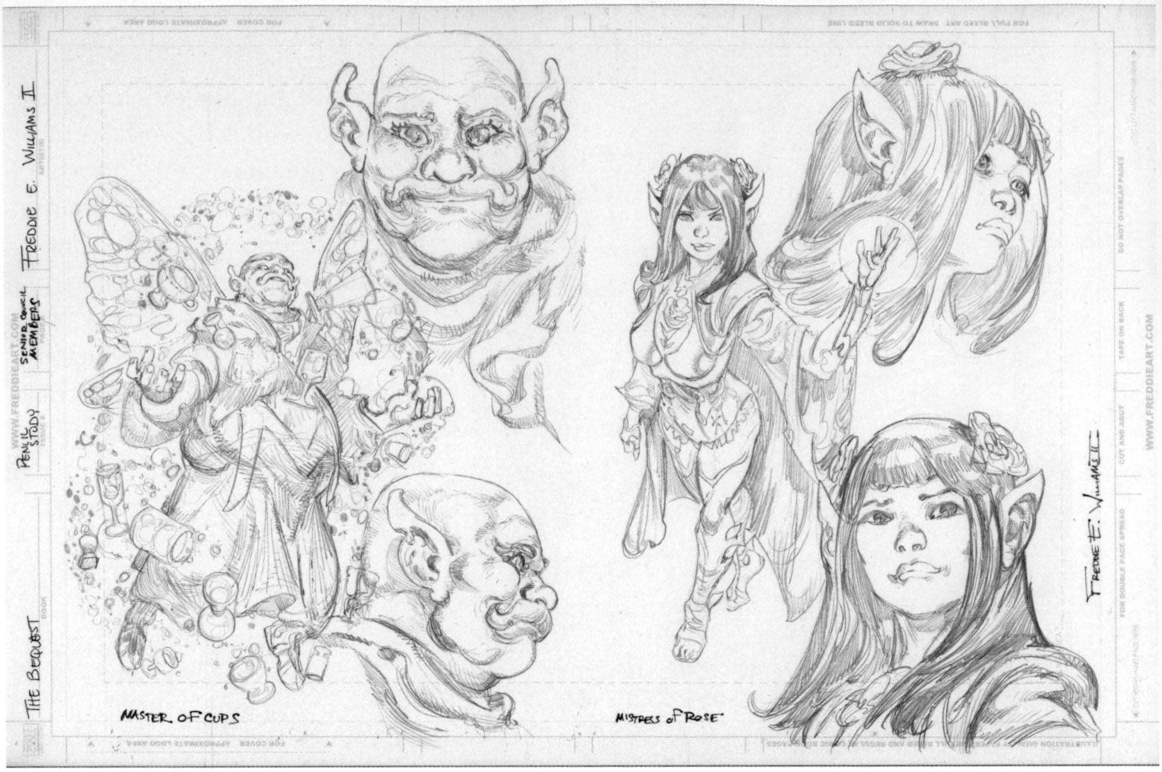
THE BEQUEST
PENCIL STUDY
SENIOR COUNCIL MEMBERS
FREDDIE E. WILLIAMS II
MASTER OF CUPS
MISTRESS OF ROSE
WWW.FREDDIEART.COM

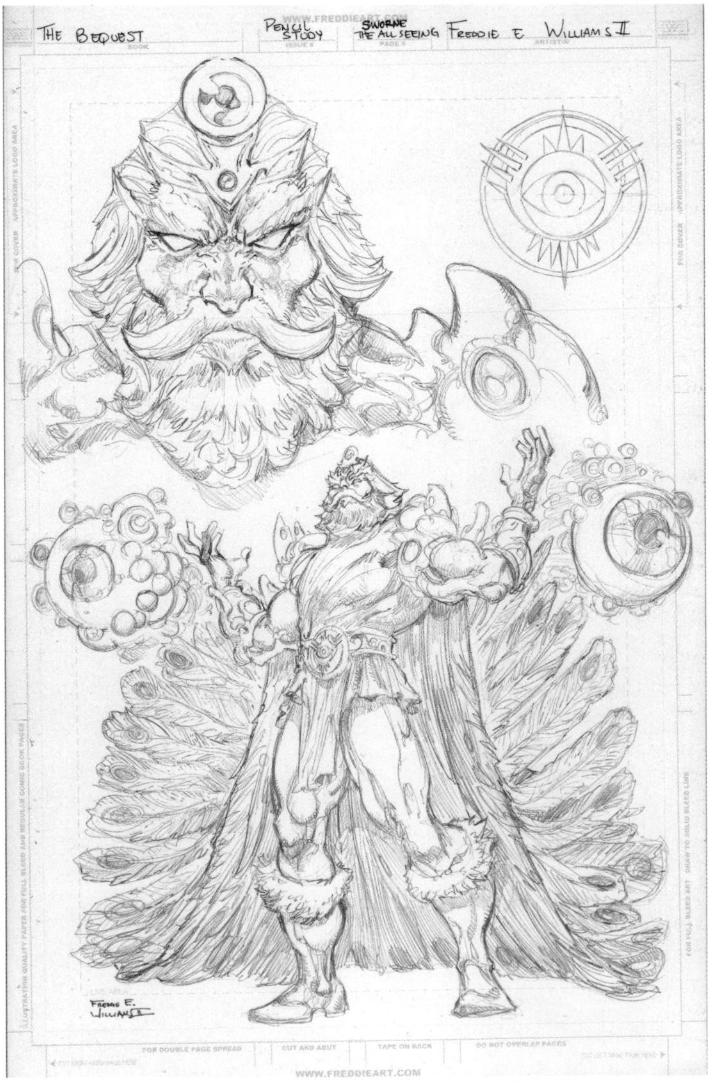
THE BEQUEST
PENCIL STUDY
SWORNE THE ALL SEEING
FREDDIE E. WILLIAMS II
WWW.FREDDIEART.COM

THANK YOU

Once upon a time, a comic book series didn't even find its legs until about issue #78. These days, most comics wrap it all up in five, before the attention of the readers can be taken by Twitter or Netflix or a really good taco.

So, look, clearly these four issues of THE BEQUEST (I mean, technically, at twenty-four pages an issue it really is the same amount of story as most five issues runs!) were meant as an introduction. A foray, if you will. Because Freddie, Jeremy, Marshall, Christina, Mike and I built two goddamn worlds here, and we need another 74 issues to even find our legs.

I hope by about midway through issue two you realized what kind of story we were making here, and that you thought that whether or not the concept was fully unique, our approach was. I hope you enjoyed the hell out of this fusion of sword and sorcery tropes and modern American life. I REALLY hope that if you enjoyed THE BEQUEST, you'll tell friends, family and mortal enemies to pick up the trade. And I hope most of all that Freddie, Jeremy, Marshall, Christina, Mike and I can come back and tell more stories about the War Party and their not-so-politically-correct adventures through a not-so-sane world.

Thank you so much for joining us here at AfterShock Comics, and may all your journeys be good ones.

Tim Seeley!

THANK YOU to everyone who has been supporting THE BEQUEST. The reviews and response has been so nice, and we really appreciate it!

What a blast it's been working on THE BEQUEST! Although Tim and I didn't know each other in high school, we would have been best friends if we did! (Secretly) playing Dungeons and Dragons as well as our common love for He-Man and all things fantasy made us click just a couple years ago on Injustice vs Masters of the Universe, which led to this book!

(Most of) The War Party members are actually Tim's high school D&D characters, and it was a blast getting to play in that neighborhood of the toy box. I hope to again soon! There is a lot of life and love in the characters of THE BEQUEST, so I don't think this will be the last time we see them. I sure hope not!

Also, as a quick aside, I've worked with Mike Marts at DC, Marvel and now at AfterShock—what a great editor and awesome guy! And Christina Harrington is not only an awesome editor, but a really GREAT DUNGEON MASTER, I am impressed by her, at every one of our interactions!

Freddie E. Williams II

ABOUT THE CREATORS OF

The BEQUEST ™

TIM SEELEY writer
🐦 @HackinTimSeeley

Tim is one of those "slash" people...a writer-slash-artist. He has drawn a number of different comic book series including *G.I Joe*, *Halloween*, *Wild C.A.T.S.* and *Exsanguine*. His writing work includes NY Times best selling *Hack/Slash*, *Grayson*, *Batman Eternal*, DARK RED and the critically acclaimed *Revival*. He resides in Chicago, Illinois and works at Four Star Studios where he is never far from his 80s action figure collection.

FREDDIE E. WILLIAMS II artist
🐦 @FreddieArt

In 2005, Freddie began work with DC Comics on the Eisner Award-winning series *Seven Soldiers: Mister Miracle*. He's probably best known for illustrating a series of fun and improbable crossovers: The New York Times best-selling *Batman/Teenage Mutant Ninja Turtles*, *He-Man/ThunderCats* and *Injustice VS Masters of The Universe*, as well as writing the *DC Comics Guide to Digitally Drawing Comics*.

JEREMY COLWELL colorist
🐦 @Jeremy_Colwell

Jeremy Colwell lives near Portland, OR. Thanks to COVID he spends pretty much all his time at home with his three cats, two boys and one loving partner. He listens to a lot of music, watches a few movies, plays the occasional game, likes to put together puzzles and daydreams about hanging out with friends again after the pandemic. He loves good food, wine, hugs and laughter. He also colors comics.

MARSHALL DILLON letterer
🐦 @MarshallDillon

A comic book industry veteran, Marshall got his start in 1994, in the midst of the indy comic boom. Over the years, he's been everything from an independent self-published writer to an associate publisher working on properties like *G.I. Joe*, *Voltron* and *Street Fighter*. He's done just about everything except draw a comic book, and has worked for just about every publisher except the "big two." Primarily a father and letterer these days, he also dabbles in old-school paper & dice RPG game design. You can catch up with Marshall at firstdraftpress.net.